D0394923

750

IN THE FOOTSTEPS OF
JOHNSON AND BOSWELL

OTHER BOOKS
BY ISRAEL SHENKER

As Good as Golda (co-editor)
Words and Their Masters
Zero Mostel's Book of Villains
Harmless Drudges
Noshing Is Sacred

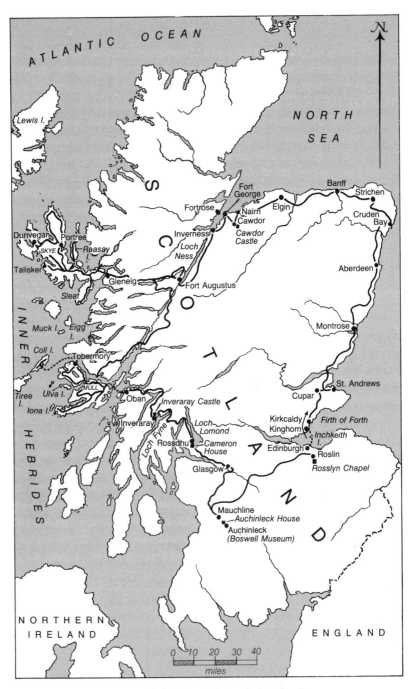

Map of the Tour Through Scotland

IN THE
FOOTSTEPS OF
JOHNSON
AND
BOSWELL

ISRAEL SHENKER

Boston
HOUGHTON MIFFLIN COMPANY
1982

Illustrated with maps
by John V. Morris

Copyright © 1982 by Israel Shenker

All rights reserved. No part of this work may be reproduced
or transmitted in any form or by any means, electronic or
mechanical, including photocopying and recording, or by
any information storage or retrieval system, except as
may be expressly permitted by the 1976 Copyright Act or in
writing from the publisher. Requests for permission should
be addressed in writing to Houghton Mifflin Company,
2 Park Street, Boston, Massachusetts 02108.

*Library of Congress Cataloging
in Publication Data*

Shenker, Israel.
In the footsteps of Johnson and Boswell.
Includes index.
1. Scotland — Description and travel —
1951–   . 2. Shenker, Israel. 3. Johnson,
Samuel, 1709–1784 — Journeys — Scotland.
4. Boswell, James, 1740–1795 — Journeys —
Scotland. I. Title.
DA867.S53   914.11′0473   81–7193
ISBN 0–395–31856–4   AACR2

Printed in the United States of America

V 10 9 8 7 6 5 4 3 2 1

I wanted to speak of courage and humor
and of strengths even less tangible,
but sometimes a book is too little
and a page is too much.
So now, simply:

For SUSIE and MOSHE ZIRKEL

PREFACE

I had desired to visit the Hebrides, or Western Islands of
Scotland, so long, that I scarcely remember how the wish was
originally excited; and was in the autumn of the year 1773
induced to undertake the journey, by finding in Mr. Boswell
a companion, whose acuteness would help my inquiry, and
whose gaiety of conversation and civility of manners are sufficient to counteract the inconveniences of travel, in countries
less hospitable than we have passed.
　　　　— Samuel Johnson,
　　　　A Journey to the Western Islands of Scotland

SETTING OUT through Scotland in the footsteps of Johnson
and Boswell, I did not expect to find a people shrouded in
ignorance, benighted and brutish, lacking curiosity, and bereft of confidence. Nor did I plan to draw grand conclusions
about the state of souls or the nature of achievements or the
intensity of loyalties. It was the entreaty of humble curiosity,
not a desire for scholarly discoveries, that led me on, and I
expected not hardship but pleasure. With my wife as enthusiastic ally, I would go to the places Johnson and Boswell
had been, see what they had seen, and seek out descendants
of the people they had visited. If they had spoken with the
local minister, so would I; if they had inquired into the
customs of the country, so would I. Their interests would be

mine — farming, education, religion, language, clans, emigration, the rigors of the land, the character of the race.

In the eighteenth century, travel in the Highlands and islands of Scotland was an arduous enterprise — primitive transport in an exotic area far from centers of culture and refinement. Roads were poor and scarce. With increased distance from Edinburgh, commercial lodgings were rare, and Johnson and Boswell had to depend on the hospitality of friends and strangers; while there were cases of comfort, there were also stretches barren of the arts of gentle life.

I wanted to follow the course as precisely as possible, but my plan was not to be willfully archaic. There was now a network of good roads and ferries, and, except in the busy months of summer, no shortage of hotels and inns and bed-and-breakfast accommodations and cottages to rent. So it was not going to be beds of straw; there were few of them around. It would not be travel by horse-drawn diligence — that would have been difficult to arrange; or on horseback — that would have made *me* the object of curiosity; or in small boats hauled about by straining oarsmen — hardly feasible, given the prevailing prejudice against cruel and unusual punishment. I was less interested in reproducing the hardships that Johnson and Boswell faced than in seeing the changes effected by two centuries: it was the present that intrigued me.

I scarcely remembered how my wish to undertake the journey was originally excited, but one stimulus was a desire to emancipate myself from voluntary servitude as a reporter for *The New York Times* and to cast adrift from that stately galley.

During the strike that closed down the newspaper in 1978, I was liberated from daily addiction to reading the contributions of my colleagues and from the much more onerous obligation of writing my own; it seemed an opportune moment to change course for good and to bob along in my own fragile craft. I considered the perils long enough to decide that when publication resumed, I would return in order to resign.

My admiration for Johnson played a role. I came late to his work, when the vagaries of newspaper reporting brought me to Yale University to prepare an article on what was known as the Boswell factory; academics there had been working for years to convert riches of Boswelliana and Johnsoniana into popular as well as scholarly publications. On reading Johnson's *Journey* as well as Boswell's *Journal of a Tour to the Hebrides with Samuel Johnson, LL.D.* and his *Life of Johnson,* I surrendered completely, uncritically, to the glory that was Johnson, to the majesty of his prose, the wealth of his imagery, the rigor of his wit, and the acuity of his intelligence. What a pleasure it would be to sail in his wake!

Since Boswell, in 1773, had written to tell friends that he and the great Dr. Johnson were about to venture into the wilds of Scotland, I sent word ahead that my wife and I were going to follow. Some correspondents heeded the warning and disappeared without trace; others generously replied with invitations to visit them. My next move seemed clear. With *The New York Times,* that zealous master, finally back at work, I waylaid the executive editor and told him I was resigning. After sobbing incontinently, he regained control of his emotions and gamely decided to keep the newspaper going without me.

Scorning half-measures, my wife and I sold our New York home and came to live in Britain. On arriving in Scotland, I called on John A. Smith, the retired deputy principal of Glasgow's Jordanhill College. My letter to him was like the others I had sent: my wife and I planned to follow the itinerary of Johnson and Boswell, to see what they had seen, and to see what they could not see — how things had changed since their day. The letter was three short paragraphs. His reply was three long pages — closely handwritten, detailed, and suggestive.

An antiquarian who seemed to know every other antiquarian in Scotland, he was a genial enthusiast of Scottish history and of the trials of his native Gaelic. With his address book at his side, and with volumes of history about us, he settled back to offer both encouragement and an introductory course in first principles. We would be visiting a part of the country where oral tradition was strong and accurate, he suggested, noting: "My grandparents, both sides, were illiterate, but full of history and literature. It's quite possible that you'll pick up things about Johnson and Boswell that will surprise you."

Mr. Smith recalled that Johnson and Boswell were favorite reading in the schools he had attended. "We were angered, of course, at Johnson's joke about the tragedy of losing his walking stick on Mull, because Mull is very thickly forested. Perhaps it wasn't then. I think Johnson dealt very soundly with Macpherson, perpetrator of the Ossian hoax, who passed off compositions of his own as translations into English of an ancient Gaelic poem that he somehow never managed to produce. Gaelic literature suffered a lot from fantasizers — fabricators — adding to legends to make them more coherent. It's not the falsifying of records; it's just touching things up a bit.

"The journey was a great feat for Johnson, for a man sixty-three years old. He and Boswell made a big impression here. Johnson was known as Doctor Mor — Gaelic for Big Doctor. I have a great admiration for him — he was a little like Churchill, I think. He didn't suffer fools gladly, but his heart was in the right place. I much prefer him as a person to Boswell. I don't like Boswell at all — a priggish, conceited man."

When I next saw Mr. Smith he had more names and addresses and advice to give me. After setting off, I heard from him time and again; once I even received a short letter, a mere two pages. There were always suggestions of people to call on: "I stayed overnight on Friday night with my cousin Mrs. Fraser in Kyle. She has been warned that you are in the neighborhood and may call. There is no obligation to call but do if you need help. Mina is her first name . . . If you do not have a car hire one from Duncan McGilp, Tobermory. This is the village that I was brought up in and lots of the older people remember me. Your two predecessors stayed here overnight on arrival from Coll. Mull is a lovely island, and you will enjoy it . . . I could go on and on but have mentioned Torloisk, Iona, Lochbuie previously, as well as Coll, of course."

In addition to John Smith, there are others to whom I am grateful for guidance or wisdom or tolerance, and often all three. Professor Frederick A. Pottle, foreman of the Boswell factory and author of the Topographical Supplement detailing the itinerary of Johnson and Boswell, merits the gratitude of all who follow the trail. Dr. Irma S. Lustig, Professor Pottle's collaborator, gave meticulous scholarly help. Richard B. McAdoo, my editor, joined the arts of diplomacy and patience to the skills of advice and criticism. My wife, Mary, was the peerless traveling partner, quick in sympathy, wise in counsel, firm in resolution, enduring cheerlessness and homelessness and brooding silences. She proved capable of the ultimate sacrifice by forgiving the moody and impetuous author of her trials — Dr. Johnson. I am indebted also to the indulgence of those, named in the account that follows, who, when importuned by a visiting castaway, stood their ground and never cried halt. Our experience of this kindness, and the other pleasures of our journey, encouraged us to abandon our plan to go south and live in England. Instead, having come to the end of Dr. Johnson's Hebridean jaunt, we did what he, with his attachment to England and his love of London, would have considered unthinkable, and settled in Scotland.

IN THE FOOTSTEPS OF
JOHNSON AND BOSWELL

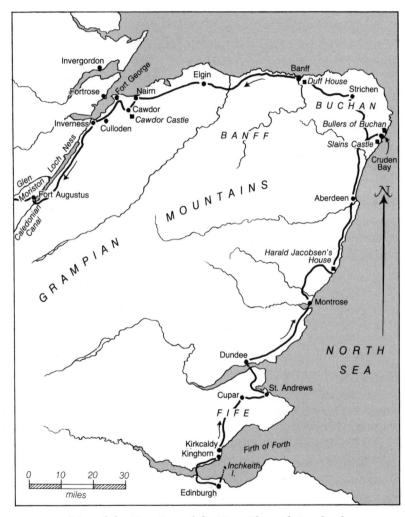

Map of the First Part of the Tour Through Scotland

CHAPTER 1

As there subsists no longer in the Islands much of that peculiar and discriminative form of life, of which the idea had
delighted our imagination, we were willing to listen to such
accounts of past times as would be given us. But we soon
found what memorials were to be expected from an illiterate
people, whose whole time is a series of distress; where every
morning is laboring with expedients for the evening; and
where all mental pains or pleasure arose from the dread of
winter, the expectation of spring, the caprices of their Chiefs,
and the motions of the neighboring clans; where there was
neither shame from ignorance, nor pride in knowledge; neither curiosity to inquire, nor vanity to communicate.
— Samuel Johnson

JOHNSON AND BOSWELL set off from Edinburgh on August
18, 1773, and they returned on November 9. It was not the
best season for a journey through Scotland, with the days
getting shorter and the weather growing worse. Since I did
not have to return, as Boswell did, for the resumption of
court sessions or, as I might have had to do in my earlier
incarnation, for the next day's newspaper, my wife and I
spent more time on the trip and traveled in all seasons.

We found that people often had strong opinions about
our predecessors. Johnson, notably, was too considerable a
force of nature to have his renown altogether silted over

by the flow of years. He was a great bear of a man who carried a vast baggage of learning and theory, a stern believer capable of intolerance as well as magnanimity, subject to bouts of repentant melancholy but also to intoxicating flights of conviviality. Forceful in speech, with a powerful talent for debate, he could pronounce solemn good sense or paradoxical better sense on either side of an argument. To oppose him demanded foolhardiness, or intelligence of the toughest fiber: he disputed not for the pleasure of the joust but for the joy of victory, not to wound but to annihilate. His conversation had the fluency and verve, the artistry and persuasiveness, of the most carefully deliberated writing, with a mastery born of quick intelligence apt for leaps of insight but also hospitable to chastening skepticism. Poised athwart a minimum of supporting evidence, he could spin a vast fabric of speculation or unravel a skein of theory with a single slashing riposte. Some of his conclusions about the Highlands and the Hebrides were more like axioms packed before he came to Scotland, as when he declared that these "primitive people," endowed with "a barbarous tongue," were capable only of thinking grossly, with no interest in the past. But he was also discriminating in judgment, as when he dismissed ancient vivacities of narrative, noting that "to count is a modern practice, the ancient method was to guess; and when numbers are guessed they are always magnified."

Avid for celebrity, Boswell collected friends whose luster would descend on him. He was companionable, witty, tactful, observant, and high-spirited — except when *he* was melancholy. In Johnson, Boswell found a noble spirit capable of exciting his admiration, worthy of service, a resplendent candidate for immortality. And so he devoted himself to memorials that would ensure the fame of them both, and he produced a life of Johnson that is commonly held to be the greatest biography written in English.

Boswell had suggested the trip to Scotland, for he wanted

to have Johnson all to himself, and he was eager to show his country to the great man who was known for raillery at the expense of the Scots. It was Johnson who said that "the noblest prospect that a Scotchman ever sees is the high road that leads him to London"; it was Johnson, in the dictionary whose composition confirmed his eminence, who defined oats as "a grain, which in England is generally given to horses, but in Scotland supports the people."

Introducing his *Journal*, Boswell noted that Dr. Johnson had for many years encouraged him with the hope that they would go together to the Hebrides, to see "simplicity and wildness, and all the circumstances of remote time or place, so near to our native great island." Boswell wrote that there would be "some inconveniences and hardships, and perhaps a little danger; but these we were persuaded were magnified in the imagination of every body. When I was at Ferney, in 1764, I mentioned our design to Voltaire. He looked at me, as if I had talked of going to the North Pole, and said, 'You do not insist on my accompanying you?'—'No, sir,'— 'Then I am very willing you should go.'"

Johnson did not get the idea of doing a book describing the trip until two weeks after the departure from Edinburgh, and he wrote it after returning to London. His *Journey to the Western Islands of Scotland* has the settled flavor of wisdom precipitated, conclusions pondered in tranquil recollection. Boswell's *Journal of a Tour to the Hebrides with Samuel Johnson, LL.D.* is livelier, chattier, several times as long as Johnson's account, and, though edited and amplified later, was written as the trip progressed, with the vividness of fresh reporting. Johnson's book was first published in 1775, Boswell's in 1785, the year after Johnson's death. Johnson was not intent on writing the life of Boswell; it was Boswell who was intent on writing the life of Johnson. As a result, Johnson dealt more single-mindedly with what they saw, and Boswell with what he heard.

Though nation and people inevitably had changed since 1773, I suspected that much had remained constant, land and climate still enforcing their rule. Was it not likely that characters formed in adversity showed as much? But now, bound to the outside world by ties of modern communication, Highlanders and islanders surely had lost their innocence about what lay beyond their borders, and perhaps had abandoned their resentment about what had occurred within those borders — military defeat, oppression by foreign power and native authority, indignities of contempt and poverty and unemployment.

Were Highlanders and islanders, even within Scotland, a breed apart? Would Johnson still see them as primitives? What would he make of the people? What had they made of themselves?

CHAPTER 2

To the southern inhabitants of Scotland, the state of the mountains and the islands is equally unknown with that of *Borneo* or *Sumatra*: Of both they have only heard a little, and guess the rest. They are strangers to the language and the manners, to the advantages and wants of the people, whose life they would model, and whose evils they would remedy.

— Samuel Johnson

JOHN MACINNES, specialist in Gaelic poetry and senior lecturer at Edinburgh University's School of Scottish Studies, had hardly admitted my wife and me to his study before he proudly revealed that the desk, acquired by his grandparents, was one Johnson and Boswell were supposed to have sat at. A morass of papers had acquired squatter's rights there, and fugitive pieces seemed to be floating weightlessly. Dr. Mac-Innes himself appeared to be hovering insubstantially in midair, lean and disheveled, with the look of the absent-minded professor whose thoughts rose above pedestrian concerns. In one heady exercise — actually, it went right above my head — he dilated on the transmutation of the letter p into f, or at least this seemed to be the issue. My eyes glazed, and I wondered how to lower this flight of erudition to my level. Meanwhile, I forced myself to take notes. When I consulted them afterward they resembled a patch of nettles, and I shied clear, frightened of becoming hopelessly impaled.

Eventually Dr. MacInnes moved from cloudy heights of alphabet to the very dawn of language. Recalling the time when Gaelic was triumphant vernacular instead of endangered relic, he said that people in Scotland once believed that Gaelic had been spoken all over Europe. Some even held that it was the language of the Garden of Eden, and Alexander Macdonald, a Gaelic poet, wrote about Gaelic coming from the lovely lips of Eve. "There's a dictionary of Gaelic where every word is glossed with a Hebrew word," Dr. MacInnes said. "I took a course in modern Hebrew with the local rabbi, and the sound system I found quite congenial."

Exhibiting extraordinary recall of Scotland's literary controversies for the past thousand years or so, Dr. MacInnes flung out the names of heroes and culprits with such abandon that I feared he was causing whole clans to crumble. From the springs of his agile memory tumbled a cascade of names — MacLeods and Macleans and Mackinnons and Macdonalds, surnames appended to first names that seemed indistinguishable from one another, locations that appeared to merge into one locus, universal and remote. Dr. MacInnes rushed on, speaking as though I had spent a lifetime clumping through the bogs of Hebridean controversy, and warning me to tread carefully. "Even in a subordinate clause you can give the impression of a hinterland of ignorance," he suggested with delicacy, and I wondered how he had pierced my disguise so quickly.

As I struggled to gain a footing I sank deeper, until I was firmly mired. "You're going to run into certain feuds — that's usually true with a small people or a broken people," he warned. "Lachlan Mackinnon, on Skye, is a Tory, and Sorley Maclean, the poet, is a left-wing socialist. You must get both sides of the coin, or, so to speak, all sides. You've heard the clearances described as the time when the land-lords could no longer afford their tenants, but that has been countered by those who say that the time had come when tenants could no longer afford the landlords. You will hear people say that Calvinists and Calvinist ministers were great destroyers — they supported the clearances. All Protestants in the seventeenth century were Calvinists. What they fought bitterly over was not theology but the structure of church government. The Church of Scotland in the High-lands was moderate, worldly, if not top crust then certainly upper class, like the English squarsons — squire-parsons. Against that came a very intense evangelical religion, a re-cluse religion, like the Amish in Pennsylvania. Leaders of the evangelical movement tended to be against the estab-lished Presbyterian Church and against the landlords and chiefs, holding that the Lord had given the land to the people. The peasantry justified themselves with the Bible.

"The impression that Johnson left with was of such extra-ordinary elegance; people who could talk, if not on his own level — after all, who could? — at least very well. He was convinced that the peasantry weren't like this. Johnson, being a Tory, saw the value of the upper class. If he returned to the Highlands and the islands, the biggest change he would see is the disappearance of this class that entertained him. Johnson and Boswell stayed at the homes of minor gentry, a class that — when they haven't gone — have become angli-cized and are no longer part of the community. John Mac-Leod of Dunvegan may be head of the MacLeod clan, but he is as anglicized as anyone from Sussex."

Dr. MacInnes suggested that we visit the veterinary sur-geon Donald John MacLennan on the isle of Skye; Alistair Nicolson on the isle of Raasay, for he had a burning interest in his country; and Mary Gillies and her father, George Gillies, since they had pointed views on the condition of Raasay. As the names poured forth, I began to despair of seeing the end of the trail, and I said as much. "Bash on!" he exclaimed.

I bashed right on to see the successor of William Robertson, the eminent eighteenth-century historian and principal of the college that became Edinburgh University. Dr. Robertson had welcomed Johnson and Boswell, and in showing them about the place had observed that strangers could easily mistake the buildings for almshouses. But the university now had more than ten thousand students and buildings that could be called handsome.

John McIntyre had arrived in his office at the Old Quad before his secretary, and he led me through her large outer office into his own cavernous inner chamber. Straining my eyes to see its outer limits, I dismissed the notion of suggesting that the university's basketball team could practice in one corner while the soccer team shared the rest of the room with those who fancied lacrosse.

Professor McIntyre told me that he was holding office until his successor, a professor of rural economy at Oxford University, finished the term there before moving north. At Scottish universities the principal is the counterpart of the vice-chancellor at English universities, and, as in England, the office of chancellor is honorary. Edinburgh's chancellor is the Duke of Edinburgh. Until about a century ago the principal was traditionally a minister, but now the principal can be from any discipline, even rural economy. As chance would have it, Dr. McIntyre was a minister in the Church of Scotland and a professor of divinity.

Edinburgh's theology faculty is the largest in Britain, with twenty-three full-time staff members, Professor McIntyre told me, and I told myself that since Scotland had a history of tormented, often acrid religious controversy, this did not appear at all excessive. Though Scots Presbyterians had a reputation for dourness, for seeing life sober and evil endemic, the professor of divinity seemed tolerant and good-natured. I asked him how religion had changed in Scotland since 1773.

Church membership had declined, he told me, and there was now greater openness than during the severe Calvinism of the eighteenth century. "If you find the parish records, they were almost prurient with regard to sin," Professor McIntyre said. "Almost all sin was sexual, and they just rooted it out hither and yon."

But then there was what Dr. MacInnes had warned me about — the other side of the coin. "The Calvinism of predestination — a person believed himself called — gives a man license, particularly with relation to sin and morality," Professor McIntyre said. "If he's going to be called, he can do what he pleases. We've moved a long way from that, in the church's sensitivity to political and social problems, and ecological awareness finds a strong support in religion." The Church of Scotland body dealing with the relation of religion to technology "has a file as thick as this," he noted with pride, holding thumb and forefinger of his right hand as far apart as they would go, to indicate the bulk of the dossier.

I asked Professor McIntyre what would be considered grievous sins nowadays, and he said that "things like racialism would be very high on the roll, and hypocrisy," adding, "What in young people is regarded as forms of irresponsibility can properly be called an intense form of sincerity."

From the principal's office I set off to consult Edinburgh sheriff J. L. Martin Mitchell, who was said to be highly knowledgeable about the itinerary of Johnson and Boswell. Following the itinerary that he had outlined for me to reach his office, I soon found myself in a stately courthouse. My impression was that the sheriff, moderately extended, was equally imposing. A shaggy colossus of a man, he strode with giant step, and, with eyes cast upward, seemed to draw his wisdom from some occult source in the heavens. He spoke peremptorily, never at a loss for words, as though he would brook no quibble, on or off the bench, and I silently thanked the fates who had preserved me from appearing as a prisoner in the dock.

Sheriff Mitchell had spent two vacations helping the Scottish National Library prepare an exhibit on Johnson and Boswell by visiting the places in Scotland where they had been. He laid before me a photograph album with small black-and-white photographs of the holy places. As he thumbed through the book, keeping pages open long enough to set his memory racing but hardly long enough for me to see more than a blur, he reeled off quick oral annotation: "Abbey of Fort Augustus . . . Johnson altered the inscription . . . Go through Broadford and take the next road to the left . . . Red rusty roof, a rubbish tip in the middle of it . . . roofless church . . . There's a sheep track that goes to the right . . . A low hill . . . Just two holes in the ground. Och, when I was a boy we would have a *ceilidh* [party] in there, but you can't go there now."

The last sentence was spoken with mock Highland accent. Resuming his Lowland Scots, the sheriff galloped on: "The tree he sat under at Talisker House . . . From Iona went to Lochbuie Castle. The proprietor of the house at Lochbuie is a ———." Coming from a man of the law, the expletive sounded shocking, and doubly so when proclaimed from the summit of Mount Mitchell, in tones stentorian and unequivocal. If reported, the word would land him or me or both of us in sheriff's court, defending a suit for slander or libel or both.

"He let us photograph when we yelled 'National Library!' at him," the sheriff continued. "Nice Georgian stables . . . Point two miles out from car speedometer reading — drive along road looking left."

By this time I was forty-two miles behind, but in the pause accompanying the turning of a page I caught up. Sheriff Mitchell acknowledged that he had followed the meticulous directions in the Topographical Supplement by Yale's Professor Frederick A. Pottle. Professor Pottle was the maximum authority on Boswell, and his Topographical Supplement accompanied the edition of Boswell's *Journal* that he had co-edited. But suddenly — it was almost more than I could credit — I heard Sheriff Mitchell say that in the case of "point two miles out," he had found what he was looking for by *not* following Professor Pottle's directions.

"You mean Pottle got it wrong?" I asked, my incredulity plain in each syllable.

"No," said Sheriff Mitchell, equally aghast at the very idea. "They altered the road after Pottle was there."

CHAPTER 3

On the eighteenth of August we left Edinburgh, a city too
well known to admit description, and directed our course
northward, along the eastern coast of Scotland, accompanied
the first day by another gentleman, who could stay with us
only long enough to show us how much we lost at separation.

— Samuel Johnson

CONVINCED, as was Johnson — this was the second paragraph of his *Journey* — that Edinburgh was sufficiently
known to make description superfluous, we prepared to head
northward. Between Edinburgh and the north lay the broad
mouth of the River Forth. When David Hume, the eighteenth-century philosopher, contemplated what he called
"that great gulf," he was overcome with "horror and a kind
of hydrophobia," and he could not bring himself even to
venture across for a visit to his eminent friend Adam Smith.

In crossing the Forth, it was not terror that assailed Johnson, but curiosity. Seeing the island of Inch Keith — Inchkeith today — lying ahead, he suggested landing there. The
travelers struggled onto the shore and, as Johnson wrote,
"made the first experiment of unfrequented coasts." He concluded that "Inch Keith is nothing more than a rock covered
with a thin layer of earth, not wholly bare of grass, and

very fertile of thistles." Boswell wrote that there were sixteen head of black cattle and one ruined fort. "Dr. Johnson examined it with much attention. He stalked like a giant among the luxuriant thistles and nettles."

Johnson reflected on how different would have been the attitude to this island had it been near London. People would have bid against one another for the privilege of purchasing it, and then would have lavished money and industry to cultivate and adorn it. "I'd have this island," he mused. "I'd build a house, make a good landing-place, have a garden and vines and all sorts of trees. A rich man of a hospitable turn here would have many visitors from Edinburgh."

In Edinburgh I called the office of the Northern Lighthouse Board, which now exercised hegemony over the island, to see if the board was of a hospitable turn. The commissioners of Northern Lighthouses went back to 1786, and their motto was an optimistic *In Salutem Omnium*. I explained that I wanted to visit Inchkeith, since Johnson and Boswell had stopped there when they left Edinburgh, and I was following in their footsteps. With a rich Scottish accent, the woman on the phone relayed my message to her colleague or colleagues, adding, obviously not for my benefit, that somebody wanted to follow in the footsteps of Johnson and Boswell, "whoever they were."

The next day I received a letter of authorization to visit Inchkeith lighthouse, "provided that you do not land after the navigation light is in operation, or when the landing is in use for lighthouse business . . . You will, of course," the letter added, "appreciate that the visit is entirely at your own risk and that the Commissioners cannot accept responsibility for any injury or accident which may befall you during the visit."

Meanwhile, I had been preparing the way with Douglas Shepherd, chief boatman of the Royal Forth Yacht Club, who said that he would be glad to run me across to Inch-keith — once his boat was repaired. He was waiting for a gasket. On successive days I called back to ask if the gasket had arrived, and finally he said that the boat was ready. Consulting the times of the tides, he suggested that I come to the middle pier at Granton, on the Firth of Forth, at 1:00 P.M. the next day and look for him in a boatshed at the right of the pier.

The shed was deserted when I arrived, but from a smaller building blared a transistor radio tuned to Radio Forth, a commercial station specializing in popular music and humor that lost something in transistoration. Within point-blank range of the sound bombardment, sitting rapt as though worshiping the great god Cacophony, were two young men who, when we noticed one another, introduced themselves as assistant boatman and part-time assistant boatman. The assistant boatman, who knew that I was expected, raised his voice to make himself heard and gave me a quick preview of Inchkeith: "There's a lot of wee hoosies and tunnels, and lots of seals. Thousands of seals.

"Hundreds of seals," he said, after a moment's reflection, tempering his exuberance as he realized that I would be seeing and counting for myself.

When Mr. Shepherd arrived, he and I went aboard the *Poseidon*, a 19.5-foot motor cruiser, and as he took the wheel, he put on a yachting cap, somewhat sheepishly, I thought. "It's a fine boat," he said, "but like everything else — we've just started the season — everything went wrong with her." He ducked into the cabin and returned with a maritime chart, which he spread out for me. "You've got to be careful here," he said, indicating our course. "There's rocks, and if we're lucky we're going to see some seals."

We passed through the gap between breakwaters, and instead of steering between the black buoy at starboard and the yellow buoy at port, the prescribed channel for vessels to and from Edinburgh, Mr. Shepherd headed directly for Inchkeith, more than four nautical miles away; he kept an eye on the depth indicator to make sure that we avoided submerged rocks. While the boat made slow headway, Mr. Shepherd told me that he had served twenty-seven years in West Africa as shipping agent for a British line, and had seen service in Ghana, Gambia, Sierra Leone, and Nigeria. "I had a more elevated post than this," he said. "Arthur's Seat and Salisbury Crags," he interrupted himself, pointing back to landmarks in Edinburgh.

The sun glinted on the lighthouse, tiny in the distance, and the island, about a mile long and a quarter of a mile wide, resembled the hump of the Loch Ness monster. Mr. Shepherd looked about him with contentment. "You'd go an awful way in the world to get scenery like this," he said. "That's my opinion." I asked him why the lighthouse was not automated. "I should presume," he began, and then stopped. "To tell you the truth," he said, "I don't know. It's an anachronism, I should imagine."

We tied up at the high, concrete pier and climbed the rusty iron ladder onto the shore of Inchkeith. Two signs warned visitors to stay off the island, and set into the rock face was a huge plaque: "In remembrance of Sidney First Lord Herbert of Lea. Born 1810, died 1861. Twice Secretary of State for War who was the first member of government to perceive the necessity of protecting the shores of the Firth of Forth from the inroads of hostile cruisers . . . He was the steadfast supporter of Florence Nightingale and the friend of the soldiers of the British Army."

As we walked along a path leading to the lighthouse looming above, gulls by the hundreds wheeled and cried overhead, and the occasional bird swooped low in mock attack. "Gulls seem to have taken over the place," Mr.

Shepherd said. "Sometimes there's a cull and everybody shrieks and yells about it. But the gulls have destroyed all the exotic birds, such as the puffins."

Seeing a stairway that seemed a short cut to the lighthouse, we climbed the steps, seventy-eight of them, rough-hewn, and Mr. Shepherd appeared to make heavy weather of it. He explained that he tried to keep fit but drank too much beer. "Not an unreasonable amount," he added quickly.

At the top of the stairs we trudged along a winding path, and suddenly we spied, moving toward us with the rolling gait of a sailor, a man in sunglasses, wearing faded jeans and a navy pea jacket. His face was grizzled, and perched jauntily on his head was a straw hat, rainbow hatband festooned with cloth cutouts — a tiger much like the Exxon tiger, and a lion less awesome than the British lion. "I wondered why you were coming this way instead of the direct way," he said, and when we looked toward the short cut *he* was indicating, we blushed at our mistake. Then, with the accomplished fluency of the veteran guide, he launched into an unsolicited account of the island's history, beginning in the second century, when, he said, this was part of the kingdom of Bernicia. "That was King Ossian, and the island was called Alana," the lighthouse keeper said, and told us that *he* was called James Combe and that he was sixty-three years old. Oddly enough, he said nothing about events during the reign of James IV. In 1497 Edinburgh was stricken by the plague, and many of the victims were transported to the Inch, there, as it was said, "to remain till God provide for their health." When the island was plague-free, the king had a dumb woman and two infants put there as sole inhabitants, in a celebrated experiment to learn what language the children would speak, for this obviously would be man's primordial tongue. It turned out, of course, that they grew up speaking good Hebrew.

When we came to the ruins of a modest building, Mr.

Combe said, "This was a stronghold, and there must have been a portcullis here. I can see it in my mind's eye — a small stronghold." Closer to the lighthouse were the substantial remains of a fort built just before the First World War. Inchkeith had once been a source of water for passing ships. "It's got a sort of brackish taste," Mr. Combe observed, "but they say it's good for you." He drew our attention to a small neighboring island and said it was known as "the Iron Craig" because it was the scene of so many shipwrecks; a ship had come to grief there the previous winter.

Mr. Combe and two colleagues stayed on Inchkeith a month at a time and were then relieved by three other keepers. When the Forth was too rough for boats, the keepers flew to the island; the large **H** of a helicopter pad was painted just next to the lighthouse. There was a gateway nearby, with a brightly ornate coat of arms and the date 1564. Mr. Combe said that arms and date commemorated the visit of Mary of Guise, mother of Mary Queen of Scots, who, contemplating the bodies stacked there after a battle, is supposed to have observed "I never saw such a lovely sight." "But I don't believe that," Mr. Combe said.

He told us that he spent a good deal of time reconstructing events of the past and imagining difficulties encountered by previous residents. Mr. Combe pointed to a steep gradient — one in two, he estimated — and said that it was too difficult for horses to climb and that it must have been men who dragged heavy loads up the slope. There were cottages in ruins and long, desolate structures that had served as barracks during the Second World War. At the northern tip of the island stood a solitary ruined house. "I thought there were about three thousand soldiers here during the Second War," Mr. Combe said, "but I met a chap who told me he lived in that promontory at the edge and that there were only two thousand, and I think he's right. He's now selling that double-glazing."

Inside the lighthouse we began climbing the spiral stairs. Mr. Combe opened a cupboard at one landing and showed us that there were many old books there. "Quite a lot of them are Bibles," he said. We looked into several empty rooms and from a window peered out toward Kirkcaldy, across the Forth from Edinburgh. "I sat here and was doing a crayon drawing," Mr. Combe said. "I was going to paint it afterwards. But every half-hour the whole thing changes. Do you see that big gray building? Come back in half an hour and it's disappeared, and there's nothing but those woods. Come back a half an hour after that and the woods have disappeared."

At the top of the stairs was a metal catwalk circling the light, and Mr. Shepherd and I exclaimed over the gleaming equipment and over the craftsmanship that had fashioned the gears and bearings. Mr. Combe explained that a weight slowly descended, turning the gears that caused the lenses to revolve; a mixture of paraffin and air produced a white light that flashed every thirty seconds. "Every hour and twenty minutes you have to come up and wind it up again," he said. "It's not so difficult if you're young, but it's a bit hard for me. It takes about a minute to wind up. Half a gallon of paraffin will keep the light running for a whole night."

From a drawer he took an old ledger, marked *Album,* that served as a visitors' book. The first signature — April 22, 1901 — was that of the secretary of the Northern Lighthouse Board, and there were pages and years to go before another ledger would be required. I added my name and refrained from noting that I had seen no seals and that the island could use a few cows.

When we left the lighthouse I asked Mr. Combe what he had done before serving on Inchkeith, and he said that he had been in a parachute regiment and then had driven cars for a rental agency. Summoning my courage, I asked if it would not make sense to automate the light and the foghorn. He took no offense. There were plans to automate, he said, and everything was ready for the changeover. "I think they're just a bit lackadaisical," he declared. "I think they're wondering what to do with the men. But this thing's aching for automation. The only trouble is vandalism. On another island someone smashed up the lenses. Then they tried to bring this big glass from France — you can hit it with a hammer and it bounces off."

In the nineteenth century, when Thomas Carlyle visited Inchkeith, he described the lighthouse keeper as "by far the most life-weary looking mortal I ever saw," with every feature of face and voice suggesting "Behold the victim of unspeakable ennui."

I asked Mr. Combe if *he* enjoyed his work. "Some days, when you get a good day, it's like being on the Riviera," he said. "Only you wish you could get off it."

He was to get his wish — with a vengeance. The Northern Lighthouse Board decided that it was indeed time for a change and put the island in the hands of a real estate agent, offering it for sale. Now if only there were a rich man of a hospitable turn . . .

CHAPTER 4

When we landed, we found our chaise ready, and passed
through Kinghorn, Kirkcaldy, and Cowpar, places not unlike
the small or straggling market-towns in those parts of England where commerce and manufactures have not yet produced opulence.
— Samuel Johnson

FERRIES no longer plied the Firth of Forth, so after returning to Edinburgh and crossing the Forth via road bridge, we
drove along the north shore eastward toward Kinghorn;
since chaises were rare on the ground, we had acquired a
1.3-liter Ford Escort. The road that Johnson and Boswell
must have followed had become a hard-surface, two-lane
highway. At the entrance to Kirkcaldy, which now had
about fifty thousand inhabitants and apartment houses fifteen
stories high, taller than any building Johnson and Boswell
saw in Scotland, the town sign did not mention the two
illustrious eighteenth-century travelers, but it did identify
the royal burgh of Kirkcaldy as "the Birthplace of Adam
Smith." From a parking lot just inside the royal burgh a blue
truck pulled out, on its sides the words TUDOR CRISPS and the
likeness of King Henry VIII.

In Cupar — Johnson's Cowpar — we inquired at a bakery

for a pleasant tearoom and were directed to the Copper Kettle. Johnson and Boswell stopped in Cupar to drink tea and talk of Parliament, and from the three women at the next table we heard talk of church but not of state. One woman said to the others: "The last time the church had a sale I gave some clothes away. I've regretted it ever since." "When I go out I change everything down to my hose," her partner across the table said, and the third woman rejoined, "I get dressed in the morning, and that's me."

We drove out of town in the wrong direction, and finally asked advice of a man helping schoolchildren across the road. He suggested a U-turn, and then I heard him say, distinctly I thought, to turn left at the lollipop lady. At the first sizable intersection stood the statue of a unicorn perched atop a slim pedestal, and I decided against its being the lollipop in question. The next statue was an angelic figure complete with wings, and since she seemed susceptible of being described as lollipoppish I turned left. Only later did I learn that "lollipop lady" or "lollipop man" was colloquial for the traffic attendant at a school crossing who hoisted a stop-and-go sign resembling a giant lollipop.

Ahead lay the town of St. Andrews, and it seemed to be slumbering in the warmth of late afternoon. Behind it dazzled hundreds of tiny white dots that later appeared in the splendor of reality as two trailer camps.

My first visit the next morning was to Robert N. Smart, the university archivist, at the library of the University of St. Andrews. Set into a vast campus quadrangle, the library was strikingly modern, light stone and clean lines, a twentieth-century implant surrounded by dark structures of past centuries and former styles. Inside the library, all was brightness and clarity. The walls of Mr. Smart's office were glass; even the door was glass. It was hardly the sort of place that one associated with archivists at stately old academies.

Mr. Smart said there had been controversy over the design of the new library: "The local preservation trust made such a fuss that the university modified the plans, to ensure that the library would not be visible from the street. The architect of this library wanted a building constructed on engineering principles — a collection of girders with walls built into them, with partitions placed here and there. No doubt the old place had great inconveniences; in the end, it was a string of buildings, difficult to manage. But they spoke of extending the old premises, and I would have preferred the old place."

Johnson had written that

from the bank of the Tweed to St. Andrews I had never seen a single tree, which I did not believe to have grown up far within the past century . . . There is no tree for either shelter or timber. The oak and the thorn is equally a stranger, and the whole country is extended in uniform nakedness, except that in the road between *Kirkcaldy* and *Cowpar,* I passed for a few yards between two hedges. A tree might be a show in Scotland as a horse in Venice. At St. Andrews Mr. Boswell found only one, and recommended it to my notice; I told him that it was rough and low, or looked as if I thought so.

"Dr. Johnson was a very funny character," Mr. Smart observed. "It's no surprise that he characterized this as a treeless landscape, since he went through the county of Fife at ten o'clock at night. We have a holm oak or ilex in Saint Mary's quadrangle. Saint Mary's thorn must also have been there. The oak fills practically the entire quadrangle."

When Johnson visited St. Andrews, the university was struggling for survival; one of the three colleges had been dissolved, and students were few. Johnson wrote: "Had the University been destroyed two centuries ago, we should not have regretted it; but to see it pining in decay and struggling for life, fills the mind with mournful images and ineffectual wishes."

"There's no doubt that Saint Andrews wasn't what it had been, but I don't think it was quite so badly off," Mr. Smart said. "Johnson is a source for the state of the town, but there are other descriptions that could have been quoted and that differed quite radically. Johnson was just a curiosity here, and Saint Andrews has been visited by curiosities since time immemorial. The great Italian physician Cardan visited here in the sixteenth century, and he was impressed. Cardan actually cured the archbishop's chest complaint — he hung him up by the heels. Now, it's curious that this treatment is still carried out. An eminent surgeon from Liverpool assured me that it is."

Mr. Smart was not an archivist for nothing. He turned quickly to a biographical dictionary and read aloud the entry for Jerome Cardan (1501–1576), who wrote over a hundred treatises on a range of subjects beginning with medicine and ending with theology, just as life did.

When I asked Mr. Smart to characterize the present state of the university, he complained that this was an awesome task. "I suppose it's still a relatively small university — three thousand five hundred students," he ventured. "It's not in the smallest league, but it's still a small university. It probably comes close to the idea of an ideal university, of a closely knit circle of intellectuals, of a community of scholars. Yes, I think you could reasonably say that it was flourishing, within the constraints of not being in a large populated center or a large industrial center, which would allow the expansion of certain branches of the university."

If the town of St. Andrews was now a flourishing community, it was perhaps more through golf — the Old Course was the world's oldest golf links — than through the university. Indeed, golfers had boasted that what scholars had not been able to achieve by industry, *they* had managed to accomplish by idleness.

Mr. Smart said there were no plaques in St. Andrews commemorating the visit of Johnson and Boswell, but there was a memorial by Robert Fergusson, a precursor of Robert Burns, who took a jaundiced view. Within two minutes Mr. Smart located a copy of *The Poems of Robert Fergusson*, printed in Philadelphia in 1815. The commemorative poem took principal and professors of the university to task for obsequious attentions to Johnson, and another poem, satirizing Johnson's penchant for lexical sesquipedalianism, began:

> Great *pedagogue*, whose literarian lore,
> With *syllable* and *syllable* conjoin'd,
> To transmutate and varify, has learn'd
> The whole revolving scientific names
> That in the alphabetic columns lie,
> Far from the knowledge of mortal shapes;
> As we, who never can peroculate
> The miracles by thee miraculiz'd,
> The Muse silential long, with mouth apert,
> Would give vibration to stagnatic tongue,
> And loud encomiate thy puissant name,
> Eulogiated from the green decline
> Of Thames's banks to Scoticanian shores,
> Where *Loch-lomondian* liquids undulize.

It was a short undulation from the library to the castle, and there I went directly to the bottle dungeon, down seven stone steps, through a portal about eighteen inches wide, into a cryptlike room. In the center was a thick, low, circular wall about five feet in diameter, much like the portion of a well visible above ground. An electric light set into the ceiling illuminated the dungeon floor, about twenty feet below. Prisoners used to be interned there, hauled up like buckets of water when their final hour came, and then executed with a great show of barbarity, to the delectation of Cardinal David Beaton, a prelate of surpassing worldliness and severity. Installed as Archbishop of St. Andrews in 1539, he gave church lands liberally to his mistress, mother of seven of his children, and presented churches to two of his many sons. It was Cardinal Beaton, first Scottish cleric to become a Roman cardinal, who picked suitable wives for the King of Scotland, and who opposed England's Henry VIII to such effect that Henry's army put Edinburgh to the torch.

The cardinal's way with heretics was no less terrible and swift. When George Wishart, later known as the martyr, stirred dissent with eloquent preaching of doctrines subversive of the church, the cardinal had him seized, and looked on approvingly as Wishart was burned at the stake. Three months later a group of Beaton's enemies invaded the castle, murdered the cardinal, and hung his body from a castle window by an arm and a leg. Those who had taken the castle were joined by others, including John Knox, who had imbibed his Protestantism from Wishart. After a siege of many months, the French sent a fleet to take the castle, and the small band of holdouts surrendered on condition that they be spared and taken to France. Those of superior birth were imprisoned there. Being of inferior condition, Knox, who was to become the principal instrument for the spread of Protestantism in Scotland, served two years as a galley slave.

As it now stood, well lit, carefully maintained, with never a prisoner inside, the bottle dungeon had lost most of its power to oppress the mind or to rouse the sympathy of the onlooker. Nearby, along a portion of the ruins next to the sea, waves crashed against the foundations of the castle, eroding the very fabric of the structure. It was easy to see why the castle was now only a dispersion of fragments and why there should be destruction even without the complicity of man.

But man had done his part; in the seventeenth century, for example, stones from the castle were used to repair the harbor.

It was more difficult at first to see why the cathedral, which Johnson described as "poor remains," should have fallen into so dilapidated a state that, except for isolated gable and tower and odd, miscellaneous portions, little survived of what had once been the premier house of worship of Scotland's archiepiscopal and metropolitan see. In fact, the cathedral was more or less as Johnson saw it, except for some nineteenth-century repairs financed by Lord Bute. So that His Lordship's contributions should be distinguished from the somber gray of the original, they were built in red sandstone and were distinctive enough to constitute an offense to architecture, if not to religion.

According to legend, the cathedral owed its existence to a Greek monk who had a vision in which an angel instructed him to take relics of St. Andrew and travel west to the end of the world. The monk, whose name was Regulus, or Rule, took with him bones of St. Andrew's arm and fingers, and he was shipwrecked roughly where the tower of St. Rule now stood, in the center of the cathedral grounds. But there was no trace of the saint's relics, though their purported presence once endowed the town with a reputation for miracle cures. After fire, storm, Reformation zealotry leading to the willful destruction of books and images and altars, and outright theft, the citizens of St. Andrews had treated the cathedral with the ultimate form of contempt — outright neglect. Eventually, what remained was entrusted to the nation, and the government had made the place about as tidy as ruins could be.

There was greater consolation to be drawn from the state of St. Leonard's Chapel. In the eighteenth century, when St. Leonard's College was swallowed up by the two other colleges, St. Salvator's and St. Mary's, the chapel of St. Leonard's was excluded from the takeover, "in case it shall ever be repaired and again used as a church." Johnson complained that whenever he tried to visit the chapel of what he called "the alienated college," he was, "by some civil excuse, hindered from entering it." He was subsequently told that an attempt to convert it into a greenhouse had failed. "To what use it will next be put I have no pleasure in conjecturing," he wrote. "It is something that its present state is at least not ostentatiously displayed. Where there is yet shame, there may in time be virtue."

The reward of that virtue was a handsome chapel, restored and reopened. Neatly set at each place were the *Scottish Psalter and Church Hymnary* and *The Office of Compline,* which opened with lines for the minister: "May the Lord Almighty grant us a quiet night and a perfect end." Apparently interrupted in her devotions, the chapel's cleaning woman had left behind, at the foot of a pulpit, one pair of rubber gloves, two dusters, and a can of polish — appropriately enough, Johnson's polish.

Just as the chapel had been restored, so now had St. Leonard's College itself been revived, as a center for graduate students. I asked its provost, Ian Kidd, if Johnson's impression of St. Andrews — an institution in decline — would be different today. "Oh, very different," he said. "The reverse process is taking place. This is a new college that is growing in strength."

Since the provost was also professor of Greek, I inquired about the vitality of his own discipline. "I think we're going through a transitional stage," he replied. "There was a period, beginning in the nineteenth century, when the classics were the most important study in school. They were the base of British humanistical education. Things have changed since the war, with the reorganization of education in the state schools, forcing minority subjects, if you like, onto the sidelines. Latin and Greek, particularly Greek, have suffered considerably because of this. Greek is being taught less than it was, and in some schools has disappeared altogether. But we're finding more and more boys and girls coming up to university and saying they want to start Greek and Latin."

When I asked if it made sense to continue studying Greek, he took my provocation in good spirits, replying: "In Johnson's day, Greek was recognized as part of an education, in England and in Europe generally. You will find Greek books that were part of the furniture of an educated man's library. I'd say that the continued study of Greek is one of the keystones of Western civilization. But if it were only that, it would be an historical study of historical interest. The Greeks were a people of quite extraordinary intellectual and esthetic ability. To study them now is to study human potential. Their masterpieces are as great today as they were then. Asking whether it makes sense to study Greek is like asking whether one should study Shakespeare or admire Velásquez or cherish Mozart. The time element is irrelevant. It's the content that matters."

From Professor Kidd's office I went to see Robert M. Ogilvie, the university's professor of humanity. At St. Andrews, "humanity" meant Latin, and Mr. Smart had told me that the professor of humanity was interested in Johnson's use of Latin. Professor Ogilvie's office was lined on two sides with bookshelves, a wealth of Greek and Roman authors in the original languages — the likes of Aristotle, Plato, Euripides, Thucydides, Livy, Caesar, Lucretius — and a leaven of modern works, including *Martin Chuzzlewit* by Dickens and *H. M. Ulysses* by Alistair Maclean. Perhaps it was the title of Maclean's book that appealed to the classicist in Professor Ogilvie.

"Johnson's acquaintance with the classics was very, very

considerable indeed," he suggested. "He knew Horace, Virgil, and Ovid backwards, and these date from his schooldays in Lichfield, when he would have had the ordinary grammar education. All English schoolboys until recently were expected to write Latin verse in imitation of classical verse. It was the education I had. From the age of eight I used to write two twelve-line poems a week. The phrases trip off your pen, and you can put the phrase in classical form. So when Johnson came to write he found it necessary to go to Latin to express emotion — his poem on going blind, and his ode to Skye."

With accents of indignation, Professor Ogilvie suggested that because of the doctrinaire views of certain political leaders and the nefarious decisions of the Schools Council and similar bodies there was great pressure to regard classics as irrelevant and to squeeze them out of state schools. "It seems to me that classics are no more and no less relevant than the study of the eighteenth century," he said. "They are of themselves of interest. They teach you a lot about how people at different stages have thought and expressed themselves, and this helps one articulate one's own idea of oneself and the world. Fundamentally, I think the justification is that it's fun. You get a kick out of it — the sheer fun, or the fun of saying, 'Yes, that's what I thought, and he said it so much better.'"

When I asked Professor Ogilvie if there was a chance these days for a Johnson to turn up at St. Andrews, he replied: "I think it's very difficult because of the enormous increase in literature as a whole and the emergence of the scientific revolution. I don't think it's feasible, even if you're a Chomsky, to be more than an amateur in a great number of fields. The one who would come closest would probably be Isaiah Berlin. The world was that much smaller in Johnson's day. There was France, yes, and Italy to a very limited extent, and Germany hardly at all except for places like Brunswick.

"Johnson would see great differences here. Whether he'd like the changes, I don't know. I'm not sure he'd like the way the undergraduates dress, and I don't know what he would feel about student involvement in university government. I'm not sure how he'd feel about some of the things being taught. I'd love to know his views on sociology."

CHAPTER 5

If a man is to wait till he weaves anecdotes into a system,
we may be long in getting them, and get but few in comparison of what we might get.
 — Samuel Johnson,
  in *The Journal of a Tour to the Hebrides*
  with Samuel Johnson, L.L.D. by James Boswell

SINCE JOHNSON AND BOSWELL called on local gentry,
I thought it appropriate to visit Harald Jacobsen, a retired
industrialist who had settled on a farm between Montrose
and Aberdeen. Johnson was interested in the reading habits
of his hosts, and I had heard that Mr. Jacobsen had a substantial collection of first editions.

It was not difficult to find his farm, but quite easy to miss
him. Bent over in the garden, he was planting a row of sweet
peas that — as he said at once — he had promised himself
he would have in the ground before we arrived. He straight-
ened up, welcomed us, and from that moment until we left
he was all energy and motion, never walking like a seventy-
year-old subdued by age, but always bounding from place
to place as though there were no time to let a foot settle,
meanwhile talking virtually nonstop, his white goatee bob-
bing, his words erupting with an exuberance he made no

effort to conceal. After introducing us to his wife, he turned rapidly left and right, uncertain what to show first, then grabbed me by the sleeve and hurried me down the hall into his library — floor to ceiling of works venerable and rare, ponderous volumes that seemed to promise solemn intelligence. Once in the library he was as troubled as ever, since he had to decide which books to single out. Dismissing all thought of a peaceful approach, he attacked, seizing book after book at random, launching into an account of what it was and how he had acquired it, then dropping it — gently — and bubbling into a saga, quickly truncated, about the next. *The Old Country Houses of the Old Glasgow Gentry* was one of the first books he extricated from the tightly packed shelves. Next, he pulled down works by John Knox and by Sir Walter Raleigh, then an old volume describing a trip to Russia, with engravings that unfolded to a length of four feet, and following that a 1688 edition of *Paradise Lost.* "I wanted that Milton," he said, "and the dealers all stood down and let me get it. It was the desire for knowledge that led me to buy books. But I was never humble. I never let myself be humble." Another book had a double set of engravings so that the bibliophile could withdraw one of each pair for framing. Mr. Jacobsen said that in his spare time, when he had any, he framed pictures. There were two copies of a journal published by Queen Victoria, and he told me that on the grounds of one of his former homes, in Aberfoyle, was the big oak that she had sat under. In *More Leaves from the Journal of a Life in the Highlands,* I read the queen's account:

> We went on perhaps a quarter of a mile, and, it being then two o'clock, we got out and lunched on the grass under an oak at the foot of *Craig More.* It was very hot, the sun stinging, but there were many light white clouds in the blue sky, which gave the most beautiful effects of light and shade on this marvellous colouring. After luncheon and walking

about a little, not finding any good view to sketch, we got into the carriage (our horses had been changed), but had not gone above a few yards when we came upon *Loch Ard*, and a lovelier picture could not be seen. *Ben Lomond*, blue and yellow, rose above the lower hills, which were pink and purple with heather, and an isthmus of green trees in front dividing it from the rest of the loch. We got out and sketched. Only here and there, far between, were some poor little cottages with picturesque barefooted lasses and children to be seen. All speak Gaelic here.

The queen had come to open the Glasgow waterworks, which Mr. Jacobsen called — and his voice swelled as he announced it — "the biggest engineering project in the world!" "In the world!" he repeated, as though daring me to express doubts, and his goatee shook with the fervor of the moment. When Queen Elizabeth II was crowned, the Jacobsens wrapped red, white, and blue bunting around Victoria's oak, and they festooned the tree each time their sons came home from boarding school.

Mr. Jacobsen was so eager to recount the story of his life that the orderly flow of narrative, from early to late, was inadequate to the torrent. He therefore opted for the anarchy of simultaneity, anecdotes pouring out in headlong disorder. After tossing about in a whirlpool of introductions, he took hold of himself and began: "My mother was a superior person, although she was near penury." As he spoke the word "superior" he mimicked an upper-class accent.

"She was a proper snob. When my father drank himself to death at forty-five, he had two racehorses. We were in absolute penury, and the day before he died he was at the races in Ayr and won forty-five pounds and left it with a former Celtic [soccer] player who had a pub, so he'd have the money to drink. By this time my mother in fact was doing millinery in order to earn money. Someone said to my mother, 'If you would feed them better, instead of just getting them dressed up!' She would see that I was dressed with a soft hat, spats, and a gamp, and she always thought I ought to have a coat with an astrakhan collar, but that was reserved for my Jewish friends. Eventually, all my suits were made in Savile Row. This lad who was here the other day gets his suits at the same tailor, and tells me they cost three hundred and twenty pounds now. Three hundred and twenty pounds! I was known as the last of the big spenders — I would buy two or three suits a year. Now we get about thirty-eight pounds a week social security. My mother wouldn't have taken social security. When she was dying, the doctor asked her how old she was. 'Don't tell him,' she said. There she was — 'Nearer My God to Thee' — and she wouldn't tell her age.

"I went to apply for this job when I saw an ad in the *Glasgow Herald* — 'Youth for Design Office.' I thought it would be art they wanted, but it was engineering drawings. It was the Kelvin Construction Company. The man who interviewed me asked if I was related to Thelma Jacobsen, and I said that was my sister. Well, Thelma had been his typist. 'If you're as good as your sister, you'll do,' he said. 'Take off your coat and start.'

"I used to work two nights a week late for one-and-eight tea money. We spent about a bob of that on cakes, and I worked with another draftsman on Friday nights. We would start work at nine on Friday morning and work till the regular closing time, at five in the afternoon. Then we'd go on working till noon on Saturday. They said it was too costly for overtime. I got three-and-six for that. We had to take our sandwiches with us, never leave for a minute — and white light and the paper was terrible."

Miming the act of shielding his eyes from the glare, he interrupted his account to observe "I've had a very, very cruel life," then gleefully added, "I've had a great life, with impertinence."

On free nights he went to technical school and took every course — mathematics, engineering, design, architecture — qualifying in none but becoming expert in all. "I was always buying technical books, and I used to buy books off the barrows in Glasgow. The first year I was courting Ina, I used to have three-and-six to spend and I took her to a picture house in Glasgow and I bought her a rose for a bob and she would wait for me at the corner and I was always late because I was always stopping to buy books at the barrows. On my thirtieth birthday I was on the Kelvin board. I had a salary of a thousand a year and another thousand as a bonus. In those days you didn't get on the board unless you were two feet in the ground. When I was thirty-six I was managing director, and I was in the business fifty-one years. Eventually I bought the business, and then I sold it to Hawker Siddeley and I stayed on as the big boss. The chairman of Hawker Siddeley wrote me a letter, saying, 'You'll get two thousand five hundred pounds a year. We'll pay in a thousand for pension scheme and we'll run your salary up a thousand pounds a year. You'll spend time in London and you'll stay in the Savoy. I'll recommend you to be a member of Ciro's Club, and I suggest you get a Bentley.' So I ran a Bentley after that. I was a bit dominant in my ways. But I still touch the forelock when necessary." Suiting act to word, he touched his forelock to ward off evil.

"I bought this place eleven years ago. I've only been retired for five years. We looked at umpteen farms all over the place. I put up buildings here — now there's room for two hundred cows. There are six hundred and sixty acres — four hundred forty arable, two hundred twenty hill and rough. I'm not going to tell you the price I paid for the farm, but it's worth a hell of a lot more now. I wouldn't sell it for a million — and I don't mean dollars."

One of his two sons farmed the adjoining property as well as his father's, and the second son, who lived in Glasgow, was an architect and racing driver. Mr. Jacobsen said that he was leaving his library to his sons, with instructions that it be kept intact unless they agreed otherwise.

In the sitting room, to which Mr. Jacobsen escorted me at his customary scamper, Mrs. Jacobsen served coffee, smiling indulgently while her husband spoke. When I asked her what she thought of him, she said: "A very remarkable fellow, but recently he's become so powerful I call him a clever Dick. He's really got a bit overpowering."

Mr. Jacobsen beamed, and as he escorted us back to our car he seemed to bound even higher than usual.

CHAPTER 6

I received the next day a very kind letter from Sir Alexander Gordon, whom I had formerly known in London, and after a cessation of all intercourse for near twenty years met here professor of physic in the King's College.

— Samuel Johnson

DURING HIS STUDENT DAYS in Edinburgh, Donald J. Withrington had been warned that specializing in Scottish history was a direct road to unemployment. But now he was director of the University of Aberdeen's Centre for Scottish Studies and co-editor of *The Scottish Historical Review.* "When I was at school, what you were taught in Scottish history and heritage was the romanticized account of Mary Queen of Scots, the Jacobites, and the like," he said. "That has all changed now, and if you're going to study the industrial revolution, why study it in England? We had the same kind of industrial revolution in Scotland. In the last twenty years we can see academics coming to believe in the correctness and value of work based on Scottish history."

In the crowded office at King's College, shelves overflowed with volumes devoted to Scotland through the ages and in all sorts of revolutions, not only industrial but also linguistic, religious, political, social, and cultural. Mr. Withrington spoke of a determined effort to emancipate Scotland, at home and abroad, from the tartan image, and of the distinguishing characteristics of the country's people. One could not define Scots by race, religion, or even by geography or environment, he said, but rather by the influences and consequences of historical development. Before the Second World War there was a deep sense of cultural inferiority in Scotland, and there were still feelings of defensiveness and sensitivity. "You'll find among Scots a worry, a more essential worry, anxiety, than you'll find in many places in England, about the relationships between social classes," Mr. Withrington said. "I don't want to push the idea of the democratic ideal, but there's a softer relationship here between classes, between social groups. Perhaps one of the reasons is that the characteristic mode of Scotland has been neighborhood schools, where you get pupils of different social classes and aspirations attending classes together."

He suggested also that the Scottish attitude toward unemployment differed from that in England. In Scotland, people were quicker to recognize that when the able-bodied were out of work, it was often for reasons beyond their control. For a long time, the democratic socialism preached within the Labour Party had a strong Scottish accent. "Many of the Labour moderates were Scots, and they brought into their thinking a lot of the older idealism," he said. "Many, if they weren't themselves active churchgoers, drew on church traditions. You find this in Keir Hardie [1856–1915]; if you read some of his Parliamentary speeches, you'll find them larded with references to the Old Testament. He was against what he called 'churchism,' but not religion."

At the end of the 1960s came "a huge flourish of Scottish nationalism," Mr. Withrington said. "Large numbers of the students doing Scottish history were card-carrying members of the Scottish National Party. The bubble burst in the mid-seventies. Things simply got better. It's sometimes said that

Scottish nationalism, as a formal movement, has always fed on economic distress and tended to disappear in periods of economic success."

For all its devotion to humanities and to chronicles of the past, King's College had known so much recent construction that, though it was in Old Aberdeen, it seemed rather to be in a city newly risen. Marischal College, on the other hand, thrust as it was into the commercial center of the new town, endowed its surroundings with an air of age and tradition. When Johnson and Boswell visited Aberdeen, the colleges were not associated with each other, but in the nineteenth century they joined to form the University of Aberdeen, and Marischal now concentrated on technical disciplines, like engineering for the oil industry, so vital to the economic well-being of the city.

Set apart from King's and Marischal was the large Foresterhill medical center, most of it owned and operated by the National Health Service, but one part constituting the university's school of medicine. When I learned that there was a professor of medicine, holding the chair that Johnson's old friend Sir Alexander Gordon had occupied, I went to call on him.

Professor A. Stuart Douglas began by handing me a copy of his 1970 inaugural lecture, which included a brief history of his predecessors. There had been a "mediciner monk" from the foundation of King's College in 1494, and a chair of medicine beginning in 1503. Before Aberdeen, only universities abroad, such as Basle and Padua, had chairs of medicine. There was no professor of medicine at Oxford or Cambridge until the middle of the sixteenth century, and none in Glasgow till the seventeenth. Sir Alexander had been professor of medicine from 1766 to 1782, and Professor Douglas said that in those days medicine "was just a herb garden . . . I would think that it was medicine in the sense of an art rather than a science. If you go back to seventeen seventy-three, there really weren't any effective medicines. It's not until you get well into this century that there were drugs that were any use at all."

In the eighteenth century, the professor of medicine was not expected to train doctors, but to provide "a suitable background," he noted. Until the close of the nineteenth century, medicine was understood as "a branch of scholarship, an intellectual pursuit."

> The responsibilities of the Professor of Medicine have by now almost gone full circle [his lecture observed]. The explosion of scientific knowledge has almost, but not quite, forced him back to the role of these early occupants of the Chair. Each of the specialties within medicine has become so complex with scientific fact that the modern Professor of Medicine had to appreciate, at an early stage, that admission of ignorance in large areas is the only honest course left to him.

"It's hard enough to keep up with the younger people working in the wards," Professor Douglas complained to me, "let alone be up on all the branches of medicine in an age when you have specialists in gastroenterology, endocrinology and diabetes, clinical genetics, clinical pharmacology, respiratory medicine, and cardiovascular medicine." He thought that if the professor of medicine could be expert in a specialty, and preferably one with clinical problems, he could maintain his self-esteem. It was research rather than care of patients or teaching, and certainly more than administration, that gave *this* professor of medicine his greatest pleasure. Teachers at the medical school were in an anomalous situation, he said. The university did not demand of professors of English that they write good books, or of professors of divinity that they have the cure of souls, but it did demand of its professor of medicine that he do research and heal the sick.

What qualities did the professor of medicine need? I asked, and Professor Douglas replied: "You need wisdom, humanity, experience, and a degree of discipline that I think has to be discipline administered by example. I don't think you can motivate a young man or a student by taking a stick to him. If he hasn't got it, he hasn't got it. I hope that the students and the younger men learn by example rather than because a certain discipline was forced on them. I run my department with a lax rein, but I don't think you get the best out of people by adapting tougher government."

At Foresterhill, only about a fifth of the doctors in internal medicine drew their salaries from the university, and the rest were paid by the National Health Service. There was an unwritten understanding that those on the university side would look after patients as well as teach, and that doctors paid by the health service would teach as well as look after patients. "It's a sort of knock-for-knock gentleman's agreement," Professor Douglas said.

Aberdeen's medical school took in a hundred and thirty students annually, and they trained on a population of half a million people. "You can only teach on the patient supply that's available to you," he said. "Glasgow will have an intake of perhaps two hundred and twenty students, but they have a population base in the west of Scotland of three million. No two patients are identical, and therefore if you have a problem that has twenty different ways of presentation, the student experience is all the greater."

He suggested that the local student was much less articulate than his English counterpart. "In an oral examination he'll have trouble. This community has been remarkably static over the years. The non-Scot, by and large, is more extroverted. It's terribly important that the Aberdeen student doctor and graduate get away and see what the rest of the world is like."

Professor Douglas was about to leave for Buffalo to confer

on his specialty, blood-clotting and thrombosis, having just returned from a visit to Saudi Arabia, where he had been surveying the progress of women medical students. Only recently had women in Saudi Arabia been admitted to the study of medicine, and they were still finding equality elusive. They were not permitted to attend classes taught by male teachers, and were relegated to video recordings of the lectures. When they completed their medical training they would not be allowed to treat male patients — not, that is, in Saudi Arabia. Professor Douglas said that he thought these bars to equality would eventually crumble, as had the original ban on women in medicine. He believed that Saudi women students were more highly motivated than the men, precisely because of the difficulties imposed on them, and also because the men had so much money.

Just then, Aberdeen's professor of surgery came in to talk to Professor Douglas about the year's academic awards. It turned out that half of each entering class at Aberdeen's medical school was made up of women and that the women regularly carried off most of the prizes.

CHAPTER 7

Upon these rocks there was nothing that could long detain attention, and we soon turned our eyes to the Buller, or Bouilloir of Buchan, which no man can see with indifference, who has either sense of danger or delight in rarity.

— Samuel Johnson

AT CRUDEN BAY, fishermen were pulling in their nets, just as men like them had been doing over the centuries. But there were also scenes alien to the distant past. Cruden Bay was now landfall of an oil pipeline from a North Sea field over a hundred miles distant, and long lines of dark brown, two-story wooden structures that had housed pipeline construction workers stood almost derelict, the best effects of sunshine unavailing to endow a rustic charm.

Four miles to the north, on a promontory beside the sea, stood Slains Castle, in 1773 a seat of great luxury with a gallery of Hogarths, a full-length portrait of its owner, the Earl of Erroll, by Joshua Reynolds, an extensive library, and elegant accommodations. Below, the sea sent great waves crashing against the rocks on which the castle perched: Johnson thought the view the noblest he had ever seen.

A terrible washboard road now led to Slains, and as we

bounced along it, birds overhead screamed a message difficult to decipher, though the raucous strains seemed devoid of any note of welcome. As I entered the castle grounds, only an owl appeared to take umbrage, and it flew out of the ruins. The great building, inhospitable to men, barely adequate for birds, was now a dull red huggermugger of decay, and the ground was strewn with stone and brick, a jigsaw puzzle only one-third assembled, awaiting a Goliath who would gather the pieces and restore them to prouder service. Though the place appeared to have been abandoned for centuries, I learned later that the castle had been inhabited until the 1920s. When the owner left, he removed the roof to avoid the tax levied on covered buildings. Weather did the rest, reducing a noble monument to a desolation of lowly fragments.

From Slains it was a short drive to the Bullers of Buchan. A sign near a group of freshly painted cottages that sparkled in the sunshine directed nonresidents to leave their cars and proceed on foot. There was also a notice, white letters on red, with the warning THESE CLIFFS ARE DANGEROUS. Hundreds of gulls flew overhead, and others warmed themselves along the craggy sides of the cliffs, evidently indifferent to danger. Some appeared to cling to the rock face where it was smoothly vertical, with no apparent foothold, and there were frequent squabbles between birds contesting a minimal perch.

"Bullers" came perhaps from a Swedish or Danish word signifying "roar" or "tumbling noise," or from the French *bouilloire,* meaning "kettle." The Bullers of Buchan (Johnson's Buller of Buchan) was a rock chasm about a hundred feet wide and twice as deep, with an entrance to the sea. Centuries ago the chasm was probably a high cave, and then its roof must have collapsed, leaving a lofty circular margin along which one could walk and observe the water below, churning and foaming with savage turbulence. "This monstrous cauldron," Boswell called it.

"He that ventures to look downward sees, that if his foot should slip, he must fall from his dreadful elevation upon stones on one side, or into the water on the other," Johnson noted. "We however went round, and were glad when the circuit was completed." Boswell said it was "somewhat horrid to move along," and "it was rather alarming to see Mr. Johnson poking his way."

As I poked my way along the narrow, grassy path, I had for the first time the sensation of being precisely where Johnson had been, and it delighted me to be treading in his footsteps — and then to transport his memory and myself to safer ground at Strichen. Johnson had been curious to see a Druids' temple there, so we followed a local road to the gray ruins of the "new" Strichen House. Of the old Strichen House that Johnson and Boswell visited, all that remained were fragments of a circular tower and a ruined column. Nearby, surrounded by a rough picket fence, was a plot about a hundred feet by sixty; inside the plot were the stones that made up the Druids' circle, no longer in circular array. I made a mental note to find out why the geometry was wrong, and we retreated to the bed-and-breakfast where we planned to stay for several days.

Across the street was the All Saints Church, which belonged to the Diocese of Aberdeen and Orkney in the Episcopal Church of Scotland. It hardly sounded like a cozy congregation of Druids, but I decided to inquire how this circle was doing. As though heaven-sent, the minister turned up almost immediately, saying that he wanted to see if there were flowers for Sunday service. He told me that he was also rector of St. John's in Longside and of St. Drostan's in Old Deer, and that all three of his congregations were tiny. "We have twenty in the congregation in Strichen, when they all come," he said. "At Longside the church has room for four hundred and fifty, and only a few people turn up. It's like preaching in the desert — you squirm round trying to see if someone's sitting behind a column."

An old church stood on a height above Strichen, and the minister said that the building was now used for storing grain, though the churchyard still served for burials. "The church was used till the Philistines decided to close it and use this horror down the road," he said, referring to the Church of Scotland's house of worship. "They would have done better to build a pub there — not that we need more pubs — and gone on using the old church." He said that Strichen, by and large, had been blessed with poverty. "Others were unfortunate enough to have money," he suggested, "so they changed."

That evening the nine hundred and seventy inhabitants of the village were invited to attend a meeting to discuss development plans of the Banff and Buchan District Council. The council served a population of eighty thousand, and one of its aims was to give people a sense of participation in decisions affecting them. After supper we went along to the community center and found Gordon Mann, who represented the council, reporting to an audience of ten people. When Mr. Mann spoke of plans for new industries, one man asked why factories of advanced technology were concentrated in the larger towns. Mr. Mann replied that Strichen unemployment was only 2.5 percent, but unemployment in the district as a whole was 5.5 percent.

Some of those at the meeting expressed apprehension about the prospect of what they called a superquarry, suggesting that it would remove a natural resource merely to make money, with no concern for the needs of local construction. Mr. Mann said that Germany had used up its hard rock in building *autobahnen* and was now looking abroad for an additional supply. It had already imported stone from

Sweden and a little from Britain. He told of a man who had applied for permission to open a big quarry at Cruden Bay. The fellow had stood up in a meeting and said, "All I want to do is move the cliff face back from where it stands, back to the main road." Mr. Mann added, in tones of wonder, "He said it in such a bland, reasonable way."

When the Strichen gathering considered housing needs, a local resident urged that neighborhoods be built on "the old sensible gridiron plan" — streets running perpendicular to each other, as they did in the heart of Strichen, where a rectangular area was bordered by streets named North, South, East, and West. Mr. Mann suggested that there were other good models, perhaps not so boring when the neighborhood expanded. But the local man insisted that, with streets running every which way, "people all get lost on the way home nowadays . . . A lot of these planners run mad — streets off streets off streets again. You never know where you are. It's a great thing — straight lines."

Another man brought up the problems of the football — that is, soccer — field. "There are seven different football teams fightin', all aimin' to play on the one field here," he said, and all this fuss over a field with terrible drainage. "The linesmen have to run with Wellingtons on."

During the tea break, Mike Brydon, the head of the Strichen Community Council, came over to say that he was glad to see visitors from outside the village. He himself had been in Strichen eleven years — he worked as an electrical engineer, his wife as a teacher at the local school — and the local people had been very welcoming. "This village, when I came here, was an aged community, totally apathetic," Mr. Brydon said. "There was one man who galvanized the place. He was the foreman of the sand and gravel works, and he had the gift of speaking to people and of motivating them. He simply got the village together and said we're going to have a gala. I admit to being one of the skeptical people — 'This damned place, they'll never have anything.' They ended up the gala with fifteen hundred pounds. They said we need a hall — the town hall is no good. So we ran more galas and minigalas, and in six years we've raised twenty-three thousand pounds out of a population of less than a thousand. We've thrown our talents into the community interest. If you're prepared to show an interest in them, they respond very warmly."

The next evening the Brydons had us over for tea, and when I asked about the noncircular Druids' circle, Mr. Brydon said that about fifty years earlier a timber contractor had bought the Strichen estate, felled the trees, and left the stumps. When the estate changed hands again, a second contractor pulled out the stumps, and in his zeal to do a thorough job he knocked over the Druidic stones. But the stones had been knocked down even earlier, in about 1810, and the laird of that day had put them back more or less as they had been. "He kind of titillated them a bit," Mr. Brydon said. "And now we're trying to arrange them in the prehistoric, pretitillated setting. There's the recumbent stone and the two flankers and about seven others. We have glass slides — photographs made in the early nineteen hundreds used to make postcards — that somebody found on a rubbish tip. They show the stones as they were placed formerly."

Before we left, Mr. Brydon urged us to visit Robert Bandeen, the village's retired schoolteacher, retired librarian, retired registrar, and virtually retired justice of the peace. Mr. Bandeen lived at the edge of the village in an old house that incorporated a chapel, now also retired. Round about were gardens and fields, two ponies, two cats, a dog, and twenty-seven sheep. "The perimeter of this garden is my limit now," Mr. Bandeen said. "I occasionally wash my face and go to the village." In recent years he had suffered two coronary thromboses and a cerebral hemorrhage, but at seventy-two he looked in good health, with a paunch that he patted contentedly while paying tribute to his wife's cooking.

He spoke so expansively of the old Strichen House — "The place was infested with lice, children, and dogs" — that I almost wondered if he had seen it when Johnson had. Mr. Bandeen said that old Lord Strichen, father of the man who had welcomed Johnson and Boswell, had been sixty years in the College of Justice and was the prototype for the judge in *The Heart of Midlothian* by Sir Walter Scott. It was Lord Strichen, sitting in the circuit court at Dumfries, in 1737, who committed Isobel Walker for trial on a charge of murdering her natural child. In Scott's novel the woman was Effie Deans, and her sister Jeanie walked all the way to London in quest of a pardon. The Duke of Argyll sent Jeanie to Queen Caroline, and then Jeanie walked back from London, bearing the royal pardon.

"The Duke of Argyll was Lord Strichen's brother-in-law," Mr. Bandeen said. "Lord Strichen was a very fine old man, but he succumbed to the vices of the parish and had a few illegitimate children himself. There were six circuit judges, and it was said that two ate, two drunk, and two did neither. It didn't say which was which, but I have an idea that it was Lord Strichen who drunk."

Perhaps the most celebrated occasion for Lord Strichen's indulgence was the case of the English sergeant Arthur Davies. "He was with two other soldiers, and he told them to go ahead without him, and then he never arrived," Mr. Bandeen began. "Now this Gaelic woman was sleeping in bed when she was shaken rather roughly by a ghost. The ghost told her where to go to the hills and find the body indecently interred. She went with two friends and disinterred the body with some buttons missing from the uniform. The two soldiers were then found with the sergeant's buttons in their pockets. Lord Strichen was about to pronounce sentence when the defense counsel asked how it was possible for the Gaelic woman, who had no English, to understand a ghost who knew no Gaelic. The opposing counsel replied that Gaelic was the language of heaven, and that was what the ghost spoke. Lord Strichen accepted that and found the two soldiers guilty. The case has been a bone of contention in Scottish law ever since."

Our bed-and-breakfast landlady had told us that when someone asked Mr. Bandeen what initials belonged after his name he had replied, "B.L.U.F.F." Mr. Bandeen confirmed the story. I asked him to tell us about his life, and after protesting — "I'm the person I'm least interested in" — he agreed to do so.

"It was the time of the Depression I lived through," he said. "I was the second in a family of eight children. My father was unable to go to war in nineteen fourteen because of bad eyesight, and had to live at home, rather impoverished, so that there wasn't money to provide education, although education was as cheap as it was in the whole of Britain, and still there wasn't enough. As a result of which, I had to pick up just where I could and went to the Workers Educational and then associated myself with Aberdeen University for a winter term.

"Before the war, for ten years, I lived at Insch. I learned to be a tailor's cutter with my father, and then I worked in firin' a hospital some time, I worked on a threshin' mill, I worked also as a greenskeeper on a golf course, and then I became a farm servant, and then I went and qualified sufficient to become a member of the Amalgamated Engineers Union. When I came home, Mother had flitted to Strichen, where she belonged. And when I came to Strichen, well, it was the same problems, because when we were married at Insch, Mrs. Bandeen was referred to as Bob Bandeen's wife, but when I came to live in Strichen, I was referred to as Alice Stephen's husband.

"When I left school, I left with little knowledge but a

great desire to learn. After the army, I was recommended for an educational course at Aberdeen. But after having left my wife and children five and a half years — they were growing up and rather wild and requiring my presence — I went back to the head of the school and told him the circumstances at home, so he said, 'We've never turned anybody away from the trough yet, so you come back when the time is ripe.' As the years went by I returned, went to the training college, qualified, and taught music, English, history, and geography, taught at four schools. As after that there was a scarcity of music teachers, I dropped the other subjects — humanities — and taught music. My next adventure was thirty years as a librarian, while teaching. It was genteel poverty, but I loved it. I was prepared, at least Mother was prepared, to make sacrifices.

"As a librarian it wasn't so much the issuin' of books. It was the fact that it opened up vast regions of knowledge and interest. And one day a man said there were a lot of papers in the loft above the cattle court, and they were Lord Pitsligo's papers. The warmth of the beasts underneath kept them warm. Because of the moisture, some of the parchments were like porridge. I dried them, restored them, and dealt with them, more or less, twelve thousand different manuscripts. The canons of spelling and punctuation were not established, and each one had his own type of shorthand, as a result of which it was worse than reading a foreign language, because you had always to read all that one man wrote and then go to the next man and find a different style altogether."

For the same thirty years that he was village librarian, Mr. Bandeen was also its registrar, and he told us that there were few skeletons in cupboards that he did not know about. He was still a justice of the peace. After age seventy, justices were put on the supplementary list and continued to be available for service. "But when they see obvious signs of senility they tell you you can stop," he said. "You die from the neck up. As long as the mind is active you're living. I would have been an undergraduate all my life if I could have been. Education is not something that you acquire and it's not some quality that you possess. Stevenson said, 'To travel hopefully is better than to arrive.' There is no such thing as an educated man. There is a man in the process of being educated. You never arrive. You travel."

I asked Mr. Bandeen what his travel consisted of these days. "Well, more or less with my hands now," he replied. "The finest and the most intelligent person is not the person who's purely involved in scholarship, because scholarship at one time was an education in breadth. The finest and most cultivated man that I know of is a man who has worked with hands and with mind. Yes, I'm now enjoying a fuller life than I ever did before, because I have to apply my knowledge to plant breeding. The flowers in my garden I like best are the ones I'm responsible for from seed, the ones most difficult to propagate. For example, I've just sown the noble fir, great big cones. Mother says I'm still looking to see if there's any clay in the ground to make bricks and houses. The family says that the curse of the father is that he believes in occupational therapy."

When I asked him if he still did a lot of reading, he replied: "Not a great deal, apart from the Bible and Robert Burns and *Johnny Gibb of Gushetneuk*. It's a book written in the language of the northeast of Scotland. It's pure Buchan, the local dialect."

Mr. Bandeen told us of a local professor who fell ill while visiting Leeds, and reverted to his native dialect, so that neither doctors nor nurses could understand him. Mr. Bandeen came to visit, found him reading quietly, and said, "Heely, heely, To, ye glaiket stirk," and the professor replied,

"Ye hinna on the hin shelvin o' the cairt." The two of them had assembled the first sentence of *Johnny Gibb of Gushetneuk*, which told of a man who every year took his wife and sickly bairns to the wells in the town of Macduff to drink the ferrous water that cured everything from whooping cough to housemaid's knee. And with the first sentence the farmer was being told that he was stupid; he had lost the tailgate of his cart.

"Buchan is at the end of the North Sea, and you're not passin' through," Mr. Bandeen said to us. "You're goin' there and comin' out of there, as a result of which, between two seas with the gray mists of the North Sea a good lot of culture is drawn, and some of the more ancient parts of the language."

That took care of *Johnny Gibb*, so I asked Mr. Bandeen why he read the Bible. "Because it is the first and best of books," he said. "I can read into it so much of human experience. There is not an experience or a moment of a person's life, in thinking or acting, that has not found its counterpart in the Bible. And then of course there is nothing emotional, in the human situation, that is not in the Bible, that cannot help you, advise you, direct you."

And Burns? "Well, apart from the fact that I have the same initials as he, along with Robert Bruce and Robert Boothby," Mr. Bandeen began, and then cut himself short to be serious: "I find also in Burns, in colloquial phraseology, that he also expressed much of the same experience and life as most people. If I say that I read these three books you can almost define my character. However, they're not of any value unless what you're reading influences you or somehow directs your way of life, first in thinking, second in attempting to emulate them — their better teaching."

He told us that for the past forty years he had been a lay reader in the Church of Scotland. "Not that that's any great recommendation," he suggested, "but at the same time, as the man said, if you want to get off with murder, become a member of the kirk session. So maybe it's insurance against fire."

I asked Mr. Bandeen what he thought of Johnson and Boswell. "Consider the marvelous things that Johnson said off the cuff," he responded. "To get the balance of his sentences I would have had to write and rewrite and rewrite. It always gave me the feeling that I was standing in the presence of a man who I would have loved to listen to, but I would have been dead frightened to open my mouth. I hold nothing against Johnson for his bitterness against the Scots. I think more of him than I do of the sycophantism of Boswell. But if you read some of Boswell's other stuff, he knew what he was. I would not have liked Johnson as a friend. He was too irascible. Ursa Major. I rather think he wasn't so bumptious and bombastic as you would have read in Macaulay. And I think Boswell wrote one of the best biographies ever written, but I rather think there should have been more warts. And of course Boswell was on the make."

As we were getting ready to leave, Mr. Bandeen showed us a photograph of his family, taken a few years earlier when the six children and their parents gathered for the first time in twenty years. In honor of the occasion Mr. Bandeen had had a friend give him a haircut with sheep shears. But the children got their own back. They gathered all the animals — sheep, dog, cats, and ponies — and had the menagerie waiting in the chapel as a surprise for their shorn father.

When I expressed admiration for the chapel, Mr. Bandeen said that he and his wife had come to the house originally to buy a pound of strawberries; the owner complained that he was trying to sell the place, which was worth five thousand pounds, and that he just had been offered only three thousand. Mr. Bandeen continued: "I said, 'Will we split the difference?' Then I wondered if I'd done the wrong thing.

There was never more than a week's wages between me and the poorhouse."

As though he wanted to erase everything he had said, or perhaps simply provide the fitting context, he offered final words: "It all comes to six feet by two feet, and that is the leveler."

CHAPTER 8

We got at night to Banff . . . but Earl Fife was not at home,
which I regretted very much, as we should have had a very
elegant reception from his lordship.

— James Boswell

AT THE ENTRANCE to Banff, in spacious grounds next to
the golf course, stood Duff House, commissioned by William
Duff, the first Earl Fife. Though the earl was out when
Johnson and Boswell came to Banff, we decided to try our
luck. Up the old stone stairs was an imposing entrance, and
inside a nearby window we could see a teakettle, cup, and
saucer. A padlock hung on the door, and just as I was about
to retreat, foolishly assuming that the place was locked, the
door opened and a man invited us in. It was not the earl,
but an entirely satisfactory substitute, Douglas Paterson,
caretaker and guide. He suggested that we look around, and
suddenly I had misgivings. Despite a fringe of rococo cor-
nices, the house looked desolate, as though it had been left
to slumber into decay without interference from commoner
or lord. But there was also a modern graphic display —
colored charts, text, and illuminated drawings. The government's Department of Ancient Monuments had taken over

the building and, for the edification of visitors, had prepared an account of the history of Duff House.

The contractor engaged by the first Earl Fife to construct Duff House was William Adam, whose fame as builder and architect was eventually overshadowed by that of his sons Robert and James. But Adam *père* had many illustrious clients, including the Duke of Hamilton, for whom he built a hunting lodge with accommodations for hounds in the central portion, leading the duke to refer to the whole lodge as his "dog kennel." Since Adam did not believe in skimping for man or beast, the stonework for Duff House was painstakingly carved in his construction yard at the port of Edinburgh and hauled at great cost all the way to Banff. By 1745 the first earl had paid out seventy thousand pounds, or so it was said, and only the central block of Duff House was finished. Appalled at the expense, the earl halted construction before the flanking wings could be added. There was not even a kitchen yet, but enough was enough, and he refused to pay another penny. In 1743 Adam sued.

The exhibit in the entry hall offered a sample of what the courtroom dialogue must have been like:

Counsel for His Lordship: "Why, having produced such elaborate stone carvings, did you place so much of it where it cannot be seen?"

Counsel for Mr. Adam: "You engaged Mr. Adam to design a house fitting to your high estate. How can you quibble over mere trifles? Even in its least conspicuous parts, your house should display greatness of mind and flee any shadow of parsimony . . . What, sir! Would you count the cost?"

Adam won that suit, but litigation continued for years. The earl was so disenchanted that he never lived in the house, and when he drove by he is supposed to have drawn the blinds of his carriage. James Duff, second Earl Fife, was less sensitive, and in 1763 he took up residence. The sixth earl married the Princess Royal, daughter of Edward VII.

Until 1907 Duff House was the seat of the Earls of Fife, and then it was presented to the borough council. Subsequently it became a hotel and then, until just before World War II, a sanatorium and nursing home. Requisitioned by the army, it housed British, Norwegian, and Polish soldiers, as well as German prisoners of war. During the war a bomb fell on the house, demolishing the post-Adam, Victorian east wing and thus doing great service to purity of line and nobility of purpose. The Nissen huts erected on the grounds survived the bombing; later they were removed by friendly forces.

Now, very slowly, the Department of Ancient Monuments was beginning to restore the interior. On looking through a glass door, I was startled to see white figures standing in the next room, very much at ease. One was holding what appeared to be a glass of sherry. "I get a fright, too, sometimes," said Mr. Paterson, coming up behind me. He said that the plaster group had been put there to give visitors an idea of what they would have seen in the eighteenth century. When I asked if he believed in ghosts, he replied: "The older I get, the less sure I am of what I believe. When you're young, you're brash. Everything's fixed — black and white. Now everything's getting gray."

The central block had about forty rooms and more ghostly figures, two of them in what was identified as a family retreat or withdrawing room. Spiral staircases connected bedchambers, and stairs as well as rooms seemed to have been stripped to a state of positive indecency. "You can nip from bedchamber to bedchamber undetected," Mr. Paterson said. "I'll let you draw your own conclusions."

While it dealt with interior amenities, Ancient Monuments was also repairing the roof, and Mr. Paterson told us that three outsize lead figures had rested there. "I can identify Hermes-Mercury," he said. "I'm just judging by the accouterments and my rusty knowledge of Latin and Greek." The gods had been taken down to await a suitable fate, and Ancient Monuments finally stumbled onto one of its own plumbers, in the depot at Fort George, who said he could restore them. But the statues were beyond even his competence, so the department was going to decorate the roof with surrogate gods of fiber glass.

I asked Mr. Paterson how he came to be working at Duff House, and he said that he was "a middle-aged drop-out" who gave up his job as engineer with the General Post Office because it was no longer possible to use one's brain. Formerly, one followed a circuit with the help of a meter and one's intelligence, he said. But then everything changed: one was given a card with the circuit on it, and there was no need for intelligence. "You could have a chimpanzee to do that," he suggested. Since his wife came from the Banff area and was unwilling to leave, he had taken the job at Duff House.

When we left, Mr. Paterson accompanied us outside, and there he seemed very much at ease. "I could stay here forever, as long as he lets me," he said, looking heavenward. "I think I might even open a French bistro here."

CHAPTER 9

I could for a little fancy myself a military man, and it
pleased me.
                                        — James Boswell

ONE COULD DEPEND ON Johnson for the account laconic,
on Boswell for the narration expansive and circumstantial.
In writing of their visit to the minister of Cawdor and to
Cawdor Castle, Johnson allowed himself fewer than ten
lines; Boswell luxuriated in detail. Johnson noted that he
and Boswell went from Nairn to the house of Mr. Macaulay,
the minister who published a book about St. Kilda; the minister urged them to visit Cawdor Castle; the drawbridge was
still there, the moat was now dry, the tower was ancient, the
walls were thick and arched with stone and surrounded by
battlements, and the rest of the house was built later but
was not modern. That was all. Boswell reported at length
Johnson's contempt for the minister: *"Crassus homo est* [He
is a coarse man]," Johnson said; they suspected that the
minister was not capable of writing the history of St. Kilda
that had been published under his name; there were other
guests at the manse that evening, so the boredom that Boswell had feared was avoided; it was a comfortable manse
and they had a good dinner; since Macaulay had promised

to suggest a route for the rest of the tour, Johnson and Boswell stayed the night; Macaulay's route went from Inverness to Fort Augustus, Glenelg, Skye, Mull, Icolmkill (Iona), Lorne, and Inverary; but before leaving Cawdor, Mr. Macaulay said, they should visit the old castle of Cawdor, residence of the thanes of Cawdor since the fourteenth century, the very place where, in Shakespeare's *Macbeth,* King Duncan was murdered by the wretched Macbeth.

Had Johnson and Boswell taken their trip in the last part of the twentieth century, they would have been urged toward Cawdor almost everywhere they stopped. The engines of publicity had been turning overtime, and virtually every hotel had advertising flyers urging visitors to come to Cawdor FOR A GRAND DAY OUT — RAIN OR SHINE. "There's more to Cawdor than just its past," the invitations noted. "Four nature trails, colourful gardens, pitch and putt course, picnic area, snack bar, licensed restaurant and Gift Shop make it a great place to spend a day."

It would have been difficult to go astray, since at every turn on the road there was a sign with a stylized sketch of the castle and a pointer to the approved direction. We followed the signs into the car park (FREE PARKING), and then walked toward the castle proper. Outside the entrance turnstile (no free entry, which the flyers did not indicate) was a Gypsy-style wagon selling chances to play pitch and putt on the castle grounds: sixty pence for adults, forty pence for children. Near the top of the wagon, barely visible in small letters, was the handsome tribute: "Three out of four ghosts prefer Cawdor Castle." Another sign listed facilities offered the visitor, winding up with — just before "Pitch and Putt" — "Put and take fish pond."

Instead of fighting our way directly across the drawbridge, we launched a diversionary attack on the gift shop, whose style suggested that it might have been transported intact from America, where it would have been called "gift shoppe."

CAWDOR was printed, engraved, or emblazoned on almost all possible surfaces, and I casually noted Cawdor Perfume, Cawdor color slides, Cawdor address books, Cawdor woven badges, Cawdor ashtrays, Cawdor bookmarks, Cawdor buttons, Cawdor toy Highland cows and sheep and thrushes and sheep dogs, Cawdor key rings, Cawdor Castle notepaper, Cawdor shortbread, Cawdor Scotch Whisky, Cawdor Scotch Whisky–flavored marmalade, Cawdor mugs and candles, Cawdor cuckoo-bird tea cozy and matching egg cozy and mitts, Cawdor T-shirts and "afternoon aprons," and, just for show, or maybe also for sale, copies of *Macbeth* and, perhaps inspired by Lady Macbeth's problem with red, unsightly hands, Anti-Wrinkle and Skin Rejuvenation skin food based on seaweed.

In the castle itself, a route was prominently marked — hardly any danger of a false step. In the master's bedchamber there was no clue to the present preoccupations of the present Earl of Cawdor except by extrapolation from his bedside reading. A copy of *Harpo Speaks!* ("The riotous autobiography of Harpo Marx") lay atop the riotous technical manual *Waste Management Paper No. 4: The licensing of waste disposal sites.*

Each room had a clearly printed page-length guide, framed and on display. In the Tapestry Bedroom — tapestry showing Moses and the Israelites — the printed guide noted that "the musical box is Victorian, made in London by Metzler, and plays See-Saw, Faerie Voices and similar soothing stuff." The Blue Room guide concluded with a minatory "Mind your head, unless you are a Papuan pygmy."

In the Thorn Tree Room stood a venerable hawthorn tree. "The tower had been built round it by a strange conceit," Boswell wrote. But he had come a couple of centuries too early for the discovery made in 1979. While mortar joints of the room were being repointed, workers probed a "cow-bar" — perhaps it was really a crowbar — into the thick south wall of this room to see if the stonework was solid. It was not. The wall concealed a dungeon, and the Earl of Cawdor faced up to his responsibilities and added it to the wonders available for public viewing. The dungeon — about six feet by twelve, with the crown of the elliptical vault about eight feet high — was now illuminated by incandescent light, with two large mirrors arranged so that visitors could see what otherwise would not be visible. Archives were mum about this dungeon, so it ranked as a full-blown novelty. Coyly, the revised guide to the Thorn Tree Room said that enough remains of dead mice had been found to satisfy any man's appetite for the remains of dead mice.

The other rooms of the castle had a lived-in air. To save old rugs from the tramp of marching thousands, a tartan runner had been laid along the tourist route, and a corridor leading from room to room had been strung with cords to keep visitors from marauding forays. This had been done right into the family kitchen, installed in 1971, complete with wall oven, modern range, and washing machine. The kitchen that Lady Macbeth had known was farther along, with old irons and ancient pots and primitive machinery for turning the spit.

At Cawdor, Johnson and Boswell were given a letter of introduction to the master of stores at Fort George, and at the fort they were welcomed by Sir Eyre Coote, commander of the 37th Foot, an infantry regiment. Sir Eyre invited them to dinner, and after a polite refusal Johnson accepted the invitation. Then the visitors went off to inspect the fort. Johnson delivered a brief informal lecture on the manufacture of gunpowder, and at three o'clock the drum announced dinner. Boswell's *Journal* gave a detailed account of the dinner conversation and conveyed delight with the place. When Boswell spoke effusively of his enchantment at finding on such barren soil so impressive a collection of buildings, so fine a dinner, so charming a company, Johnson said that he was not astonished at the place or the experience, "because he knew here was a large sum of money expended in building a fort. Here was a regiment. If there had been less than what he found, it would have surprised him. *He* looked coolly through all the gradations. *My* imagination jumped from the barren sand to the good dinner and fine company." Johnson's account was bare bones: "Of Fort George I shall not attempt to give any account. I cannot delineate it scientifically, and a loose and popular description is of use only when the imagination is to be amused."

In 1773 Fort George was one of the grandest examples of artillery fortification in Europe. Scotland had been poor in bastioned earthworks, for their construction required great sums of money, but after the Highlanders' 1715 rising, the government commissioned additional infantry barracks, the largest at the south end of Loch Ness. This was replaced by Fort Augustus, and near Inverness Castle rose a military emplacement that served as the first Fort George. In the 1745 rebellion, the Highlanders simply ignored the forts, but the next year they began to tunnel under the fort at Inverness and mounted an artillery battery overlooking it. The fort surrendered. Fort Augustus was in turn reduced when a shell hit the powder magazine. After final victory over the Highlanders, in 1746, the authorities determined to ensure a defense against possible renewal of Scottish intemperance. Plans were prepared for a new Fort Augustus, but reason prevailed when the military recognized that the site was indefensible. The fort therefore was rebuilt almost as it had been, an exercise in nostalgia, impressive architecture, inadequate fortification. A new Fort George was designed by William Skinner, the engineer for North Britain. As work was about to start, the Inverness Town Council demanded compensation for damages to its new harbor; Skinner abandoned the site in favor of the peninsula at Ardersier, east of Inverness, where the only possible claimant for damages would be the proprietor of the only building, a simple hut.

There was plenty of room in which to build, and the position was defensible. Skinner's fort, which took twenty-one years to complete, beginning in 1748, covered more than forty-two acres and included a full panoply of eighteenth-century fortification: bastions, demibastions, terrepleins, parapets, places of arms, lunettes, batardeaux, barbettes, traverses, sallyports, casemated curtains, ravelin, magazine, glacis, ditch, scarp, and counterscarp. In 1760 the fort got modern armament in place of obsolete guns, which were then sent into honorable retirement at the Tower of London. At the height of construction there were probably more than a thousand men at work on the fort, the largest engineering project ever undertaken in the Highlands. Not till the building of the Caledonian Canal, in the next century, was there anything bigger.

By the time the fort was finished, it was evident that the enterprise was a colossal waste, since the Highlanders were pacified and in no condition to threaten anyone with anything more potent than stale haggis. Moreover, improved artillery, including the shrapnel shell, made the place obsolete. Fort George was therefore converted into a garrison and used also for army training. About a hundred years later the government decided there was finally good reason to keep the fort as a military installation, and put a coast defense battery on the north and west ramparts. Then new weapons made the defense battery obsolete. In 1964, though soldiers were still stationed there, the Department of the Environment took over the fort, and it was opened to the public as an Ancient Monument.

One of the modern amenities provided for those still obliged to languish in fortified isolation was the telephone. I phoned Fort George to ask if I could see the governor — or whoever passed for governor. My knowledge of how such an installation was run depended entirely on Johnson and

Boswell, and I hoped to find a counterpart of Sir Eyre Coote.

The man who answered the phone told me that the lieutenant colonel who commanded the regiment or the battalion was away with his troops in England, and the soldier holding the fort was the adjutant, Captain Alistair H. Cunningham. I asked to speak to him, and it took several more calls before he could be located within range of a phone. "I'm here with two men and a dog," he reported, agreeing to see me. He said I was to ignore posted directions to the visitors' car park and, instead, enter through the gate designated for military transport. "You'll find some dozing civilians and a very smart soldier," he said. "I'll tell them you're coming."

There were signposts to the fort, which stood at the tip of a spit of land north of the road between Nairn and Inverness. At the gate there was no soldier, but only a civilian, unarmed except for a clipboard. He flourished it and admitted me. I saw other civilians strolling about, and at last a soldier as well, and I asked all of them, in turn, where I could find Captain Cunningham. Each person vaguely suggested a different direction, except for those who had never heard of the captain. Finally I spied an especially smart-looking soldier, his cap flattened on his forehead as though it were a pancake, tossed from the skillet, that had landed short of the target. He ordered me to fall in behind him, and I marched forward as he did, wondering if I was under close arrest. We entered an unmarked building, and he led me upstairs. Barring the way and standing at the open door of an office, he announced in stentorian tones that a civilian wished to see the captain. I was admitted to the presence.

Captain Cunningham turned out not to be forbidding at all, indeed quite genial, though a mere stripling in the profession, having just turned thirty, with only ten years' military experience. But his composure was total, and he answered my questions with assurance, after apologizing for having been so difficult to reach. He had been out inspecting the muster parade, and he admitted there were really fifteen men left to guard Fort George — not two men and a dog. Just that morning, at the parade, he had reprimanded two of the men. "One guy had a dirty cap badge," he said, "and another guy needed to get his jersey changed. Normally on Wednesdays the whole battalion is on parade here. In the old days we used to have parade every day, but it takes about twenty minutes. It's a valuable exercise, but not so valuable that we want to spend twenty minutes on it."

Lots of tourists came to Fort George, he said, though it was not allowed to publicize itself, since officially there was always a regiment here even when there was no regiment here. I could not conceal my bewilderment. "They are here," he said of his regiment, "except they're away for two weeks' training to go to Northern Ireland."

"We're the First Battalion of the King's Own Scottish Borderers," he said, and when I raised an eyebrow and hesitantly suggested that the country was ruled by a queen, not a king, he explained that the unit had been formed under a king, in 1689. The battalion had about six hundred men, and it never stayed in one place long. He was with it during honorable service in British Honduras, and it had performed valiantly during a month of public duties in London, when a hundred of its men had been detached for the occasion. The pipe band accounted for about twenty, the military band for another thirty, and that left fifty for marching up and down and guarding Buckingham Palace, St. James's Palace, and the Tower of London. The duties were principally ceremonial, Captain Cunningham acknowledged, though at night the force did have a security function, always under the supervision of the Metropolitan Police.

The captain said that Fort George was mainly a place for the training of recruits. "It was built following the Battle of Culloden as a secure garrison for the Hanoverian troops who were loyal to the king, to keep the Highlanders at bay," he said. "We are a Scottish regiment; we come from the Borders. At Culloden in seventeen forty-six we were fighting against the rebel Jacobite Highlanders, and they were brutally, savagely repressed. We didn't have a very important role in the battle — we were in the second rank. But I think we fired the first shot. There was some affray whereby one of the Highlanders rode through the ranks to murder the Duke of Cumberland. It was a suicide mission, and one of our guys popped him off as he came through. The government was terrified of the enemy and didn't understand him. They indulged in this mass persecution of the Highlanders and built this enormous place. The Highlanders could never have started to take this place — it was using a sledgehammer to kill a bee. Now you could drop just any sort of bomb on it."

I asked him how things had improved at the fort since Johnson's time. He pondered the question. The plumbing was the same, he suggested tentatively; in fact, the buildings were also about the same. Though there was now central heating, winds still roared through the barracks. But a group of architects and surveyors had been assigned to work at Fort George, since the government had decided to improve soldiers' housing by converting barracks into apartments. Ten or twelve soldiers would live in an apartment and have, as the captain put it, "a wee place to cook and a wee ironing room and a wee recreation room."

Fort George had the outline of an enormous recumbent rocket pointing across the water at the village of Fortrose. Tracing the outer defenses on a drawing, Captain Cunningham asked if I would like him to explain "the philosophy of construction of this place." I invited him to proceed.

"Old fortifications were tall — you could pour boiling oil on people who were attacking," he said. "This was changed by the invention of cannon, and then buildings were sunk below ramparts. Moats were built round this place, and every time the tide went out, the moats dried up. The chap who designed the fort had put the moats there as an important part of the defense, and when the moats didn't work he got quite depressed and I believe he committed suicide."

Captain Cunningham seemed so relaxed — as though no enemy were anywhere within range — that I asked him if he would mind reading what Boswell had written about Fort George. He said he would be delighted, so I marched back to my car, got the *Journal*, and infiltrated back to the captain's office. He took the book from me, held it in his hands open to the passage I indicated, rested his arms on the tartan cloth covering his large desk, and proceeded to the engagement at hand. First he read the section about the discussion over dinner concerning the loyalty of Arabs defending someone in their charge. "I think nowadays our soldiers do act more out of loyalty than out of fear of punishment," he said. "It's exactly the sort of conversation we might have. We're always comparing our own soldiers and life to other people, especially abroad. We've got quite a lot of graduates at the mess. Raises the tone a bit — speaking as a graduate."

He then read of the dinner discussion concerning drama and acting, and of the dinner service — the fine wines and excellent linen. "I couldn't say we talk a lot about the theater," Captain Cunningham said. "We talk quite a bit about travel, about the places where we've been. We certainly talk about politics. We don't have expensive French wines. We have cheap Italian wines. We don't have fine linen. We have a polished table and our regimental mats and some regimental silver. When the battalion has a formal dinner, with distinguished guests, the pipers come in and play round the tables. As adjutant, I ask the guests for their favorite tunes, and the pipe band plays a medley, with tunes such as 'The Barren Rocks of Aden' and 'The Black Bear' and of course the pibroch. I used to find it a great strain to sit in silence listening to the lament of the pibroch, which lasts ten minutes. I've been in the regiment now ten years, and I love it. It is something that is quite stirring, and I look forward to it. The military band plays in a room adjacent to the dining room. They'll certainly play the regimental marches of any officers dining with us. And they'll play other things — it may be Sousa marches or Gilbert and Sullivan or it might be *My Fair Lady*."

Putting on his tartan cap and taking up his swagger stick, Captain Cunningham asked me if I would like a tour of the battlements. He took me on a lightning sweep, but also pinned me down with a drumfire of military terminology. Finally he led me to safety inside a gift shop. Alexander Duffus, who ran the shop, was a veteran of twenty-five years in the army. He told me that the fort had about thirty-five thousand visitors a year, and that most of them came to the gift shop, which featured a modest line of guidebooks, postcards, and toy cannon.

After thanking Captain Cunningham, I advanced on my own to the museum, which was crowded with soldierly relics of regiments formerly stationed at the fort. One room was devoted to medals; there were showcases and picture frames crammed with them. Another room had regimental trophies — cups, plates, miniature cannon and cannon balls, as well as the head of a ram with chased silver horns. There were lots of uniforms, regimental ties, and portraits of late, lamented commanders. When I left the fort there were no guards at the gate, civilian or military. If Highlanders were in the mood for belated revenge, this was obviously the moment to strike.

CHAPTER 10

Of the Earse language, as I understand nothing, I cannot say more than I have been told. It is the rude speech of a barbarous people, who had few thoughts to express, and were content, as they conceived grossly, to be grossly understood.

— Samuel Johnson

AT INVERNESS there was now a society devoted to the growth — perhaps simply the survival — of the Gaelic language, which Johnson spelled Earse and which appears more commonly as Erse. An Comunn Gaidhealach (The Highland Society) had settled into Abertarff House, reputedly the town's oldest building, and the venerable structure had been restored, as though this were a first step in elevating Gaelic to former splendor. On the ground floor was an exhibition promoting the language, and an introductory note proclaimed: "Were it not for the Gaels there would be no country called Scotland, no people calling themselves Scots. Sentimentality, commercial exploitation as well as ignorance and, indeed, prejudice, have obscured the story and culture of the Gael."

In an office one flight up a steep, stone staircase, wall posters encouraged right-mindedness: "Let Your Child Be Bilingual" and "Keep Skye Bilingual." Entrenched beneath the posters was Colin Spencer, a young man devoted to plain speech and stalwart hopes, education director of An Comunn. Born in England, he had learned Gaelic during ten years as an art teacher on the isle of Harris in the Outer Hebrides, and now, like Abertarff, had a new façade, signing himself not Colin but Cailean, a Gaelic version. "Gaelic is still a spoken language, as it was in Scotland for centuries, although much diminished geographically and numerically," he said. "If you entered from the south, two centuries ago, you heard Gaelic in the Lowlands. After Culloden, the English were an army of occupation and English was the language of the ruling class. In fact, the ruling classes in Scotland adopted English and Norman French from the powerful neighbor to the south as soon as English became the language of the court and the king and his nobles. Scotland became two countries — a Lowlands area becoming commercial, with burghs going up, and the Highlands, pastoral, organized on tribal lines. By degrees, as the English took over the country, English became the dominant language.

"There are still communities in which Gaelic is the daily language of the majority — in the Outer Islands from Lewis to Barra, in parts of the Inner Hebrides, and in enclaves on the mainland. Today you'd have to say that the gates of Gaelic as a community language were in Skye. In communities in the West Highlands a large proportion of older people understand the language but don't use it. The Western Isles were once part of Norway, but we don't have much in the way of Norwegian there. Gaelic wiped out Norse in Scotland, and wiped out Pictish, but it didn't wipe out English."

Mr. Spencer said that Gaelic was now spoken by about eighty-nine thousand people, and that the census of 1971 was the first to record an increase. "After seventeen forty-five, it was extremely unprofitable for anyone to identify with Gaelic," he suggested. "You were classified as a rebel, belonged to the wrong religion, and were socially inferior. It's like wearing cloth caps. A person who wanted to get on in the world wouldn't go around wearing the worker's cap or with a scarf tied around his neck. The only way you could get on was by speaking English.

"These social attitudes have a remarkable persistence. It's like the attitudes surrounding sex equality — you can still get the old attitudes of men to women or women to men remaining after conditions change. Gaelic continued to be a low-status culture into this century."

Mr. Spencer noted that *teuchter,* used by the Lowlander to express contempt for the Highlander, meant "yokel" or "hick": "Anyone not speaking or understanding English — there's something wrong with him. Just as I've heard people talking about Welsh wogs, and talking that way about the Irish. It's a basic fault that British people are never taught about the worth and pleasure that other cultures can give. There's a sense of these cultures being only interesting, colorful aberrations. I think [Scottish] Gaelic and Welsh and Irish should not only be encouraged but recognized officially."

He suggested that in the nineteenth century the suppression of Gaelic and the propagation of English were means of manipulating the character of the people. "In eighteen seventy-two, when state schools were set up, they were totally English and as a matter of policy ignored the language of the country and set out to deracinate the people. Gaelic-speaking teachers in the lowest grades were to acclimatize children to speaking English; if the children didn't learn, they were punished. One person referred to the same process in Ireland as 'the murder machine,' and it murdered the language, except in remoter areas. It has only remained as the language of hearth and home where the community has remained remote and strong, where even the school was unable to shake its hold.

"Within the last thirty or forty years there has been some

distinct change for the better. Nowadays, certainly in the Western Isles, the official policy is to encourage the use of both languages in school. For children speaking no Gaelic, the policy of Gaelicizing is not as strong or thought out. English must be taught — it's a necessity of life — that's the policy. But it's now recognized in the Western Isles that it's not only possible but commendable to educate the child in both languages.

"The most valuable richness of Gaelic is that it's a spoken language used by people who have a distinctive way of life. If the language were not spoken, there would be very little reason to learn it. And with the oral tradition you get amazing feats of cultural transference from one generation to another. It's only within the last hundred years that the process of recording has started. There were stories in verse form that scholarship has established go back centuries in Europe, stories that last for three nights — folklore, gods and demigods, heroic sagas and cycles."

When I wondered how Gaelic dealt with the innovations of modern life, Mr. Spencer said: "Only use will bring forth the new words. I could sit here all day and invent words for modern concepts, but unless people spoke them they wouldn't enter the language. A prime case of it is the use of Gaelic in religion. When the Reform religion came to Scotland, Gaelic had to develop a new way of speaking, a new code for expressing new religious ideas. In the nineteenth century a whole new vocabulary had to be invented to deal with agricultural developments. Since English is the dominant language, it often sets the tone and provides the vocabulary for new notions and things."

A great deal of his work was conducted through Gaelic, and this had helped to spawn an administrative vocabulary exclusive to An Comunn. Mr. Spencer said that the society now had words for "committee," for "subcommittee," for "proposition," for "seconding a proposition." *Comhairle,* which meant "advice," was used for "committee"; a "sub-committee" was *fo-chomhairle,* aspiration and prefix (*fo* being Gaelic for "under") constituting the modifiers. "When the language was in a state of monoglottism and in a period of growth, a lot of neologisms came in out of necessity," he said.

Others had told me that Mr. Spencer spoke excellent Gaelic, and I asked him what had attracted him to the language. "At one time I would have said I liked Gaelic because it was a beautiful language," he replied, "but now I think all languages are beautiful. It's a very rich language, the living representative that can take us back to six hundred A.D., when the Gaels came to Scotland. It's linked with Wales and Ireland and the whole of the British Isles."

In the afternoon I returned to see Donald J. MacCuish, a solicitor who called himself president pro tem of An Comunn Gaidhealach, since he was already beginning the second year of his three-year presidential term. Tall and white-haired, he spoke in a careful, deliberate way, a mode that seemed characteristic of native Gaelic speakers using English. An Comunn, he told me, was founded in 1891 by a group of men in Oban. "At that time the Gaelic Highlands were very well populated, in fact grossly overpopulated, and the language was in a healthy state," Mr. MacCuish said. "When An Comunn started, there was no need to put in a great effort to ensure that the Gaelic would survive. So they turned to the expatriate Gael in the urban, industrial areas, to keep the native Gaelic speaker in touch with his own culture, and the *mod* [a Gaelic festival, often with music, drama, and recitations] became very much a central part of An Comunn's work. They had *ceilidhs,* published a magazine, ran a youth movement, ran a summer camp, and held local *mods* as well as national *mods.*

"With depopulation and growth of urban life, it became clear that Gaelic was being pushed back. The Comunn began to see that if the language was going to have a future, they would have to see what was going on. About twelve years ago we brought the headquarters up to Inverness, and about eight years ago opened an office in Stornoway. We saw it was necessary for us to lend our weight. When you get newspapers and radio and, most deadly of all, television — because television can catch pretty well from the cradle — you have a difficult struggle. When the Western Isles got its own government region, that really created a climate in which Comunn activities and various other authorities could operate. In a few weeks we will open an office in Oban and come full circle."

He believed that to a great extent the bias against Gaelic had died out. "It's not so much a question of prejudice as of not understanding fully that the language is here, that it is basically a Scottish language, that Scotland was once Gaelic and has a character and culture of its own. I think it's not a lack of sympathy but a question of not knowing. One of Comunn's initiatives is to interest members of Parliament, local government, and the community. One of the things I do, in canvassing Members of Parliament, is to say 'If you have a genuine interest in Gaelic, let us know and become a member of our Parliamentary lobby.' I was surprised at the number who had a latent interest. It remained latent because they didn't come across Gaelic every day. But they were prepared to be interested."

When I asked how Gaelic dealt with contemporary life, how, for example, in Gaelic he would say "antiballistic missile," he replied: "I don't as a rule talk about interwhatchemacallits in Gaelic. Most of the terms in English are taken from Latin anyway, and I think it would be fair to Gaelicize the English."

Mr. MacCuish said that he championed Gaelic precisely because it was his native language. When he began primary school he knew not a word of English. "I must have been six or seven," he said. "I don't remember it was unpleasant; what stands out is the fact that you spoke Gaelic at home and in the playground, and at school — shutters down on Gaelic. What I do remember quite vividly, if you slipped into using a Gaelic phrase you really felt you'd dropped a brick, but you wouldn't get punished. It's only as one gets older that one realizes the iniquity of a person who had a language like that, and a language as good as that, being shut out. You're the richer with bilingualism and trilingualism, and the better educated for it."

Pursuing that judgment, the Inverness Royal Academy invited students at age twelve to select a second language to study, either French or Gaelic. In the most recent group, of 290 students 272 chose French. That was regrettable, suggested Mary Gillies, an assistant rector at the academy, but there was not much one could do about it.

We had gone to see Miss Gillies on the advice of John MacInnes, and by good fortune her father, mother, and aunt were all visiting, in her new home outside Inverness, beside the Culloden battlefield. The family was drawn up in a circle in the living room, and at first I felt doubly the intruder, imposing alien English on their Gaelic.

Miss Gillies spoke of "dilettante resurgence" of Gaelic — people coming up to the Highlands to take summer courses, or expressing interest in their roots. Interest from the top instead of the bottom, she called it. Her aunt, Kate Gillies, insisted on the economic advantages of English: "What good is it to people if you don't have good English? It wasn't in my favor that I hadn't good English when I left home. No one ever praised Gaelic except if they could speak English correctly."

I asked Mr. Gillies, a tall, slim, white-haired man who exuded an air of reserve and dignity, whether he had ever encountered prejudice against Gaelic. It was his native language, and in replying he stopped occasionally to search for elusive English expressions. "In my experience," he began, plainly weighing his words, "perhaps the Gaelic wasn't looked down upon, but perhaps the people who had the Gaelic were looked down upon." Pointing out that his native isle of Raasay was state-owned, he called the Hebrides a colony. "The Secretary of State for Scotland is the landlord, so you haven't got much say against the Secretary of State."

He and his sister expressed suspicion about all forms of government authority. They believed, for example, that there were plans for establishing a naval base on Raasay, and without anyone consulting the local people. "Why are they making good roads?" she demanded. "Why all this expense — the pier and three landings? A hundred and fifty people could be told to move out."

Mr. Gillies said one had to be careful not to be too outspoken. "You see, the ruling people, the people in authority, are very jealous of their authority," he explained. "If you cross them, they'll keep an eye on you."

"I'd praise them up," his sister said. "It's the only way to get what you want."

Mary Gillies spoke of the Highlands as a stamping ground for government agencies, for the Highlands and Islands Development Board, the Forestry Commission, the Crofters Commission, the Land Court, the Scottish Office, and the Highland Regional Council. On the one hand, she and her father and aunt welcomed grants and subsidies; on the other hand, they suspected the government of evil intentions and of not being interested in the people of the Highlands. But when her father and aunt spoke about economic hardship, Mary Gillies could not help interjecting, "There's nobody poor in Raasay."

Her father belonged to a successful sheep cooperative; there were nine shareholders and he was the only surviving founder-member. "When we started we had a shepherd," he said, "and we were sending the sheep out to the mainland, to Inverness, for wintering of them, and we had to pay for them and for the shepherd. Now the cooperative keeps the sheep on the island in winter. At the time of the snow on the high ground the sheep can exist on heather. Heather is good, and it's better than nothing at all. We hand-feed them hardly at all. We clipped five hundred and eighteen ewes in nineteen twenty-four and about sixteen hundred and fifty last year."

He recalled bygone years, when Raasay's men sought employment in the fishing fleets while their wives stayed home to work the croft. "I was nine years an assessor with the Crofters Commission, and the woman crofter was never mentioned," he said. "But I remember my mother hoeing the patches and of course milking the cows, and then the peats had to be lifted up and they had to be stacked and my mother was out with us cutting the hay."

"It was a blessing there wasn't a family allowance to encourage even larger families," his sister suggested, laughing.

Mary Gillies recalled that when she went to school in Raasay, there were two teachers. "I remember Raasay having *three* teachers, and now it has just one," her father said. He said that the population was in such steady decline that eventually no one would be living on the island.

Mr. Gillies gave me the feeling that for him history was not an account of the past but a claim on the present. When he spoke of the gentry who once owned the island, his tone implied that villainy could not be forgiven simply because a century had passed. He recalled the case of George Rainey, a Lowlander who made his fortune tea-farming, and who purchased Raasay in 1843. "Rainey developed Raasay House as a shooting estate," Mr. Gillies said contemptuously. "His kennels were better than the houses people lived in. He had running water and beds for the dogs, and his dogs are buried with tombstones."

Offering his views of the nineteenth-century clearances,

when crofters were driven from their homes, Mr. Gillies spoke solemnly, and at least initially in the present tense. "That's very, very wicked in deed and very sinful. The Scottish Confession of Faith, the Westminster Confession of Faith, in the longer catechism, says 'Thou shalt not steal.' There is in it depopulation — 'Thou shalt not add house to house and field to field.' It was wicked what they have done. There was as much land in Scotland as would have kept these people, and Her Majesty's subjects they were, and this was allowed to go on all the time. It's even galling yet when I think of it."

People talked about the plight of refugees from Vietnam and from Africa, he said. "And quite right. But not a mention in the Scottish schoolbooks of what happened in the clearances."

"There is now," his daughter objected, but he shook his head and suggested that I read a book called *The History of the Working Class in Scotland*. "I had a read of it myself," he said.

CHAPTER 11

We soon came to a high hill, which we mounted by a military road, cut in traverses, so that as we went upon a higher
stage, we saw the baggage following us below in a contrary
direction. To make this way, the rock has been hewn to a
level with labor that might have broken the perseverence of
a Roman legion.

— Samuel Johnson

FROM FORT AUGUSTUS, as Johnson wrote, the travelers
were to cross the Highlands toward the west coast. We could
have crossed easily on the excellent road built long after
Johnson's day, a route heading northeast from Fort Augustus
along the western shore of Loch Ness for about six miles
until it met another good road that headed west toward the
Irish Sea. On my three-miles-to-one-inch map these roads
were marked Primary Routes. They offered no difficulty, except that they were not the route followed by Johnson and
Boswell. The road they chose headed directly northwest and
was shorter than the easy highways of the twentieth century.
What puzzled me was that my map did not show the road
that Johnson described. Where was this road? Did it still
exist? Could I follow it?

At Inverness I sought advice from the regional offices of
the Forestry Commission. I phoned David Woodburn, an

assistant commissioner, and said that I wanted to walk through the forests from Fort Augustus straight across the hills to Glen Moriston. He invited me to come to his office, and when I arrived he seemed rather wary, or perhaps simply overwhelmed with work. His desk was piled high with paper — a Stakhanovite's quota of directives, questionnaires, surveys, reports, accounts, and correspondence. I explained my mission more fully: I was looking for an old military road that cut across the hills northwest from Fort Augustus and was used by travelers in the eighteenth century. Was it still there? Could I walk through his forests on that road? Mr. Woodburn rose and proceeded to his giant wall map — and the area was just off the map. Then he burrowed north, south, east, and west under the hills of paper on his desk and finally unearthed an old directory of Forestry Commission personnel. He dictated names and telephone numbers of people at the Fort Augustus office and advised me to get in touch with them. As I left, looking about me at the mounds of paper, I could not resist the temptation to say that the Forestry Commission seemed to be the biggest consumer of forest products. He was not amused.

When we arrived in Fort Augustus, I called one of the numbers indicated for the local office in the Forestry Commission. The man who answered was the chief forester, James Pratt, whose name was not on Mr. Woodburn's list. He heard me out and invited us to come right over.

If his home seemed just right for a bachelor whose first concern was not housekeeping — it was one of a group of simple, minimally furnished wooden houses belonging to the commission — Mr. Pratt turned out to be far from my preconception of a forester. He was in his thirties and seemed stalwart enough for the job of lumberjack, but in addition to being an outdoor man he happened to be an intellectual. On his bookshelves was an excellent library of books dealing with history, archaeology, mythology, biology, politics, and economics, as well as a fine collection of novels and short stories. He said that when I called he was doing homework for a course at the Open University, a state-sponsored correspondence institution featuring radio and television lectures. Before launching into an account of my own quest, I asked him about his.

Mr. Pratt told us that when he was eighteen years old and fresh from failing his school exams, his father, a surgeon, asked him with some exasperation what he intended to do with his life. Since Jim did not know, his father, who evidently had given the question some thought, suggested forestry. Having no better prospect, Jim went to the Forestry Commission and was taken on. Surprisingly enough, his superiors recognized talents that he had been careful earlier to conceal, and he was assigned to plant pathology, where he blossomed. Devoting himself to study, he acquired a first-class education not only in plant pathology but in liberal arts generally. Then he decided to get a graduate degree. But that meant first getting an undergraduate degree, though he was plainly years ahead of the usual college graduate. So he signed up with the Open University. Graduate work he planned to take at Iowa State University, which was known for its plant pathologists. He had already visited Iowa State and had given two seminars there on his specialty, *fomes annosus*, a root disease that attacked conifers. Mr. Pratt told us that the literature on *fomes annosus* was growing with daunting rapidity. Between 1880 and 1960, scientists published about six hundred papers on the disease, and between 1960 and 1970 another twelve hundred. Having reviewed this literature, Mr. Pratt had become a devout believer in the importance of observation, not statistics. "The crucial papers were written by an Englishman in the nineteen forties," he said, "and there's not a statistic in them all."

After years in a Forestry Commission laboratory, Mr. Pratt was considered ripe for practical experience, so his superiors assigned him to this outpost, where he was responsible for the felling of thousands of tons of timber, which, as he explained, "must be cut in the right way at the right time at the right place and sent off to the right mill, and I must make sure that the forests are not burned down while I'm on duty." He spoke at length of the hazards of fire, and said, "We're about the only people in the country who cannot enjoy sunshine."

Mr. Pratt took out his Ordnance Survey map — scale 1:50,000 — and spread it out on the floor of the living room. He promptly found the road that Johnson and Boswell followed, marked as a line of dashes, signifying, as the key noted, "Path *Sentier Fussweg*." Above the trace of this route were the words "Old Military Road." It turned out that the path began in the forest just about two hundred yards from where we were sitting.

Johnson wrote that he did not remember seeing any animals on the road, but he had been told that there were stags, roebucks, goats, and rabbits. I asked Mr. Pratt what I would be likely to see, or at least what would I see if I was lucky?

"Salmon and trout in the rivers," he said. "The usual foxes and badgers and three types of deer. The red deer; the sika — a Japanese deer, an introduction, an exotic species; and the roe deer — a charming little creature and extremely good to eat. You may see any of these three types of deer. Certainly you'll have a good chance of seeing a red deer. If it's a stag, he won't have cast his antlers yet, so you won't be able to tell him from a hind. There's nothing to control the red deer and the sika deer, so from time to time we have to shoot them. Red squirrels. You may see stoats or weasels. You may see wildcats — nothing to worry about — nocturnal, shy animals, generally speaking. Pine martens are present — like a large, tree-climbing weasel. Large feet, a good climber, likes chicken, and has a particular penchant for sandwiches. Edinburgh Zoo asked us if we could catch a pine marten, preferably female and pregnant. One of the chaps who is very ingenious at such things made a trap and first baited it with different birds, including a dead curlew — a moorland bird with a long beak. But he got no response. A keeper reminded him that if you wanted to see a marten you really have to try some old sandwich bread. They're very fat, very secretive animals, very rare. They used to be common in this country. The sandwich bread worked.

"Birds. You may see some black game, and you may see one or two red grouse, a relative of the willow grouse. It's the only bird that occurs only in Britain. If you're lucky you may possibly see a golden eagle over Glen Moriston way. It's big — wing span of about six or seven feet. Easy to confuse with a buzzard. Our buzzard is the equivalent of your red-tailed hawk — wing span of about three or four feet. Other birds. Raven — long, triangular beak, and it croaks, instead of cawing like a crow. If you see it, well worth watching. Its aerial acrobatics are extraordinary; it even flies upside down. You may see a hen harrier, if you're lucky — like an American marsh hen, a most elegant bird, another bird of prey. A merlin, smallest of the British raptors, but one of the fastest and one of the most dangerous. If you're incredibly lucky you may see a peregrine falcon. It stoops at a hundred and eighty miles an hour for a pigeon — knocks it clean out of the sky. There used to be about four hundred before the war. With the introduction of Dieldrin, there are now about a hundred. On the eastern seaboard, in the States, there used to be about a hundred pairs, and now there isn't one. The young are sold for about a thousand pounds each, supposedly for their hunting prowess, to Arabs. Makes a sort of *keek-keek-keek* sound. You may see a short-eared owl. He hunts rodents, has particularly buoyant wings. If you get too close to their nest, they'll come and whizz you. I've had one put his talons through my scalp. These are the animals you're likely to see on your one and a half miles over the open moorland. I suspect that the number of birds of prey at present is significantly less than it was in Boswell's day. As soon as the landlords started to preserve game, they naturally began to kill off the creatures that killed the creatures *they* wished to preserve."

Johnson wrote that the country was denuded of wood, with only stumps of oaks and firs indicating that it earlier had been a great forest. Mr. Pratt said that the area lost its trees after the introduction of sheep, and that formerly there had been a forest of great oaks and Caledonian pines and ash. He thought that the tops of the slopes had been barren probably since the Bronze Age, when the climate changed. "On both sides of the forest are odd little crofts here and there dotted on the hillside, evidence of old field sites," Mr. Pratt said. "There's a dun — a vitrified fort — a single wall around a primitive defense structure laced with timbers that burned and vitrified. From about the fourth century. There once must have been a thriving community.

"The first forestry was practiced in the seventeenth century, and the big forestry really started only after the First World War. Prior to that time the total acreage in Britain was about five million acres. It dropped by nineteen eighteen to about two million acres. The demand during the war was enormous just to supply duckboard for the trenches. We were always short of timber. In the seventeenth century one of Samuel Pepys's jobs was to do surveys for ships' timber. What he found was that forests were preserved more for game than for timber.

"The Forestry Commission was finally set up in nineteen nineteen. The idea was to ensure a supply of timber in case of war. Inchnacardoch here was the first or second forest planted by the commission in Scotland. The aim in nineteen nineteen was to establish five million acres by about nineteen sixty, so it meant acquiring land and technology. Land available was really managed. This country has led the world in afforesting lands where soil was poor and climate was poor and native species wouldn't grow. There are about ten thousand species of trees in the world, and you had to get the right one. The only conifers here were the Scotch pines, but climate and soil conditions have changed since Scotch pine was predominant. When it comes to consideration of species, you never know how a species will adapt. The Forestry Commission usually plants non-native species. It often plants Sitka spruce and lodge-pole pine from the U.S. and Pacific Northwest. The lodge-pole pine is being defoliated by the pine beauty moth — it's killing off thousands of acres.

"The species that did best came from Vancouver, from climate conditions similar to those here, a species that grew fast on the relatively high ground that we have here. A thousand feet here is equivalent to three thousand in the Alps. At four thousand feet, in the Cairngorms, these trees are practically in arctic conditions. At Ullapool you could go — if you had the hills — from semitropical to arctic conditions as you went up the hills.

"But the Second World War interrupted all this. The result of the war was that many of the plantations that grew up after the First World War were destroyed. So the target of five million was not achieved. We have about two million acres, and we're one from the bottom in Europe in trees per acre. France is first, and France is more concerned with quality than we are. A White Paper changed it all. In the sixties, with the possibility of nuclear war, the objective of a reserve for war was nonsense."

Realizing that Mr. Pratt would be an ideal expert to have on my walk — we eventually returned to the subject of the walk — I asked if he would like to come along. He said that he had too much paperwork to do, now that he was getting practical experience. Then he asked if I could read a map, and when he heard the hesitant reply, he gave me a two-minute course in contour lines — each line was a different elevation. And he asked me if I had a compass, and then lent me his, as well as a large walking stick and a haversack. He suggested also that I take along a piece of string, a knife, and sixpence, recalling vaguely that in ancient law one was not considered a vagrant if one could produce those three items. The idea, he believed, continuing to exhibit vagueness on this one subject, was that with the string one could set a trap for a rabbit, with the knife one could kill the rabbit, and with the sixpence — well, what could the sixpence be for? Perhaps the sixpence was for buying something to eat if the string failed and the knife therefore proved useless.

Mr. Pratt tried to reassure me that the walk posed no dangers, not even of shops ambitious for my sixpence. In the Highlands the dangers were not on land but at sea, he said, and proceeded to tell us about *his* travels in the islands, about storms at sea and lives in peril. He told of taking the boat — a "puffer" — to the isle of Eigg, off Skye, on a day when the waters were in turmoil. "You have to decant from the puffer to the Eigg boat," he said, and the two boats were moving, as he put it, "asynchronously." When he finished his account of survival en route to Eigg, he said that the terrors of that trip had been nothing compared with those he felt when he traveled to the isle of Muck. "The Muck boat was smaller than the Eigg boat," he began, "if that was possible."

Comforted by the realization that the walk I contemplated might be uphill or downhill, but it would never be at sea, I still felt that it would be reassuring to have a companion, and my wife insisted that I not set off without an experienced hiker. When I told Dhileas Leslie, proprietor of the Brae Hotel, where we were staying, that I wanted to find someone to accompany me, she went right to the telephone. First she tried the young man who worked at Leslie's general store, which had been her father's, but he could not get the day off. Then she tried another young man, who said he had pressing business in Inverness. Finally Miss Leslie had what, for want of a grander encomium, I greeted as a genius idea. She would see if Mrs. Forbes would like a walk across the hills.

Elizabeth Forbes worked at the hotel. In fact, except for the cook and the waitress, she seemed to be the only employee, tending bar, washing dishes, cleaning rooms, even substituting as cook on the cook's day off. Miss Leslie and I walked right into the kitchen and interrupted the dishwashing.

Mrs. Forbes said that she had heard of Johnson and Boswell, and she even suggested there were quite some stories told about them. Hearing about my plan to walk on the old military road, she said she was quite prepared to go along and would even like to go along, but she kept protesting, "I haven't got any sense of direction." She added to this refrain, "I can't read a map," and I allowed that I did not know much about that either. Mrs. Forbes struck me as a no-nonsense Scot, and I thought that would be right for the mission. She looked trim, even spry, in much better condition than I was. She told me that she was sixty-three years old and that she loved walking. I made an appointment with her for the next morning, confident that she was just the one to supplement my state of athletic prowess and my knowledge of wildlife. But she was a bit hard of hearing, and I wondered if she had heard me say that I did not have much of a sense of direction either and that I was not exactly a master of map-reading.

I walked upstairs to our second-floor room, winded by the climb of a flight of stairs, and opened Boswell to his introduction, with its description of Johnson: "He was now in his sixty-fourth year, and was become a little dull of hearing."

It was almost enough to make me believe in the workings of a benevolent providence — to have cast up Mrs. Forbes in her sixty-fourth year, become a little dull of hearing.

The next morning I found a packed lunch ready, and, fearing the worst, I added to it several chocolate bars and a large package of digestive biscuits. Mrs. Forbes brought along as the total of her rations for the forced march an apple and an orange. My wife drove us to Jenkins Park, the hamlet less than a mile from Fort Augustus, where the road began. A large iron gate marked the starting point, with a sign OLD MILITARY ROAD TO GLENMORISTON. The Forestry Commission had added another sign: PLEASE SHUT THE GATE.

By this time I had learned that there was hardly a path *sentier Fussweg* in the neighborhood that was not associated with the memory of General (later Field Marshal) George Wade (1673–1748). When, early in the eighteenth century, he was appointed commander-in-chief of Scotland, he took to building roads, helped along by five hundred soldiers who got sixpence per day extra pay. He called them his "highwaymen," and the enterprise he commanded was duly celebrated:

> Had you seen these roads before they were made
> You would lift up your hands and bless General Wade.

Later, as commander of British forces in Flanders, he spent a good deal of time on other people's roads, pursued and pursuing and singularly failing to find his way. Instead of blessings or glory, he earned the laughter of audiences as a butt in French drama. When he was buried in Westminster Abbey, a grateful nation had reason for additional gratitude: he had left money for a monument to his memory. In *Historical Memorials of Westminster Abbey*, Arthur P. Stanley, who was dean of Westminster, wrote, "It is said that the sculptor Roubiliac used to come and stand before 'his best work,' the monument to Wade, and weep to think that it was put too high to be appreciated."

When Mrs. Forbes and I set out along General Wade's road, we found that grass was growing between the paving stones and that the nation seemed to have forgotten about maintenance. Mrs. Forbes had grown up in the country, and she had the knowledge that a country girl acquired, a familiarity with plant and animal species that I woefully lacked. As we opened — and closed — the gate, I asked her to identify, during our walk, the plants and animals we encountered. She accepted the assignment conscientiously and, soon convinced, on ample evidence, that I could barely tell an evergreen tree from a housefly, she took to naming the most familiar objects as well as the least familiar. First came the chaffinch that she spotted high in a tree just inside the gate. About two hundred yards from the first gate we came to a fence, and Mrs. Forbes said that it was intended to keep deer out, for deer fed on trees. She then continued with an almost unending catalogue of the vegetation around us and underfoot, for the stony path was often overgrown. Broom, with its yellow flower, often called gorse, and thus classed together with the whin; fir trees, birch, larch, bracken, hawthorn, bramble, rowan or mountain ash. All along the road lay trees felled by Forestry Commission employees as part of the program of planting and thinning. The winds were so strong that unless young trees were planted close together, they toppled before the wind; being planted thickly afforded the trees mutual shelter. When the trees attained sufficient girth and strength to resist the wind, the plantation was thinned. Many of the trees had a short horizontal white streak painted on them; they were trees marked for felling.

Mrs. Forbes looked down and spotted the black snails popularly known as slugs. She nudged one gently with her foot, and it curled up on itself. "That's the heather starting to come out — the fresh green," she said, looking up. "It doesn't bloom till August. The bell heather blooms in July. The English call heather 'heath.' Honeysuckle. Dandelion."

Near the second waterfall she announced a moth. "I don't know what kind it is," she said. "I'm not good at moths. I just know it's moths." Then came wild violets. "Actually dog violets, some people call them."

Water poured from the heights at right, tumbling down the decline at the left of the road. Mrs. Forbes said that there seemed of late to be less water in Scotland, and that a professor had suggested the fault lay with the Forestry Commission's tree-planting achievements. As more trees were planted, they drew up more of the available water. "It's drying up the streams and rivers," she said. "That's holly," she continued. "A fire break," she said, when there was a broad swath without trees.

"Blaeberry — in England they call them bilberry. There's lovely fruit that comes on them, delicious in jams and tarts and things. A hazel tree. An oak." She said nothing when the next identifiable object turned out to be a large rusty piece of machinery used in clearing trees. A tiny concrete bridge spanned a burn. High above stretched a double line of pylons. "Unsightly things, aren't they?" said Mrs. Forbes. The road at this point was about three hundred and fifty meters above sea level, I judged, using my newly acquired skill at map-reading.

At left, far below, we could make out the trace of the Caledonian Canal, which joined Loch Ness to Loch Oich to Loch Lochy to Fort William. Fishing vessels used the canal to shorten their voyage between the North Sea on the east and the Irish Sea on the west. Summers, cabin cruisers based at Inverness and at Fort William swelled the traffic; tourists and local people chartered the boats for trips along lochs and canal. At night, boats tied up at Fort Augustus just short of the locks, which were manned only until five o'clock each afternoon. There used to be paddle steamers running excursions from Inverness to Fort William. "The *Gondolier* was the name of one of them," said Mrs. Forbes, "and *Glengarry* was the other." Away off to the left — this was early June — were mountains with patches of snow near the summit. When Johnson saw snow at the tops of the mountains he took it for bald patches of rock, until his guides corrected him.

"A wild rose — English people call it dog rose," Mrs. Forbes said. "That's willow there, hanging over the stream. Wood anemone. That's a beetle. It doesn't seem to want to fly. What's that?" It looked like a green fly, immobile on the ground, and it had a carapace green with orange dots. Mrs. Forbes took a magnifying glass from the pocket of her anorak and slowly approached the fly, which began to move slowly along the ground. But Mrs. Forbes remained puzzled: she had never seen that sort of fly before.

Water cascaded over rocks on the right, tumbling down step by rough step, then disappearing below the path and continuing downward at left. Another tiny concrete bridge. Half of a sign stood there: WEIGH RESTRIC 32 TONN. "Speedwell," Mrs. Forbes said, pointing to a purple flower. There was a carpet of moss on the forest floor. In the center of our path grew stalks that Mrs. Forbes identified as rushes. "You get them growing in a very wet field," she said. "Not the same thing as water reeds, you know." She tore off part of one and held it up. "See, they're solid inside.

"There's a bumblebee on that dandelion," she went on. "Look! That's not a honeybee. Coltsfoot over there — we used to call it crab's toes.

"And that," she said, pointing to a fluffy white bloom, "we used to call cotton. I can't tell you the right name of it; mosscrop is the name of it, I think. That's foxglove, with those purple-and-white flowers on the stem of them. I don't know the posh name. We used to pull them off when we were kids and stick them on our fingers. The seeds lie dormant in the ground for years and years, and then if you get a landslide or somebody comes and disturbs them you'll get these foxgloves growing up and up. That's a willow tree, but we call it a pussy willow. The weather has made it late. That's the flower of it — the catkins. Star of Bethlehem is what we call that one; I don't know the right name of that flower.

"There's been deer in the path," she said, picking out their footprints. "That's what you call bog myrtle — a nice scent off it."

With no warning, the road suddenly ended, and before us was a modest cliff that seemed to bode anything but well for our enterprise and surely would have been impassable even in 1773. But a Land-Rover of the Forestry Commission was parked there. When we inquired of the forester, he said that we had missed a turn of the road about half a mile back.

The turn was easy enough to find, though the path looked fresh for an old military road; it was covered with gravel, and simple to follow. When we consulted the Ordnance Survey map we had taken with us, it did not agree with the trace of this path, but there seemed no alternative. We headed up the path, and it once more crossed the double-pylon line. Our map indicated that here the old military road veered sharply left, or northwest. There seemed to be a path, rather like the bed of a dry river, so Mrs. Forbes and I went this way. As we walked, the path became less distinct, harder to discern. Soon we could not make out any path at all, and we were floundering in a bog. Mrs. Forbes tramped forward and back, left and right, plunging into the soggy ground, trying to pick up traces of the path. "Which way now?" she asked, but I had little guidance to offer, and very little in the way of guesswork either. She clambered — squishing and squooshing along through the mud and slipping from dry patches into wet — up to a prominence to see if the old military road would become visible. Thinking that perhaps we had been wrong to take a dry riverbed for a military road, we decided to return to the path we had left. But we could not find it. So we headed for the pylons, climbing as we did so in order to be able to follow the line of pylons downward until we reached the point at which we had left the path. We got to pylon number 6, and wished we had noted the numbers of the pylons we had seen earlier. Down we clambered to pylon 5, along the clearing that had seemed so smooth before. But this, too, proved boggy terrain, with footing treacherous. Mr. Pratt had said there was no quicksand anywhere, so that was a consolation. Finally Mrs. Forbes made it back to the original path, and I joined her there. Despite the evidence of our map, we went forward along this path, following its turns as it climbed higher and higher. We carefully scrutinized the ground at our left, hoping to find the old military road cutting off in that direction. As we proceeded, I kept consulting the compass to see if by any stretch of wish fulfillment we might somehow be going northwest, as we should. But the compass would not cooperate; we were heading northeast. Perhaps the road would still appear, but we went several hundred yards east of the pylons and there was still no road. What to do?

Suddenly there was the sound of an engine, and, mercifully, the Forestry Commission's Land-Rover came into view again. I began to suspect that orders had been given to keep track of two idiots — babes in the wood — determined to do things the hard way. But the forester seemed casual, and not part of some cosmic plan to save us from ourselves. In response to our question, he said that the old military road was ahead, first on the left. Just keep going, the road would go left; keep left; it was easy; we couldn't miss it. I wished he had not added that final phrase about not being able to miss it. In all my years of confused wandering, I had found those words virtually a guarantee that I *would* miss it.

We walked on, as Mrs. Forbes wondered aloud why the

Forestry Commission had not put up road signs at crucial junctions. The left turn was easy enough to find, and the road indeed turned northwest, still climbing. Mrs. Forbes identified a skylark. "That's peat," she said, lowering her glance. "If that were down around habitations, they'd be using that for fuel."

At the highest point of the road, the forester was waiting — not for us but simply for a colleague to complete some mysterious task off in the distance. "Is this the road?" Mrs. Forbes asked. "Bang on," he replied, and told us to continue straight ahead; we would come to the top of a hill, and below us we would see Glen Moriston.

We opened the fence that stood ahead and carefully closed it again, ignoring the stile erected there to allow people to use the right of way when the fence was locked. The road became progressively soggier. A large puddle stood smack in the center of the road, and in it swam hundreds of tadpoles. Since Mrs. Forbes had no confidence in my knowledge of nature's creatures, she explained that tadpoles became frogs, but that very few of the tadpoles would survive to become frogs. We sighted another, larger puddle about a hundred yards down the bog, and Mrs. Forbes inspected the wildlife there with fascination. She sighted water spiders and dutifully identified them for me.

Beyond this natural aquarium the road seemed to transform itself into an amorphous bog that swallowed puddles whole, and our direction became increasingly uncertain. Mrs. Forbes plunged on, slipping time after time and catching at weeds as she slipped. Since Achlain Farm, where the old military road was supposed to end, was northwest, we used the compass to guide us, but it did little for our footing. Eventually the ground became almost impassable, and we decided to head for a hillock to see if we could spy a road or a path or at least a passable bog. Below, we saw a thin trace of road, but nothing like a path between it and us. This did not deter Mrs. Forbes. On she went, falling, righting herself, muttering, "I wonder where we went wrong. Where did we make our mistake?" I recalled Boswell's description of the route as "eleven wild miles." Once more we headed for a line of pylons, and then I heard her shout, "A road!" She clumped forward with renewed hope and finally sat down and slid the last few dry yards to the road. When I joined her, we began walking down the curving road, both feeling much relieved. "A house martin sitting on that wire," she said. "Ash. Wood pigeons — do a lot of damage to the crops." At last we could see that our road would meet the highway, and on the highway a bus sped by. "Civilization!" Mrs. Forbes cried with pleasure.

At the end of our road, about a hundred yards ahead, a Forestry Commission Land-Rover pulled off the highway. The driver got out and closed the gate, which someone carelessly had left open. He shouted to us, asking if we would be good enough to shut the gate again when we left. "Fine!" I yelled back, and then — too late, since by this time he had returned to his vehicle and had driven off — cursed my stupidity at not asking him where we were. By the time we reached the highway, having carefully shut the gate, we had no indication of our position, except that I saw a bridge to the east and guessed that it must be Torgyle Bridge, which was marked on our map. We must have done the last part of the walk on the wrong road, but we were, as Mrs. Forbes had noted, back in civilization. Cars, trailers, and buses were flashing by. Doggedly, we began walking along the highway. It should have been a pleasure to be on level ground again, but this was the worst part of the trip. We were probably going in the right direction, but my feet felt blistered and raw. I wondered if I would have to call it quits, but the shame of that prospect kept me going. Mrs. Forbes did not complain, and in fact she seemed in fine spirits. We finally got to the prearranged rendezvous, where my wife had been waiting four hours, and she drove us back to Fort Augustus. I returned bearing some digestive biscuits and one chocolate bar. Mrs. Forbes had eaten nothing but half an orange; she had given me the other half. She had not touched the apple. I had expected the walk to take us four hours, and it had taken us seven. My wife told us that as she drove to Achlain Farm, a group of deer crossed the road in front of her. Thinking back, I remembered our luck — water spiders, tadpoles, moth, and fly. Of deer, martens, foxes, stoats, and weasels, to say nothing of ravens, eagles, and falcons — zero.

Mrs. Forbes went home, had a bath, and reported for duty at the hotel. I wanted to learn more about her, so she joined me after breakfast the next morning when her chores were done. She told me that she was born at Stronlairig, above Foyers. "Away up in the hills," she said. "It was the end of the road. The nearest neighbor was two miles away. Before he was seventeen, Father just walked off and joined the army and fought the Boer War. One thing I always remember him saying was that if he was in a tight corner he would rather have a Cockney or a Gurkha with him. He had the greatest admiration for both of them. He had no time for the French people. Then he met my mother and got married. Eventually my mother had twelve children — eight girls and four boys. I think my oldest brother was about two when they come to Strone. The estate owner, in nineteen seven, built the big lodge that's there now, and my mother and father and my oldest brother moved into what used to be the lodge. Lord Lovat, the present Lord Lovat's father, bought the estate, and my father, who was working as a gamekeeper before he was married, was his gamekeeper there for forty-five years.

"My father had to keep down the vermin, which was stoats and weasels and crows and hawks and eagles. You're not allowed to kill these birds now, but in those days they did.

And wildcats, foxes. He also had to burn so much heather every year to keep it coming up fresh for the grouse. He had to take a note if the grouse were diseased, to let Lord Lovat know. And of course he had to train the dogs, both terriers and for going to ground, for taking the foxes and wildcats out of the dens. He also trained retrievers. And he had to kill so many stags. And then about June, Lord Lovat, or if he had let the estate to somebody, he used to come up and there would be people there from June until the end of September, and of course they were out grouse-shooting first, and then towards the end of August, September it was deer-stalking. In the season time there was the young fellows and some older men as well. These boys from Foyers, they would just be, I suppose, fourteen, fifteen, and they used to walk fourteen miles in their bare feet up there, because they were too poor, they didn't have boots to put on their feet. They used to go up before the people came that had taken the estate, or Lord Lovat, was coming up. They used to have to repair the butts — they're made of turf, built up to about chest level, for the shooters to stand in. And these boys, when the season started, they took to what they called beating, and they had a line and they drove the grouse into the butts. They had flags or something to wave to frighten the birds. And of course they had to repair drains and ditches in the hill, and all that sort of thing.

"My father was a loader, and he had a fellow coming behind carrying the rifle, and a pony man to take the stags home. The fellow with the pony had a deer saddle on for the deer. And when it was beating they had paniers — big baskets — that was to carry home the grouse. And my father took the stalk. You have to be very careful stalking a deer, and you have to crawl along sometimes and go into burns and all sorts of things, 'cause deer are very sensitive, and they're very, very quick to know if there's something unusual about. And you've got to always go downwind of them, of course, so that they don't get your scent. And my father took the stalk, and then when he was ready he put his hand out for the gun and he put the cartridges in and he handed it over. My father used to get very annoyed if anybody couldn't shoot well. I wouldn't repeat what he said. He used to tell them off terrible if they missed the grouse or a deer. He would get very, very annoyed if anybody wounded a stag, and if they did wound it, they had to follow it until they got it. He was an exceptionally good shot himself, of course. He was an international clay pigeon shot, and I expect he thought everybody else should have been as good.

"My father was quite a character, actually. He was known all over Britain. Archie MacFarlane. He got to know practically the whole of the aristocracy of Britain. He read a great deal. He was a very intelligent man, actually, and they enjoyed his company. I didn't get on with him, I think possibly because I went away when I was eight, to Inverness and school. I stayed with an aunt there. And of course when I was born he was in the First World War, and I was three when he come home, and I suppose he just didn't know me when I was born and that sort of thing. We just didn't hit it off. Maybe we were too like each other.

"He got thirty bob a month when he come home from the 'fourteen–'eighteen war. But mind you, you had to take into consideration we had our own cow and milk and hens and eggs and potatoes and vegetables. We could have had sheep if we had wanted to, but we couldn't afford to buy them in those days. If someone was sick it was a case of my father taking the horse and trap or riding horseback fourteen miles down to Foyers to get a doctor. When my mother sent an order into town, it was for a huge quantity. It wasn't a case of buying a couple of pounds in those days — it was buying sacks, hundredweights we used to call them, of flour, sugar, salt, rice, lentils, split peas, barley, and that sort of thing.

And she used to get a tea box full of all the other odds and ends such as margarine — we made our own butter — syrup, treacle. A tea box did for maybe a month or two, and then she repeated it again. If she wanted to go into town, mostly she had to walk eight miles to the bus in Whitebridge and then eight miles back, carrying the things she'd bought. And before they had the bus my father and she would go into town — that was Inverness — with the horse and trap. It was thirty-five miles between our home and town, so that was actually seventy miles that horse had to do that day. I was never in town at all until I went away to school. We used to go about barefoot from April till October, but we always had boots or shoes of some kind.

"Some winters it was dreadful. We'd be blocked in for weeks at a time. And my father got a great big sled made — it was just like a great big wooden box, with runners on it — for the horse to pull if we ran out of food. It was very, very seldom we did, as my mother always got plenty in before the winter started, to do for three months, maybe. But if we did run out of anything, he would go down to Whitebridge with the horse and sled. Nowadays if there's a shower of snow the helicopters are dropping food. There was no such thing then. Nobody bothered to find out were you all right or anything in those days. Everybody prepared for it.

"My mother was the most fantastic cook. She used to make the most gorgeous Scotch broth, all fresh vegetables out of the garden, just taken out of the ground that morning. Rabbits every conceivable way you could think of. Venison, of course. And always the occasional hen, fish, grouse. We very, very seldom ate bread. She didn't bake bread, but scones and pancakes and oatcakes — we practically lived on that. Latterly we got bread once a week. A traveling grocer used to come up, when things became more mechanized.

"I really would have liked to go in for sport — running,

jumping, horse-jumping. You didn't get the chance in those days to do things like that. There was no such thing as anybody making their living out of sport in those days. They just laughed at you. And funnily enough I went into an office. I was a shorthand-typist. I've got all the certificates for shorthand and bookkeeping and typing and everything. And then of course I got married when I was twenty and went to live on a farm. I was there for thirty years. At Foyers. My second son still has the farm. I planted tatties, lifted potatoes, I helped with the hay, I helped with the harvest, threshed the corn — we had an old waterwheel, we had that before the combine harvesters were invented. And I milked the cows, both by hand and by machine. We generally had about twenty-five or thirty milking cows. And I delivered the milk, with the horse and trap, in Foyers. There used to be a British aluminium company in Foyers, and all these houses were occupied by these people, and we used to go around and deliver the milk. I had a big, ten-gallon tank, and they used to come out with jugs and you measured it. I helped with the lambing. And I skinned dead lambs to put on another lamb so that a sheep would take it. If a sheep has twins and another sheep has a single lamb and the lamb dies or is dead when it's born, and you find that the ewe won't take another lamb, another sheep's lamb, then if you skin it when it's dead and put the coat on top of the other one, she'll get the smell of the skin and she'll take it. You leave it on for a couple of days and take it off and she'll accept the lamb. I've done that, and well, I've brought up a family, two daughters and three sons.

"And I used to go ferreting for rabbits. I had one dog — he was quite marvelous, Roy was, oh, all the dogs were marvelous, really, but Roy was really quite a marvelous dog. He didn't need any training whatsoever. All he needed was command. When he was a wee, fluffy puppy he used to get the chickens rounded up, separate one out, and you had to take him away, because he would have kept the chicken there all day if you didn't. When Roy was about a year and a half I gave him to a shepherd to train—well, not to train, but to command him—so that he would come back for the whistle and that sort of thing. We used the dogs for the sheep, and we also had one for the cattle. We had anything from a hundred to a couple of hundred sheep at one time. You led them off on the high ground, the outgrazing, and then a couple of months before they were due to lamb you took them down to the fields. If the winter was open, if it wasn't severe, you left them out during the winter. Black-faces. They're bred for the hills.

"A lot of people say sheep are stupid and goats are stupid and all that. But animals are not stupid. No animal is really stupid. I remember we bought some in-lamb sheep at the cattle market, one year, and they were on the field about half-past ten at night, and six o'clock in the morning there was one missing. Well, this particular sheep came from a farm about six or seven miles away, and she had walked back to the farm she had come from to have her lamb.

"We marked our sheep with keel, a sort of paint. All the farmers had different colors. And they also had a different earmark. They took chunks out of the ear at the back or at the front, and some perhaps two bits and some perhaps one, and they all had different marks so that each person would know their sheep.

"Finally I walked out on my husband and I started working in hotels. After a while I went to Grantown-on-Spey with Miss Leslie. And I was there for almost five years, and then my mother took ill and I left and nursed my mother until she died. And then I came back to Miss Leslie, who had bought this place in Fort Augustus.

"I've got regrets. Who hasn't? Anybody who says they have no regrets, well, they can't have lived a very interesting life, I always think. But I'm not ever depressed. When I was younger, when I was married first, and when I had my family first, and they were young, then I used to worry about things a little. But I discovered that worrying doesn't do any good. I suppose I've worked things out for myself.

"I used to be very intolerant. I used to say to my own children, I used to tell them to do something, if they couldn't do it the right way I used to get intolerant with them till I stopped to think, well, how could they know how to do it unless they were shown properly? One person can't know everything and anything. There's only some things you know how to do. People weren't quick enough for me. I blame my father for that more than anything, because my father was a very, very, very impatient man, exceedingly impatient man, and he had a thing about being punctual. Everybody had to be just at the minute, and he has conveyed to me and to the rest of my family this thing — you mustn't be late. I would rather be half an hour early than two minutes late. If he said to you, 'Oh, would you do so-and-so for me,' and I'd say yes, but if you didn't do it just there and then — just like that! — he'd go over and do it himself. I suppose he conveyed this to me and to the others as well, but it's me that's talking just now, and I found that I was being the same way when I started working. Even in hotels I discovered I was being the same way to these young girls, when I expected them to do it properly and do it quickly. And I thought, 'Oh no, this isn't going to do at all.' I just simmered down, and now I just don't take very much notice. I think that's because I'm not an intolerant person by nature. Intolerance was conveyed to me when I was young, but it upsets everybody and you always come off worst if you blow the top and you have a row with somebody. I realized it's best to leave things to simmer down and then look at it from a sensible point of view before you give your verdict.

"And I also find that if you're never spiteful or nasty to

people, if you do what you can to help them — it doesn't matter how little it is — I think it's what Christianity is all about. I don't think Christianity is going to church and praying and all this sort of thing. I feel that Christianity is thinking more of other people than you do about yourself."

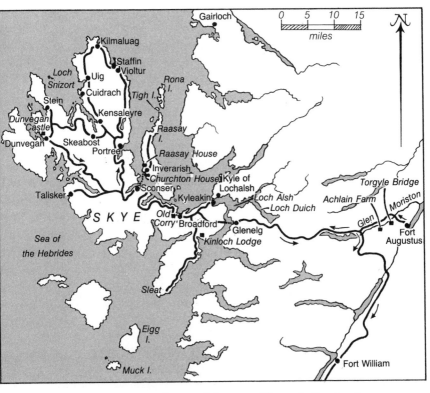

Map of the Second Part of the Tour Through Scotland

CHAPTER 12

In the morning, September the second, we found ourselves
on the edge of the sea. Having procured a boat, we dismissed our Highlanders, whom I would recommend to the
service of any future travelers, and were ferried over to the
Isle of Skye.

— Samuel Johnson

SKYE WAS A PINWHEEL of an island, long peninsulas
stretching into the sea to form tidal sea lochs; early Gaels
called it the Winged Isle, and Vikings knew it as the Cloud
Island. From northern tip to southernmost point, the distance
was about forty miles, and so it was from east to west,
though no place on Skye was more than five miles from the
sea. Volcanoes, long since dormant, had covered much of
the island with lava, producing the topographical eccentrici-
ties so striking to the eye — great crags and hills and preci-
pices. South of the Highlands, Scotland was often rich and
fertile, with a deep layer of earth favorable for cultivation,
but farmers here in the north needed wiles and perseverance
to wrest crops from soil thin and grudging. The late Calum
Maclean, brother of the poet Sorley Maclean, suggested
that the bleak, rocky island exposed "the very bones of old
Mother Earth." Trees were scarce, and seemed to grow only

where planted by man; this was scrubland, moors, and bogs — country for sheep and cattle, not for people. And yet there was a grandeur about the island; when winds were calm and the sun emerged, seas and lochs lay molten under its rays and the land basked in warmth and beauty.

Our first stop was at Broadford, to inquire about places to stay. Planning to be on the island for a couple of months, we wanted what was known as "self-catering" accommodations. The lone woman on duty in the government tourist office said that everything was already rented. But then, evidently skeptical of her own information, she sat down and called her colleague at Portree, the island metropolis with a population of about a thousand. Listening to one-half the conversation, I had my first taste of the indigenous tempo; the Broadford woman spoke slowly, almost languorously, and it seemed forever before she entered upon extended farewells. Finally she hung up and informed us that unexpectedly Anna MacLeod's place in Kensaleyre was available. She described the house in detail, gave us Mrs. MacLeod's phone number, and suggested that if there was no reply, we should try Mrs. MacLeod's mother, Mrs. Mackinnon, who lived next door.

The MacLeods' house, built for their retirement still many years away, faced Loch Snizort (pronounced *Snye*zort) and stood on a rise above the road from Portree to Uig, terminus of the ferry to the Outer Hebrides. Elsewhere in Britain, the absence of central heating would not have been a problem in summer, but here the cold was penetrating, and we sought comfort from portable electric heaters. Sunny intervals faded quickly, and I imagined chilblains rampant. En route to Skye, I had been astonished to see a pharmacy featuring patent medicines that proclaimed their efficacy in the treatment of chilblains, an ailment I had associated with nothing more recent than the reign of Queen Victoria.

We had no phone and no television. The radio in the

living room seemed to be a close relative of an early crystal set; when it was at full volume it was impossible to make out what was being said or played or discreetly gargled, and a hushed whisper was usually the best we could coax from its signal-weary innards. The nearest phone we could use was a mile away, in a call box opposite the post office. It accepted custom with an occasionally obdurate show of reluctance to swallow coins, but it never refused hospitality to moths, spiders, flies, midges, and mosquitoes. Forcing the pace of natural selection, I quickly learned to flap one arm while forcing coins into the phone with the other.

On the south side, our nearest neighbor was the Kensaleyre primary school — nine pupils, one teacher. The Mackinnons lived about a hundred yards to the north. Whenever Mrs. Mackinnon had a message for us, she strode across the field, pushed down the top strand of the wire fence separating the properties, and clambered over. The Mackinnons' sheep were faithful visitors; animals belonging to other crofters also strayed up the footpath beside the house and squeezed through the back fence to graze on nearby slopes.

We quickly succumbed to the spell of the sheep. Each morning they trooped past our bedroom window, as though summoning us to rise. The front lawn grew wild and luscious, and sheep on the way to permitted pastures made strenuous efforts to reach this forbidden treasure. The lambing season was almost over, and the young lambs — "followers" — trailed along behind their mothers. At shearing time the ewes emerged looking as though they had stripped down to long johns, and in our anthropomorphic fancy we convinced ourselves that they felt embarrassed. Huddling against their mothers, the lambs discovered that the old warmth was gone, and we imagined giant crises of identity. There were some Cheviots in the flocks, but most of the animals were Blackfaces, bred for hardiness and accustomed to spending the entire winter in the hills; during storms they hunkered down against the slopes and waited out the worst. The lambs appeared no match for the gales, and we wondered how they survived. Beside the post office one day, as the rain pelted and the wind howled, a local woman, raising her voice above the sound of the storm, told us that she could not bear the weather because of the suffering of the lambs. She had adopted two who had lost their mother, fed them from a bottle, and bedded them down at night in an old wreck of a car.

Daily we watched the tide come in and out, for we lived only about two hundred yards from the inland end of Loch Snizort. In gales the gray expanse of the loch seethed with white foam, and waves roiled the surface, as though this modest body of water were a great ocean; in calm, sunny weather the water shimmered with dazzling brilliance. Evenings we looked out at lines of cattle winding along hills and ridges, and at the ewe and two followers ambling homeward along the road, indifferent to passing traffic as they returned from goodness knows what secret paradise. Whenever the ferry from the Western Isles disgorged its cars and passengers, there was a sudden flurry of movement on the road below, and sometimes as many as half a dozen cars passed within a few minutes.

Before coming to Scotland I had written to Lachlan Mackinnon, of Broadford, and he had replied in cordial terms. "Should you be able to take me with you," his letter concluded, "I wd. be very happy to accompany you on your journeyings in the island." Johnson and Boswell had local people shepherding them about Skye, but it was hard to know how Mr. Mackinnon and I would get on, so I responded with what was intended as amiability joined to caution: "Your suggestion of accompanying me on my trip in Skye sounds more than pleasant. I'll be in touch with you when I get closer to Skye so that we can make further arrangements."

To test the waters, we invited Mr. Mackinnon to lunch in Portree. He turned out to be the retired headmaster of the secondary school at Fort William, a man of considerable reserve and, it seemed to me, total sobriety. It happened that he was also chairman of the Skye and Lochalsh District Council, and thus the closest thing on the island to a chief of state. This was an unexpected bonus, for Johnson and Boswell had been guests of the island's eighteenth-century notables, and here were we, entertaining contemporary gentry. Over coffee we decided the outlines of a first joint sortie.

On the agreed day I picked up Mr. Mackinnon, and we drove off to see Donald John MacLennan at Old Corry, formerly Coirechatachan, just a couple of miles from Broadford. Johnson and Boswell had been guests at Coirechatachan, and, as coincidence would have it, their host was named Lachlan Mackinnon. A rocky, difficult track led from the main road, and as we drove along, jostled all the way, the latter-day Mackinnon noted aloud that he would see if the roads department could do something about improving the surface; surely there was free time between major projects.

Mr. MacLennan came out of his farmhouse to greet us. Knowing that I was interested in Johnson and Boswell, he took me immediately to the ruins of the house where they had stayed, less than a hundred yards from his own home. About all that remained were gray stones forming a fragment of what had been the north gable. Three rowan trees grew nearby, much like sentries who had not been relieved of duty though nothing remained to be guarded. The rest of the stones may have been removed to build a sheepfold, but Mr. MacLennan believed that they were used to construct a *caibeal*, a wall enclosing a burial plot, in this case for the Mackinnons.

Since he was born on Harris, in the Outer Isles, and had been on Skye only twenty-one years, Mr. MacLennan described himself as an "incomer" or "white settler." One of Skye's three veterinarians, he served the southern part of the island and the mainland nearby. After he had treated us to a succinct account of exotic cattle diseases, he listened patiently to Mr. Mackinnon's complaint that crofters neglected their sheep and no longer bothered to dip them in pesticide or to smear them. Dipping was the modern practice, but for centuries sheep farmers had protected their animals against vermin with a pomade of butter, tar, and grease.

"There isn't the same attention," Mr. MacLennan agreed. "I cannot really blame the crofters, because the croft is very much part-time and can't provide a livelihood, and consequently the crofter doesn't have the time to take the same care of the sheep. I would blame it on the type of tups — rams — that are used. The Scottish Blackface was reckoned one of the hardiest sheep you could get. But they mollycoddle them — keep them inside and blow them up for marketing to fetch a big price. Instead of having a smaller, hardy type of tup, you're using a big type. I think you can breed hardiness out of them. The same thing is happening to our cattle. We had the hardy, small Highland beast there, which was slow maturing. Then people in the so-called name of improvement began crossing with the Shorthorn. They then went one stage further and started crossing with the black-polled Aberdeen Angus. It's an excellent animal, but meant for lower ground. Now they're using the Hereford, which is even more of a low-ground animal."

By this time Mr. Mackinnon was suggesting that we had to keep our next appointment, so we said a hasty goodbye and made our rocking way back to Broadford. Continuing south along a road little frequented, we finally entered the parish of Sleat, home of Godfrey James Macdonald, eighth Lord Macdonald, descendant of Sir Alexander Macdonald, the first to greet Johnson and Boswell when they landed on Skye. Lord Macdonald served in the district council, whose nine members were elected for a term of five years. The parish he represented had fewer than a thousand people, and the lands he owned were no longer the vast domain of his forebears.

When the seventh Lord Macdonald died, in 1969, death duties forced the family to sell off thousands of acres. Godfrey James was then twenty-one years old. His father had converted Kinloch, a hunting lodge on the shore of Loch na Dal, into a tranquilly inviting hotel, and the eighth Lord Macdonald decided that hotels were going to be the family's salvation. While we waited for Lord Macdonald at Kinloch Lodge, I looked about the public lounge. There was a portrait of Maria Anne Wyndham, wife of the fourth Lord Macdonald, and Lady of the Bedchamber to Queen Victoria from 1855 to 1863. Another painting depicted Elizabeth Diana Bosville, wife of Sir Alexander. Though Boswell's cousin, she was the hapless target of his criticism: "I was quite disgusted with her nothingness and insipidity. Mr. Johnson said, 'This woman would sink a ninety-gun ship. She is so dull — so heavy.'" Indeed, as Boswell wrote, "Johnson *took off* Lady Macdonald leaning forward with a hand on each cheek and her mouth open — quite insipidity on a monument grinning at sense and spirit. To see a beauty represented by Mr. Johnson was excessively high. I told him it was a masterpiece and that he must have studied it much. 'Ay,' said he." Despite my worst intentions, I could detect nothing of the lady's reputed character in the portrait on the wall.

Beneath her likeness, or unlikeness, was a pile of stationery for guests — red coat of arms at top, and at bottom the names of the hotel directors, given as: The Rt. Hon. Lord Macdonald, the Lady Macdonald Anne, and Lady Macdonald. Anne was the seventh lord's widow. Lady Macdonald was Claire, the eighth lord's wife. The Rt. Hon. Lord Macdonald was the man who at that moment entered the lounge.

Gangly, dressed in dark, unpressed slacks and a torn green
sweater, he did not resemble the portrait I had painted for
myself on the basis of stereotypical lords I had not known.
Nor did his accent suggest a Scot. That was the result of attending school in England, he explained. "It's not a plummy
English accent," he said defensively.

I wondered what Lord Macdonald's reaction was to Johnson's and Boswell's descriptions of his illustrious ancestor
Elizabeth Bosville, and — even more — to the scathing rep-
resentations of the first Lord Macdonald. During the whole
trip no one had been memorialized with greater scorn or
venom than Sir Alexander. Boswell wrote that the accommodations were mean, not befitting a clan chief; dinner
was "ill-dressed," without tea; and Sir Alexander neglected
the most elementary courtesies. "Sir, we shall make nothing
of him," Johnson later said to Boswell. "He has no more ideas
of a chief than an attorney who has twenty houses in a street
and considers how much he can make of them." In the manu-
script of his *Journal*, Boswell called Sir Alexander a "wretch"
and said he was vexed that "so much mischief should be produced by such an insect." The first edition of the *Journal*
offered a softer view, but Lord Macdonald — he was made a
baron in 1776 — found more than enough to upset him. He
wrote Boswell an angry letter, and Boswell had a friend call
on Lord Macdonald to describe the great care taken to excise
offensive passages; alas, some miscreant phrases had slipped
through. In the end, Boswell appointed a second to transmit
a challenge to a duel, but calamity was averted when Lord
Macdonald softened the strictures in *his* letter to Boswell.
Now, more than two hundred years later, what would Lord
Macdonald have to say about the withering comments of
Boswell and of Johnson?

I asked His Lordship, and the eighth Lord Macdonald
replied at once that he had read neither Johnson nor Boswell.
"Should I have?" he added, with an air of ingenuousness.

"There are so many books on clan history that I read and enjoy reading that I don't feel I have to read Boswell's and Johnson's visit to the Highlands."

Deciding to avert calamity, I changed the subject and asked Lord Macdonald to tell me about himself. He said that he was born in Ostaig House, where Johnson and Boswell stayed. His Lordship's account then moved directly to the middle of the nineteenth century, when the Lord Macdonald of the time sold off great portions of his land and kept only about a hundred and thirty thousand acres. Now the family owned fewer than four thousand acres and only about a dozen sheep. "The hotels are our bread and butter," Lord Macdonald said. "We still do stalking parties, stalking for red deer, but we don't do that commercially, really."

Johnson had said that if he were Sir Alexander he would have a magazine of arms, and Sir Alexander had objected that the arms would rust. "Let there be men to keep them clean," Johnson rejoined. "Your ancestors did not use to let their arms rust." Sir Walter Scott subsequently criticized Johnson for not realizing that a Highlander who went armed at this time was condemned for the first offense to service as a common soldier, and for a second offense to exile overseas. I asked the eighth Lord Macdonald how *his* armory was doing. "All I have are a pair of guns, four rifles, an air rifle, and a *skean dhu* [dirk] . . . I haven't fired my gun in anger in nearly two years." That left us free to conjecture as to the target of his wrath. "I enjoy hunting, but I just can't get time. At the time the shooting's at its best I'm too busy. There are not enough hours in a day. We run our two hotels on a personal basis. Claire supervises the cooking. I do all the bookkeeping work and keep the staff happy. You keep the staff happy by being kind to them. If you're kind to them, they'll be good to you, and that goes all through life. Gone are the days of being dictatorial — and a good thing, too. We've got a very, very good nucleus of staff. I suppose the main problem is getting people to have the insight that you provide a service which almost everyone does, so that you have to provide something more. You have to provide first-class service, first-class food, and the personal service means a lot. Make sure you meet all the guests every night.

"I do about a hundred and fifty miles a day going from one hotel to the other. I'm not complaining. I'd be very disappointed if I weren't busy. We're in the guidebooks now — *Egon Ronay, Michelin, Good Hotel Guide* — so we don't have to do any advertising. Here at Kinloch we close about the end of October. We keep Ardvasar open. There are always functions, and the winter just flashes by. You do the accounts, you do cleaning and painting, and it just flashes by. We've got three little girls, and from the beginning of March till the end of October I hardly see them. I just go home to sleep."

At least once a year there were clan gatherings, and Lord Macdonald greeted groups large and small. "Slightly less formal than visits to the Pope," he said with a smile. "Last year, as our house guests, we had over two hundred, basically from North America, but from all over, even Belgium. We've had a very active Clan Donald society in Belgium — over eight hundred. Those are the old mercenaries who fought against Wellington at Waterloo. Napoleon even had a marshal who was a Clan Donald man."

Just as Mr. Mackinnon and I were about to go, Lord Macdonald remembered that he had not told us about the latest move in rebuilding the family estate. The Macdonalds had just bought the local gift shop, a modest emporium that sold a grab bag of tweeds, plaids, and souvenirs. "All the prospective buyers who were interested in purchasing the gift shop were outside people," Lord Macdonald said. "If you can keep it to local people, so much the better. So much of the history of Scotland is passing to people who aren't the least bit interested in the local community. I feel responsible to the community. The gift shop is terribly understocked. It's fairly seasonal, and we're going to extend it and have a little bakery and make homemade bread and keep it open the year round and employ local people."

CHAPTER 13

The ancient rigor of puritanism is now very much relaxed, though all are not yet equally enlightened. I sometimes met with prejudices sufficiently malignant, but they were prejudices of ignorance.

— Samuel Johnson

HIS PARENTS, his grandparents, all his ancestors as far back as he could find their trace, had come from Kilmaluag, at the north end of Skye. After serving parishes elsewhere and the whole Church of Scotland as its moderator, James Matheson had finally returned to his native island, coming back to people he knew well.

We sat in the large study of his manse, a big house in ample grounds on a rise overlooking the street leading to the main square in Portree. I asked him how things had changed for the churches since the visit of Johnson and Boswell. "In seventeen seventy-three there hadn't been the sectarian events that happened since then, in the nineteenth century," he replied. "The Free Church broke away in eighteen forty-three, and then the Free Presbyterian Church, a tiny little body. So the Free Presbyterian schism, which is an infinitesimal thing on the world map, is quite big in church affairs here. One of the saddest things that has happened is that the communities on this island are split into three, and three almost equal parts, so that the community feelings, as far as the religious life is concerned, are broken apart. What ought to be a binding element is a divisive element. It seems on the surface that the hold of religion is much weaker than it was in the eighteenth century, because far fewer people go to church, even in the strongly disciplinarian churches — the Free and the Free Presbyterian. And yet when you dig under the surface, you find the same kind of immediate awareness of what you're talking about when you talk about religion. And a kind of respect — it's much more than respect; a kind of reverence — for the world and God and everything that is connected with religion. You find it on all seven days. The seventh day is one of the freak things about this part of the world. I suppose there always has to be some sort of focus for people's religion, and the seventh day in Skye fits in awfully nicely with the Skye character, which is not to do anything you don't need to do — at least not to do it today.

"There's a difference between the Highlander and others. This place was very remote and inaccessible for a long, long time. The Reformation, which happened in Edinburgh, didn't happen here for the best part of a century afterwards. But there's also differences that have been created by the disappearance of what was the focus of social life, which was the laird and the castle. Now the lairds, by and large, have deserted their folk in this area. You can't talk to anybody about the time between Johnson and now without talking about the evictions. It's bitten so, so deep. It comes into the religious rifts, too, in a curious way. The established church was very close to the aristocracy. After all, the ministers were paid largely by the lairds; their manses were built by the lairds. And therefore it was very difficult for any individual minister to say to his laird 'You get packing — I'm going to take a quite different viewpoint from you.' And this meant where there wasn't really strong character among the religious leaders, they tended to go with the establishment, and therefore they, too, to some extent, deserted their people. And when the Free Church rift came, although it was supposed to be on profound theological differences, it was quite as much from the fact the Free Church seemed to be out of this downtrodden portion of the people against the establishment, and that is the main strength of sectarians in this area. Memories are very long, but when there's a real concern for old people and young people, it's the Church of Scotland that takes a lead in these."

Dr. Matheson spoke at first of the other churches on Skye as "the small churches." Then he paused and asked aloud, "How do we talk about them?" Eventually he opted to call them "the other churches." "The other churches tend to be otherworldly," he said. "Members of the Church of Scotland are more upper class, more professional. When incomers come to the island they come into the Church of Scotland, if not into the Episcopal Church, which is very, very tiny. And there's hardly any Roman Catholics here. The really truly locals tend, in the majority, to be Free Church or Free Presbyterian."

I asked Dr. Matheson what the theological distinctions were between Free Church and Free Presbyterian. "None that I can find," he replied. "I was baptized in the Free Presbyterian Church, I was a minister in the Free Church, and then I became a minister in the Church of Scotland, so I've been through all three. All my old friends think the next step obviously is adherence to Rome. But it was a matter of difference between liberal theology and extremely conservative theology."

Had the notion of sin changed since Johnson's day? I asked. "I would say that as a whole in the thinking of the Western world the notion of sin has much less dominance than it had from medieval times right up to the present time," he said. "Both Marx and Freud made a profound difference to the thinking of us all about guilt and the occasions when we should feel guilty and when we shouldn't. Here, not so much. I think we would still talk about guilt, particularly in the other churches, as something purely religious, something that happens between me and God, whereas in general thought, in the Western world, America and here, it's rather something that happens between me and my neighbor, isn't it?"

When I recalled that in earlier times sin was often associated with sex, Dr. Matheson suggested that there had always been in the islands "a kind of earthiness and a recognition that that's what people do, and that's what young men and women do, and where a girl had an illegitimate child they went through the performance of rebuking her and all that sort of thing, and quite a palaver with the kirk session before the child was baptized, but it was perfectly understood and accepted in the community, and nobody really thought any worse of the person."

He found himself now referring to the other churches as the sectarian churches: "I keep using this word 'sectarian,' because what else can you say?" And he suggested that in the sectarian churches sin was still closely associated with sex, "not just adultery but premarital sex as well, much more than in the Church of Scotland."

He went on: "I visit hospitals, and I find some members of the Free Church and Free Presbyterian who are reading sermons by the Puritans, and when I listen to the sermons, which I do as seldom as I can, the sermons of Free Church and Free Presbyterian, they still have the same approach as one finds in the Puritans like [John] Owen, the serious breaking down of a particular passage of Scripture, a complete acceptance that this is the word of God, which has to be analyzed and applied and so on, heads one, two, three, and subdivisions. Yes, it's remarkable how people still put up with it. The literal word. Oh yes, they encourage Bible reading, but under authority. They fail to encourage the sort of Bible study that we think about, where you gather a few people around and you open a passage and 'What do you think?' and everybody's free to say what they think. It's rather closely interpreted and controlled study of the Bible, and completely fundamentalist, so much so that they're quite alarmed still at the kind of biological teaching that's given in the schools and try to counteract it.

"Many of the people one meets are the nicest people in the world, and you couldn't get better neighbors in any time of trouble. But there's a lack of welcome in their churches. If I went to communion service in the Free Presbyterian Church it would be impossible for me to take communion from the preacher. They're completely closed in that respect. They'd welcome you to services, but that would make no difference whatever to the kind of thunder you would get. They make no allowance for people who come from a different place. If you go to their churches, you must take it the way it is — the singing of the Psalms and the Psalms only, without instrumental music, the standing at prayers, sitting at singing, and the long, long sermon.

"Honestly, I think it's been a great deliverance to come into a much more open form of Christian faith and obedience than I knew in those churches. I was always uncomfortable in them, couldn't get quite the answers to my questions, and felt that to be tied to the Westminster Confession, which was constructed by a group of people way back in the early seventeenth century — most of them were English — to be tied to that as an interpretation didn't make sense to me. Why was *this* sacred, more than anything else? But I think it was mainly when I was a chaplain in the war I realized that the whole approach to life, the other-worldliness, the refusal to understand what was going on in the minds of people in the modern world — I just couldn't take it anymore.

"You don't want to hurt anybody. You don't want to make a rift bigger than it is already, and one of my prayers in this place has always been to get closer to the people who come from the same stock as I do myself, but what I cannot be patient with is the idea that there is one interpretation of the universe and of the Christian faith that has to be imposed on everybody, that is, I think, basically un-Christian."

What reaction do you get from them when you say that? I asked. "Just the usual patter," he replied. "They stick by the word, and the literal word, and say that I'm introducing the human element — a failure to realize that we're all doing that. The Pavlovian brainwashing technique was not invented by Pavlov. It was invented by Christian evangelists. There is the way of building up a feeling of guilt until the cracking point comes, and either you have to accept the whole package of the redemption scheme or else you're totally rejected from salvation. And this is, as I understand it, the classical method of brainwashing, to create this crisis which can only be resolved by accepting totally — communism or fascism or ultra-fundamental Christianity or whatever it is.

"The Christian faith, if it means anything, and it means everything to me, is about the life we're living in the world and whatever may come out of it. Therefore, it has to be our attitude to the most immediate things — racial prejudice and neighborliness and honesty and strikes in industry and particularly what kind of world we're giving to the generation that's growing up around us.

"Young people have been delivered from the bondage of having to think a particular way, having to reverence particular things with no reason given, and therefore their questions tend to be straight and clear and pointed and very persistent, and that is good. The questions are always stimulating, even to someone my age, and one never gets anywhere by trotting out the traditional answers. You really have got to face up to it or they just turn away."

Traditionally there was a strong anti-Catholic feeling among the Presbyterians of the Highlands, and Dr. Matheson said that it was difficult to speak about this on Skye, where there were so few Catholics. But just the other month a group of churchmen decided to organize a panel for the Portree secondary school to answer students' questions. "When they discovered there was a Catholic on the panel, the Free Church and Free Presbyterian ministers walked out," Reverend Matheson said. "They alleged that they hadn't known beforehand there was to be a Catholic. In the Church of Scotland we recognize that the main question facing us in our church life just now is our relationship with the Catholic Church in Scotland, which is very strong. And I personally have the warmest fellowship and friendship with quite a number of their hierarchy, and certainly some of the children of Catholics here come to our Sunday school. It's quite other in the sectarian churches."

One of the biggest problems on Skye was alcoholism, so I asked Dr. Matheson how the churches responded to it. "There's a much greater understanding now of alcoholics than there was before," he said. "You find that you have to spend time with them if you're going to do anything at all, and have to listen quite a bit and see if you can get underneath and discover what's really worrying them. There tends to be too much acceptance of alcoholism in the community as a whole — 'Well, this is part of life, and poor chap, he can't help it' — instead of rallying round to help and support and say, 'You've had enough, and it's time you came home with me.' There isn't the community support that one wants for the rehabilitation of the alcoholic. It's always been a feature of island life; it still is a feature, and I think now the church, instead of tending simply to condemn it, is really trying to understand it and to help people pastorally."

From Dr. Matheson's I drove out to the Free Church manse at Skeabost, to see Duncan MacLeay. He, too, was a native of Skye, and had served his parish there for ten years. His wife, who was brought up in Edinburgh, joined us, and we sat in the living room. A television set was on the floor, and an electric fire glowed in the fireplace. Mr. MacLeay was a short man, and as we talked he slumped lower and lower in his easy chair, until he was almost lying down. Mrs. MacLeay sat bolt upright, all attention and apprehension. When her husband spoke about anything that seemed to her controversial, she uttered a clearly audible stage whisper — something between a gasp and a sigh. Occasionally, in low, urgent tones, she would quaver, "Duncan!" — warning that he might be going too far, that he should be more discreet. He seemed to pay no attention. Whenever I asked *her* a question, he was almost demonstratively silent and seemed physically to withdraw, as though rejecting all responsibility for her reply.

"Today religion is declining," he said. "We have almost arrived at the state where you can believe almost anything now, and you can claim to be a church. You can see that in the World Council of Churches, where all faiths are admitted and claim to be Christian. The picture we get today is of compromise with the world and with various other sects that could not be reckoned as Christian at all. Each attempt at union has only increased the deadness and hardness and unbelief of the church in our own message. On Skye, things are better. There is more of a return of the old ways and old beliefs. There's the proof that we don't need gimmicks to attract the young, and that religion has the power to attract the young and the old. It's by the power of the Gospel and the power of God that anything will be achieved."

I asked him if it was true that his religion was dour. "No," he promptly replied. "It's a joyous religion. When I preach, I emphasize that. The man who is truly religious is truly happy. And he has the right to be happy. But no other man has the right to be happy. The right to be happy is given with the acceptance of God, who is the God of happiness, the author of happiness."

Isn't he also the author of sadness? I asked.

"No," Mr. MacLeay replied.

Then who is? I asked.

"Well, that's man himself," he said. "He brought it upon himself by his sin."

When Mrs. MacLeay intervened to ask about the sadness of bereavement, her husband said that was not the result of sin.

Mrs. MacLeay: "Christ was sad sometimes. Christ was sad sometimes."

Mr. MacLeay: "He was bearing the sins of man, but he knew the joy of constant community with his Father."

The minister acknowledged that he himself was sad sometimes, and he explained: "I attribute that to the fact that so many are going on in the world without an interest in the Gospel, an interest in the things that most concern them and that they most need. All because of their folly and their blindness. But I can rejoice in the midst of that. There is a God who can take away the sadness."

Do you believe the Church of Scotland is a Christian church? I asked, and I heard Mrs. MacLeay gasp as her husband answered. "Well, yes, we believe that she is a Christian church in that she acknowledges Christ and observes the sacraments, but there are many things in which she is not Christian. She is un-Christian in that she rejects much of the word of God in the Bible. She doesn't believe in the whole Bible. We believe in the literal word of the Bible, and that it is inspired. No, we do not believe in evolution. The creation theory is what we adhere to."

When I asked if two people, both fundamentalists, might understand a Biblical passage in different ways, he said, "You've got to take your interpretation according to the interpretation of the word of God, on the text that you're preaching." This did not seem to me a persuasive reply, but I despaired of convincing him that *he* was wrong.

What about the Catholic Church? I asked, and prepared myself for the gasp. I was not disappointed. "The Catholic Church," he said, "I would hesitate to say it was a Christian church. I know that people would disagree, but I believe that she is one of the anti-Christs, that she is one of the anti-Christian churches. Because she sets herself up as lording it over the conscience of men, and she sets herself up in the place of God and sets her tradition on an equal footing with the word of God. In the old days, when the Highlander was untutored, he was under a false view of life, he was living under the darkness and superstition of Roman Catholicism."

How had the notion of sin changed? I asked.

"Sin, to a large extent in the land today, has disappeared," Mr. MacLeay replied. "People don't believe that there is such a thing as sin. It's a misfortune, it's a disease, not sin; you're not to be condemned for it. Now that is contrary to the conception that was held with regard to sin."

When I asked if it was not true that there used to be special stress on sexual sins, he said, "Oh definitely," adding: "It was severely rebuked by the church. Those who were guilty of it had to appear before the kirk session and be publicly rebuked before the congregation. It does still take place before the session, and recently, quite frequently, it took place by public rebuke before the congregation. We don't do that anymore. I think that perhaps there was a tendency on the part of the people to revel in seeing one of their fellows being thus rebuked, and maybe to having their own sensual lusts gratified by listening to this."

Mr. MacLeay agreed that alcoholism was increasingly a problem. "There's too much money, and they're getting it too early in life," he said. "The habit has changed even in my own lifetime — of women drinking. We never saw a woman drunk on Skye, nor did we see young girls going into a cocktail bar to drink. Now we do see that. There's drinking every day of the week. That was unheard of in Skye before."

Mrs. MacLeay: "We're not teetotalers."

Mr. MacLeay: "I preach the word of God — that no drunkard shall enter into the Kingdom of Heaven. No, I don't consider alcoholism a sickness at all."

Mrs. MacLeay: "You do agree there are some people where it is a sickness."

Mr. MacLeay: "It does *become* a sickness."

He said that he was troubled by the conflict of generations, and as his wife sighed and prepared for the worst, he went on: "There's a separation between the young and the old Christian, which was not the pattern of the church in days gone by. The young Christian learned from the mature Christian; he was willing to sit at his feet. The young Christian today is more inclined to mix with his own age and leave the older Christian; just to develop on their own initiative, without the help of the older and mature Christian. And maybe in that view I might be treading on the toes of some of my brethren, but I think it is a fault of the setup in this day." Mr. MacLeay was born in 1914.

The essential, he said, was to be born again. "When I was born again it came about contrary to my wishes. But it came about by a power that brought home to me that I was a sinner, that the wrath of God was lying upon me which I couldn't put away from me, and that I was helpless to bridge the gulf between me and God. I had the conviction that I was condemned and that I could not remove that condemnation by any action I could do. And that I had to acknowledge the justness of God in condemning me. But my desire was, at the same time, that the Lord have mercy upon me. I just wanted to go the way of the world, just to live, to sample life for myself, and to live carelessly, with no restraints put upon me. That was my idea of what was going to be a happy life. I was sixteen."

He had resented it when people pressed him to return to school and study for the ministry, for he felt that it was not through the urging of man that this could be; it had to be through God. Then, one night at a prayer meeting, he felt the return of an urge to preach, and he took it as a sign from God. "And I have never regretted it, although I think my labors are very inadequate. I should have been more conscious of the preciousness of time. So many years have gone and I have done so little, and so few years remain in which to do anything at all. But the man who has done the most is probably the man who thinks he has done the least."

At the Free Presbyterian manse in Portree, the front door stood open, but the inner door leading from the entrance hall was locked. Coats hung in the entrance hall — every one black, and a black umbrella beside them. Fraser Macdonald, the Free Presbyterian minister, was dressed all in black, with half-glasses perched on his nose, and when he brought me into the manse he took his place in a small, dark study.

The Free Presbyterian Church had about five thousand members, almost a thousand of them on Skye. "We are definitely Calvinistic and stick to the old methods," Mr. Macdonald said. "Nothing but the Psalms and prayer. There's no change with us. Without gimmicks of any sort." He pronounced the word *jimmicks*.

"There is nothing like the old Gospel to draw people to

the kirk as such," he went on. "Many other devices have been tried, and in my judgment they've failed. You see the people on a Communion Sunday and you don't see them again perhaps until the next communion, whereas our people are always there. We get regularly on a Sabbath two hundred to two hundred fifty, with an influx of strangers from all the earth in summer. On Wednesday we have a prayer meeting and we get about a hundred there. We accept the verbal inspiration of Scripture. We accept the word of God as divine revelation. The holy men of God were divinely inspired by the Holy Spirit. We have no right or warrant to philosophize or speculate. Take it or leave it. It may be unpalatable and it may be what you don't like, but we stick to that. I never have doubts about the word of God, about the authenticity and the validity of the word of God as such, and that will stand forever, whatever men say or whatever generations say or whatever changes of thought or philosophers, theologians, or modern theologians say. Anybody who has a religion that is really deep does have doubts like John there in prison. John the Baptist, he had doubts, as far as I can gather. One would say, well, it was almost impossible for him to doubt. But they're not doubts reflecting on the word of God, you understand."

Do you believe in evolution? I asked.

"No, no, no, we don't have that," he replied. "We just don't accept evolution as such. We deny it as a fact, but we have to take cognizance of it as a theory. When we're working on Genesis One, creation, we believe that it is absolutely correct. And personally, I feel that ultimately all the sciences, archaeology and zoology and so on, will come to verify the statements made in Genesis One. We are not modernists, and we will not accept the higher critical theories. Definitely not.

"When we preach against sin, we're preaching basically about the total corruption, the total depravity of man. We believe that, with all our heart and soul. By all means the Sermon on the Mount and neighborliness and kindness, that's taught in the Scripture, but the basic matter is, with us, the new birth, divine, supernatural regeneration.

"The criticism leveled is that we're dour. You see, we have no organs, we have no music. Our singing certainly could be improved, and yet go to the isle of Lewis and hear a Gaelic congregation singing — a thousand voices — and it's sometimes just out of this world, it's just beautiful. An organist is just used to cover up deficiency and poverty. But in the house of God our attitude is that we have no instrumental music at all; the fruit of our lips giving praise unto God. Every individual there is allowed to sing — they can only croak or the voice is flat; it doesn't matter. If you're really singing with your heart, I think that's what matters.

"We're also told that we're always condemning. When you see the last several decades, the deterioration in morals, let alone religion, has been accelerating. What would have made one stagger two decades ago, today would hardly raise an eyebrow. So that we do speak out against abortion, euthanasia, and all these contemporary problems as they arise. I appreciate what people do in science and I respect what people do in that sphere, but after all is said and done, I always feel that they raise more problems of a moral nature than they solve. I appreciate what they do very much, in medicine for example, but there you've got this abortion, and that's ghastly to me."

I asked Mr. Macdonald how his church differed from the Free Church. "It was over higher criticism, really, and the verbal inspiration of Scripture," he said. "My theory, and it is that of the church as well, is that when you attack one portion — the Scripture is an organic whole — you are really assailing not just one doctrine, but the whole. The Free Church itself will acknowledge that there's a certain laxity creeping in. The Church of Scotland meanwhile has really gone modernistic, Barthian. They're complaining that their membership is down to under a million. They talk about commitment and all this sort of thing, but really, as far as the church is concerned it doesn't mean to them what it means to us, even to our adherents. The church means an awful lot to our people. I think it could well stem from the fact that in the home this was impressed upon them, that salvation was the one thing needful and that the church was not just an institution for social entertainment but a place for the salvation of one's soul. That's what we have, and the Free Church is pretty near to that, I would say in fairness."

Was there any chance of reunion with the Free Church? I asked. "I don't think so," Mr. Macdonald replied. "It's not a unity superimposed by man. It's a spiritual unity. I am already one with all genuine believers, truly gracious, born-again believers. I could really enjoy the fellowship, and I wouldn't for a thousand worlds deny that they were the children of God."

But the ecumenical movement was a sham, he said. "They're not asking, 'Is this man saved?' They're not asking, 'Is this according to Scripture? Is this according to the apostolic doctrine?' Their great idea is 'Look, we're kind of, well, if we could only integrate, you see, we're not cooperating sufficiently.' My simple answer to that is that the strength of the chain is the strength of its weakest link. If I cooperate with a gentleman here who doesn't believe the basic doctrines of the truth and doesn't believe in the supernatural, who doesn't believe in the resurrection, I cannot have fellowship with that man. He may be a minister, he may do a lot of good social work and all the rest of it, he may be very, very well-intentioned and very sincere, but my conscience and the word of God forbid me to have anything ever to do with him in that sense.

"Every day I pray to be preserved from Phariseeism or

being dogmatic or not being ready to listen to the other's point of view, but basically I feel there's no common ground where you're not one on Scripture. I don't think a union is likely unless one of the parties is willing to concede that he erred. In any society you've got your rules and regulations, even a secular society. If you don't toe these rules, you're out. And yet it's not a sort of thumbscrewing — you must do this and you must do that. You know, they talk about the scandal of division, but there are scandals much more scandalous than this. The way they treat the word of God itself, and praying for homosexuals. Romans One states very categorically that that's the dregs of society. So we're not on the same wave length at all, at all. I respect them and I pray for them and all that, but as you can see from our approach to the word of God, we've got to stand there, and as Luther said, 'I can do no other.' "

When I asked if he considered Catholics Christians, he said that he had great difficulty doing that. "I'll tell you why. The worship of the Virgin, for example. There are certain tenets, certain dogmas, that they must shed before there could be any possible coming together. They talk about grass roots, but as I see it, their bulls and their dogmas have not been rescinded. You see, there's such a large organization and you get one cardinal saying something and another saying another, like celibacy just now. It's on the way out. Now, time was when that would have been absolutely frowned upon. When you think of it, we have quite a large percentage of ministers who never marry. That's just that. I don't think they credit themselves with any merit because they haven't married. I'm married, and happily married. We would regard the Church of Rome as such as the anti-Christ. But I would still say, as in Revelation, 'Come out of her, my people, that ye be not partaker of her sins, and that ye receive not of her plagues.' It would hardly say 'Come out of her' unless there were some in there who were truly children of God. But the system as a whole I regard as corruption of the truth. Such things as worship of saints. It just doesn't make common sense, let alone spiritual sense."

Mr. Macdonald told me that he had intended originally to get a doctorate in agriculture, and I asked why he had gone into the ministry instead. "Oh, well, I hope the Lord converted me," he said. "I was brought up in a God-fearing home. We never went to dances or anything like that — that was frowned upon and I think rightly so, in retrospect, though I didn't think so at the time. But I never went, just out of fear and respect for my parents and their tenets. The world, and what appeals to the world and to the flesh, just living for oneself and pleasure, that isn't the be-all and the end-all. I felt myself in that category, although I was always in the church, and at home in the house we had family worship morning and evening. And we were very strict, of course, on the Sabbath as well. We hold strictly to that — that this one day in seven should be conserved for the worship and service of God, and only works of necessity like visiting the sick are allowed.

"When one emerges from this initial experience, the general norm is a profound sense of the majesty of God and our sin and our wrong relationship with God, and one finds by the power of the spirit the answer to that. There is a great sense of relief and I suppose the novelty of the joy, and life takes on a new dimension, a new perspective; there's something to be lived for, it's a reality, an objective in life. Then it's what is said in Corinthians — 'Therefore if any man be in Christ, he is a new creature: old things are passed away.' At that point, and I'm talking from personal experience, friends, associates, activities that I would take part in of a worldly nature are of a questionable nature. They just cease to make any appeal to me. Of course I believe in the devil. I definitely believe in the power of Satan, and in the corruption of the whole nature of man, so one has always to be on one's guard. But when that sort of arises again, and you feel this sort of stirring up, the flesh lusting against the spirit, well, then you really begin to doubt, well, was I really born again? It varies experimentally from person to person. Some are foolish ones always. Others may be taken aside into error for a little and come back and see the folly of their way. But I hope the Lord dealt with me in a very deep and definite manner — conviction of sin, and it wasn't just the acts of sin; it was the sinful potential, the sinful nature. The corruption of my whole nature was very real to me. We still preach everlasting punishment, heaven as well as hell, and I would say that doctrine is very important. We haven't moved. I think that would be a fair comment without exaggeration at all. I still read all these divines, and my product is my own, seventy-five percent to eighty percent my own. I also read exponents of the other side. You have exponents of one view and exponents of another view, so you're just at a loss. You're just back to square one. Whereas we accept the word of God as it is."

I suggested that fundamentalists could differ on interpretation of Scripture. He said, "We feel that we have a yardstick by which to judge which opinion is correct, and that is the word of God."

But that missed the point of my question, I objected.

"I would dig in my heels and say that my interpretation is right," he rejoined. "The relationship to God — that's the crux. Does that man acknowledge the sovereignty, the majesty, the glory of God? Does that man know the spirituality of the divine law? It's not a matter of the outside, but the motive, the heart, and all that. One could be lauded by one's fellow creatures, adulation and all that, and yet in the sight of God he's just a sinner."

I asked Mr. Macdonald if he preached about alcoholism. "Oh, dreadful!" he replied. "I just thunder at that. I just tell them where they're going. I have no hesitation in saying that the drunkard, the adulterer, the murderer are forsaking their hopes of the Kingdom of Heaven. I don't say it callously. I say it with tenderness and compassion. I know that there, but for the grace of God, go I. But I think it's a terrible blot on our society, because otherwise they're delightful people. I'm afraid that this is a feature in the Highlands, right throughout. I was in Lewis for fourteen years — the same problem there. If you have seen the misery caused by drunkards! I have several in my flock. I can talk to that man when he's sober, and say, 'Look, your wife, your child.' 'Yes,' he says, 'that's right.' Then he goes right back to drink — really outrageous, beyond it. If you begin by considering alcoholism an illness, then where do you end? If you do that with any particle of the law, or any sin to which you are addicted — it may be pride, it may be envy, it may be ambition, it may be a spiritual sin — well, society doesn't care about that, but the searcher of all hearts does. So we're really not that sympathetic. You really feel you've got to tell them in very plain terms. Ultimately, whatever I say, whatever compassion I have, it's 'What saith the Lord?' What's the word of God? If he continues impenitent, in that sin or in any other sin, we have no fear in saying to him that he shall be lost eternally. Whereas on the other hand, we do offer freely, without money and without price, the glorious salvation of the Gospel.

"I've said for twenty-five years, 'You watch, the next commandment to go will be the Seventh Commandment [Thou shalt not commit adultery]. Now in this country this is what's happening. I know that people say in the Victorian era it was condemned, but there was an awful lot of hypocrisy and it was brushed under the carpet. But really the glissade and the declension and the decadence in the last two or three decades, to my mind, morally, is just frightening and alarming. The only answer is to get back to the basics of the Gospel and the teaching of the Savior and to live it out in our lives."

Mr. Macdonald was born in 1924 at Oban, on the mainland, and English, not Gaelic, was his native language. But he learned Gaelic and now preached in it as well as in English. "Gaelic is very expressive," he suggested. "They tell me — not that I ever heard it or would know it even if I did hear it — that swearing in Gaelic is just, oh, it just takes the biscuit; that English is just nothing to it."

He told me that he and his wife were once on a train with "three young lads going at it like troopers." The boys were speaking English, so the Macdonalds had no trouble understanding. "Oh, it was vulgar — ribaldry," Mr. Macdonald suggested. " 'Look here, lads,' I said, 'do you ever think of anything but this life? Don't you realize this is not the end of it? Money, money, money, and swearing.' Then they sort of simmered down, and I said, 'Don't you realize you're sinning against your own souls and against your God?' So we got sort of pally. And I said I was a great sinner, perhaps the greatest sinner in this carriage as to my consciousness. 'I tell you to stop that kind of conduct because the end of that kind of conduct is death.'

"One of the fellows produced a picture of lovely children, and on the back was a woman's picture. 'That's their mother,' he said. 'Oh,' I said, 'is that your wife?' 'Oh no,' he said, 'she's far better. We just see each other from time to time. No bickering and no squabbles.' So then I had to tell him what the word of God said about marriage, that marriage was divinely ordained and that promiscuity was wrong and that the proper thing was laid down in the Bible. It talks about sex in its proper context and perspective and purity and dignity and all that. Oh, some of them were so far gone you couldn't get through to them. But they did stop swearing, and I could see they did have a conscience and they had some kind of hope that they would reform someday."

Mr. Macdonald rose from his easy chair and went over to a shelf, from which he took two large books resembling ledgers. He showed me that in one book he listed the subject and date of each sermon, with a note on whether it was delivered in Gaelic or English. The other book listed his pastoral visits, with dates and names. I had the impression that he was keeping these records to produce on the Day of Judgment, to transfer the accounts to God's good books. He said he really should not be showing me these records and explained that even when a person's name was listed only once the listing might represent many visits to the same person. "It's tremendously taxing on time," he said. "Well, I feel they are convinced I'm really interested in them and their souls and bodies and families. It comes through. They know that you're not kidding and that you're not just putting on an act. You're really interested that they will be saved, and we leave that to the sovereign will of God. We believe in election and all that, but nonetheless it is our duty to preach the Gospel to every creature on earth, and that we endeavor to do, but along with that there's this pastoral visitation all the time."

When I left, Mr. Macdonald came with me to unlock the vestibule door. "Do you know why I lock the door?" he asked, and answered, "In case somebody has had too many *deochs* [nips]."

I called next on John Macarthur, who was born on Lewis, in the Outer Hebrides, and was now the Church of Scotland minister at Broadford. While serving his first parish in the mainland county of Sutherland, he acted also as chairman of the county education committee. After five years in Sutherland, he returned to Lewis and spent seven years serving parishioners in the church and heading the education committee for the Outer Islands. "I've been involved long enough in the islands to see the need for a social outreach from the church," he said.

In Lewis he had been enthusiastic about the use of Gaelic in the conduct of local government, but he had decided it was not enough in the church to have only one English service a month. And he had felt it wrong that, while Church of Scotland services elsewhere were short and included hymn-singing and instrumental music, "in the rural parishes none of those things happened . . . I said to the session, 'I want to have every Sunday an English service as well as the Gaelic one — not in place of the Gaelic one, but in addition. I want to be able to sing hymns; because there's no one here to play an organ, I'll lead the singing myself.' Now, they accepted that, because it was something extra, not something in place of. Generally you can carry people with you, and changes can come gradually. Otherwise, it's a self-defeating exercise.

"Ministers will have trouble meeting the last part of the twentieth century unless they are more open to outside influences and more prepared to lead than to be led. I have a suspicion that recently they have not been leaders. They have accepted the ways of the church as decided by the parishioners rather than by themselves. As expositors, as those who are supposed to expose the word of God, I'm not sure that they have allowed its cutting edge to come through."

When I asked how notions of sin had changed during the past two centuries, he replied: "The predominant sin that I find in the old church records was what was called antenuptial fornication. The church seemed to have singled out that particular sin because obviously when the parents came for baptism it was something they could latch on to. I think the harshness associated with much of that has gone completely."

Mr. Macarthur said that on the islands there was more

preaching about sin than in the rest of Scotland. When I mentioned alcoholism, he suggested that the "sins" of dancing and drunkenness were given a place out of proportion to that given "the sins of the mind — the gossiping, the sin of the tongue, the bad relationships in families, in communities. The real problem about drinking is the lack of alternatives. If you only provide the church or the hotel, and these two are seen as poles apart, and there's nothing else for the young person to do — and that is the situation in a large part of the islands today — then obviously you have a problem. If it is the hotel, the lounge bar, that provides the billiards table, the dartboard, and if the church has looked askance at any opportunity to get out among the young folk and looks on recreation as being somehow sinful, then I think the church has to recognize its own responsibility.

"Sometimes I'm ashamed, for the church and for myself, at our lack of love, at our lack of understanding of the difficulties of young people, at our failure to grasp some of the questions they are putting to us. It's far easier for us to shake our heads and say 'How terrible!' than it is to repent. If you regard Christ as the bridge-builder between people, as well as between us and God, and he calls on us to be bridge-builders, it's a matter of shame if we're blowing up the bridges."

I asked Mr. Macarthur about ecumenism on the islands, and he said that here it was not something between Protestants and Catholics. "The problem is between the different Presbyterian denominations," he said. "And if you try to handle ecumenism the way you handle things politically, at daggers drawn rather than as brothers, then you're asking for trouble and you deserve what you get. But it's different if you allow ecumenism to grow naturally, out of love for your fellows, and gradually begin to hack away at some of the principles."

He suggested that within ten or twenty years inflation

might prove to be a powerful ecumenical instrument. "We're paid, reasonably poorly, running cars at whatever the price of petrol is, maintaining properties, paying insurance, heat, and light, and all to serve a hundred people. I don't think we're going to be able to do it much longer. We're going to have to learn a lot of things if Scotland or the Highlands or the islands are going to have a ministry at all. But if you believe in a God at the center, working his purposes out, things can go very low, down to almost nothing, before they come back. And it's not a matter then of despairing, but of being prepared to suffer that and to learn from it with an openness. I'm an optimist at the end of the day."

And during the day? I asked.

"During the day you have your ups and downs," he replied.

CHAPTER 14

A man who has settled his opinions, does not love to have the tranquillity of his conviction disturbed; and at seventy-seven it is time to be in earnest.

— Samuel Johnson

AS A YOUNGSTER, John Nicolson used to play among the boats on the loch, and ever since then he was much better known as the Skipper. Now, at age seventy-five, he spent most of his days at home in a large and venerable farmhouse in Cuidrach, a settlement that appeared to consist of this weathered house and one other. When he came out into the farmyard, he too looked weathered — a short man, lean and dark and grizzled, with hollow cheeks. He had put on a frayed jacket and vest, with a watch chain draped across the vest, and his clothes looked weathered. Inviting us into a room ancient and worn, he motioned us to eroded easy chairs. Since his language was Gaelic, with English a late addition, he repeatedly had to hunt for other words into which he could press his Gaelic thoughts, and the result was a more original speech, a sort of transliterated Gaelic. When I asked about his work as a crofter — he kept sheep and cows — he said that the sheep were less trouble. "You can always sleep with the good and bad weather," he explained. "She never troubles you. You just have to shear her and mark her lambs, but with the cattle if you house them you have to feed them daily and attend to them daily and you can't be away a night from home.

"I had three uncles who were experts at sheep," he said. "One, especially, would put a thousand lambs after their mother without a mistake. He had that instinct of knowing which lambs went with the mother. It's a thing that you can't teach or learn to anybody. It must be a gift of some kind, because you can't instruct a man how he knows it, but he knows it. The same as a forester. You can give him two pieces of timber there, with the bark and all taken off, but they tell you which is which. I've seen that, too."

He recalled his uncle standing silently beside the road as the sheep passed, and every so often undoing a button of his jacket. "And every hundred would come a button was loose," Mr. Nicolson said, rising from his chair and demonstratively undoing a button of his vest as though the hundredth sheep were passing, a second button for the two hundredth sheep, and then a third. "He kept the total number going to market, and he never made a mistake. And I've seen him, we were at the road there, and there was about five hundred sheep in all, Cheviots they were, of course, about fifteen years ago. And there was a counter beside him, taking a count of them, and he said, 'Have you got them all?' And my uncle said, 'Two missing. Maybe the shepherds have lost them in the bracken.' 'Oh never,' I said, because I thought it wasn't possible that they would. Well, at the back end of the year, what came among the sheep up at the glen there but these two that were missing. And that proved to me, who was there, that it was no tale."

In the old days, he said, crofters caring for sheep were not pressed or harried. "You were left on your own. You were left to yourself to choose when the things should be done in time. The rest of the time I would be out there fishing, for any fish that I could get. Prawns or haddocks or cod. My boys are at it just now — away at the prawn-fishing. I'm on my own now, at my leisure, but of course you have to work as hard as you can if the day is good. This was the worst year I have experienced. The winter and summer as well. The feeding wasn't there so much for the sheep. We had a touch of frost early, and that cuts out the sap of the grass and leaves it like slices of wood."

The Skipper grew up just a few miles away from Cuidrach. His father was a crofter who lived to the age of seventy-seven, and the Skipper recalled his father telling of the Highland clearances, which he had heard about from *his* father. "I remember when I was small, and the neighbors cracking away at these subjects," the Skipper said. "Well, I hadn't got the sense to observe it all, running about and such things."

He was one of four sons and four daughters, and he himself had four sons and four daughters. One of his brothers took over the family croft, and eventually the Skipper leased the Cuidrach property. "In the olden days, all your clothes and socks and everything was done at home, spun on the spinning wheel," he said. "There was nothing coming practically from the mainland but what was done on the island here itself — the baking and the fishing and the plowing and the cultivating, and it was all by manpower everything was secured. Today it's mechanical, and if it wasn't mechanical power I don't think you could secure the crops you were doing in these days. And there wasn't a blade of hay coming to Skye forty years ago. And now hundreds of tons come a year. Crofters work very less hard than they used to."

He now regretted having left school when he was fourteen. "We hadn't got the opportunities to continue, and we hadn't got the grants what we have nowadays. There was good positions to be got out of school, but at the same time I have probably done as well, what I have done, financially and such things, as I would be maybe. A fellow who went in for figures and such is not better financially than I am. But if I continued at school I would have gotten more of a cushier job and more comfort. You have more comfort than the navvy who was out day and night with all kinds of weather walking miles maybe while another man in the office was comfortable by the fire whatever kind of weather would be."

I asked Mr. Nicolson why he had not emigrated. He said it was expensive to emigrate. "And we knew of the hardship of those that did emigrate. We had our food and our clothing and we seemed contented with the way that we were. You were equal to your neighbor. And there was no envy between one another, as it is much today. I suppose it's because if you're living better than me that's no good. That's how envy works. But there wasn't so much of that in the olden days. They would help one another much more than they are today. The new incomers have changed Skye a lot. You don't get the hospitality at all now that used to be with the older folk. They weren't making strangers of nobody. Nowadays you come across a man and he doesn't want to say much to you at all. The young people haven't got as much respect for their superiors or the old people as it was. That has gone. On a Sunday you don't know it's a Sunday. In the old days there wasn't any traveling on a Sunday except the necessities and mercies, as they called it. That was if you had an animal that was sick or went into a bog or anything like that."

The Skipper suggested that he had other complaints. "I would like to see all those that doesn't occupy their land to be given to somebody that would make use of it," he said, "and grant him the house if he wants to stay in it. If he doesn't want to stay there, I don't see why he should be occupying two houses when there's a fellow without one. That is not right. I can go to the city and have a house here and have another house in the city. And you're dying for a house and you can't get it. Well, that shouldn't be. I think our rulers, they're in the wrong place, some of them. If they weren't suitable to such a job, I would put them to some other kind of work that they would adapt themselves to. You know, you can have educated fools and you can have educated wise men. But there are as many educated fools today as there is of the wise men."

Many of his own views were formed through reading Gaelic poetry, beginning with the poems of Duncan Mac-Intyre and William Ross, who lived in the eighteenth century, and proceeding to Mary MacPherson of the nineteenth century. He showed us a volume of MacIntyre's poetry, noting: "He couldn't read nor write, but today he's studied in the universities."

The Skipper thought Gaelic a wondrous language. "But whether Gaelic was spoken in the Garden of Eden is a question," he said. "That book of MacIntyre says it was. And what was very strange, Mary MacPherson, the poetess of Skye, well, she lived a hundred and fifty years after Mac-Intyre, and she'd never seen him and never heard of his work and she says the same, that Adam says to Eve, 'How are you?' when he met her, in Gaelic. And MacIntyre says that it was the language of the Garden that Moses spoke to the people, and at the time of the drying of the Red Sea and the prophets above give the tidings. So who can say that it wasn't? I think it is that old that nobody can give a date of its existence. It may have not been, but who can say no, because he said it and you can leave it like that. Whether that is right or wrong, who can say no?"

Archie Ross struck me as the sort of person who incarnated the ideal of nay-saying, of severity and disapproval; he spoke like a Biblical prophet inveighing against evil and condemning sinners to sackcloth and ashes — unless, as was likely, they did not deserve such mollycoddling. Almost eighty-two years old, tall, blond, ruddy-faced, he walked stiffly erect, as though moral rectitude were inconsistent with physical ease. For eleven years he had transported his rigid ways once a month to Inverness, where he served as a member of the Inverness-shire County Council. With the introduction in 1975 of the regional government system, he decided he had had enough, and stayed at home in Violtur, a tiny hamlet.

The oldest of eleven children, he had abandoned school at fourteen to help his father on the croft, and at sixteen he had left Skye to serve on the Loch Lomond pleasure boats. In those days there were five steamers, not just one, and no tourist buses traveled round the loch. Then he moved to what he called "the deep sea." "I wandered away from here for a while," he said of his twenty-five years in the merchant navy. "At one time at least fifty percent of the young people from here went to the sea. If you're going to sea from the time you're a wee boy going out fishing there, you loved the sea. You knew the currents, you knew how to handle boats and all the rest of it, and that came very much in evidence during wars when your ship was sunk there and you were fortunate enough to get into the lifeboat on the vast open spaces of the ocean when there's nobody there to save you.

"We had seven sons in our own family," he said, "and between World War One and World War Two they all served. I saw thousands of ships all over the world. I remember a Russian ship I saw in Port Said. I remember the name — *Kamenets Podolsk*. They took the Russian refugees, the grand duchess and what-not that were fleeing away from the land."

When his mother fell ill, he returned to Skye. "I had a necessity to come home, and I had to make a sacrifice, though anything you do for your mother is not a sacrifice. So I didn't reach the giddy heights I might have.

"Well, I joined a small cruise ship. My mother was bedridden here, and I didn't feel I should be away at the other end of the world. I joined that ship and we were cruising around the Western Islands here. And on this early June morning we were lying at Gairloch at night, and we were leaving at about three o'clock in the morning, at the start of day here, crossing over — and that's twenty miles across. This gentleman came out of his stateroom in his dressing gown and he said, 'What land are we approaching just now?' The sun was rising and peeping over the Ross-shire hills. It wasn't a true light, you see, and it wasn't bright sunshine either, but a faint golden glow on Skye. You know these rocks around here — the Needle, the Table, the Quirang, and all these — well, these rocks, at that time, in that faint glow of sunshine, looked white, and the rest was velvety green down to the sea, and the houses whitewashed, dotted here and there. I said, 'We're approaching the northeast coast of the island of Skye.' And he was silent for a moment or two. And then he said, 'I have traveled the whole world, and I never saw a scene to compare with that in all my life.' And there was me, a Skye man, but I had never seen it in the same light as I saw it that morning. I didn't appreciate it before I went away."

Eventually Mr. Ross returned to work the croft. The land between house and sea was peat, and Archie Ross's father had converted the bracken to arable soil, removing the top layer with a spade, cutting the peat, draining the land, restoring the turf. As Archie Ross explained the process: "You went down and cut the peat, and it was a slow and arduous task and took about five or six years. You made a calendar."

I was puzzled by the reference to a calendar, and he explained that one cut a quantity of peat every week, and all the weeks together made a calendar. He went on: "They had it under corn [oats], and that corn was threshed and sent to mill and grinded into oatmeal."

Before going to sea, Mr. Ross had learned a good deal about sheep and cattle, and his neighbors taught him more. "You know, when you're going to tell a fellow, 'This is the way you should do it,' maybe he'd object," Mr. Ross said. "But I wouldn't. You can always learn, till the end of your day. They taught me how to stack corn and how to stack hay. I had a fair idea about the growing; I was following their own pattern. The secret of successful crofting is if you can grow enough on the croft to feed the stock that you're keeping. If you have to go outside and start buying in, when you sell the offspring — suppose you get a decent price — you've got to subtract all that you paid for their upkeep, so your profit's very small.

"The price of cattle has multiplied about eightfold since twenty years ago. It's not easily done, restocking. Sheep are very dear, too. But we had a very severe winter here, the worst in living memory, the worst I ever saw here. We tried, during the winter, to feed those that we thought needed it most, and the others, they had to run the risk of surviving out in the hills. And they managed, not badly, not badly. But they were in weaker condition, so we lost a lot of lambs. The outlook was not very bright. Up to last year the subsidy for sheep was three pounds a head. But they're advocating far more than that now. I hope they'll do it. To make a living out of it, if you could keep about eight cows and their followers, and about two hundred sheep, you wouldn't be too bad off. I like sheep especially. They're easily handled, and I always had good dogs. Some of them take a bit of training, but some of them require very little. I had one disappointment, a son of the champion of Scotland in nineteen seventy-five. This one my grandson took back and forth to school with him, and this dog lost interest in the sheep.

"I've no time for the tractors. I used to work horses, the plowing and everything with horses, but I never tried my hand at the tractors. My son does that. But if you've got to employ agricultural contractors, that again adds up to the bills of expenses.

"It's a full-time job to do it justice. In the present day there's a big demand on your purse, and if you can't go anywhere else to earn money, no matter how much you've saved, and the pay wasn't so big when I was at sea, you feel that you're fighting against the elements ashore. Financial elements. People are striking now and squabbling and fighting for money. They're earning more in a week than I got for a voyage to Australia and back. I don't believe in going into debt if you can help it at all. I know things have changed. Some people go in for this hire-purchase business. Maybe it's all right in a sense, but it's a poor legacy to leave to your family."

Many people in the crofting community have lost interest in crofting, he complained. "You'll see it across the road — crofts are overgrown with rushes. They go in for bed-and-breakfast business, boarders and suchlike, and that's rather a speculative business. You see now, with the price of petrol people can't afford to travel. Crofting is also a speculative business, yes, in a sense, but I think it's a sounder business than depending on who should come to your house here asking for bed-and-breakfast."

I asked Mr. Ross if he ever missed life at sea. "Sometimes in your mind you wander away to Port Said and to Alexandria," he replied. "We crossed the Mediterranean more times than I can remember — Alexandria to Taranto, Port Said to Marseille. I did miss the sea at one time, but now I like living here. In reality I think of the many friends I met all over the world. Over there in the States you hardly have any sleep when you're in the ports, people wanting you to come over. I think we ought to thank God in this country, in comparison with the starving children in other countries. I was in Constantinople — it's Istanbul now — there was a whole harbor of ships, and at mealtime, when we dumped garbage over the side, they had big nets to scoop up what we threw over the side. And in India little babies lying in the streets. It widens your horizon. I never appreciated Skye before I left here, but I appreciate it now — the peace and quietness and tranquillity and orderliness of the life. You don't fear for your life at night. If there was anything happening in this house at night, you could go and waken your neighbor at any hour and he was ready to help you. When I went to sea there were lots of places where in the ports we had to go around in pairs. In Buenos Aires, if you had two dollars they'd murder you for it."

Having heard from another Skye man that Mr. Ross was "a wee bit religious," I asked him his views on religion. "You have a car there," he said. "When you go out with that car, if you make a mistake on the road and cause a collision you're tried in a civil court and you're punished. That's just. But God doesn't believe in punishment. He believes in repentance. He's a just and only God, and he would rather see you and me repent, and confess your sins — 'God have mercy on me, a sinner' — than come in judgment against you."

Mr. Ross told us about the time a foreign dignitary called at 10 Downing Street to see Prime Minister Gladstone. "A servant came to the door and said that 'the Prime Minister is spending an hour with his Master.' That man was praying to God before he took up his duties as prime minister of the nation. None of us are above that.

"I regret to say that I know how well God prospered this country. I'm not taking any sides now — we all belong to different countries — but when I was going to school there were red dots all over the map. That was when the sun never set on the empire, and that was because they revered God. On your coins it says 'In God We Trust.' Well, those were sensible people who put that on the coins. If I knew, at the start of a voyage, that the captain of that ship believed in God, I faced the elements with far more confidence. We're only just frail mortals, at the best. In dangerous times at sea I saw people who were supposed to be hard cases, and they began praying. Those who said they didn't believe in God, they were the biggest cowards when it came to action.

They were like a lot of children. It was a case of 'God save us!'

"My religion means everything to me. Faith in God. You're only here for a brief period, a very brief period, and the longer you live, the shorter the week becomes to you. I feel the week going by quicker here than a watch at sea. On a dark, drizzly night, on the bridge, four hours seemed longer than a week seems to me just now. I don't want to try to make myself appear a very pious person, but I think I would advise everyone, when you step out of your bed in the morning, to ask God to protect you and to save you from wrongdoings in that day. Everyone makes mistakes. Was it Abraham Lincoln that said, 'Everyone makes mistakes, but it's only a coward that won't admit his mistakes'? You say to yourself at the end of the day, 'Well, what did I do wrong? Why did I say this, and did I hurt this man here?' At the end of my days, I hope to God, by the cleansing of his blood, that I'll be redeemed, and many more."

CHAPTER 15

In Skye there are two grammar schools, where boarders are taken to be regularly educated. The price of board is from three pounds, to four pounds ten shillings a year, and that of instruction is half a crown a quarter. But the scholars are birds of passage, who live at school only in the summer; for in winter provisions cannot be made for any considerable number in one place. This periodical dispersion impresses strongly the scarcity of these countries.

— Samuel Johnson

THOUGH IT HAD only five hundred people, Staffin sprawled for miles along the east coast of Skye, and it seemed not a village but a sprinkling of hamlets, a terrestrial parallel to the medieval description of God as that perfect Being whose center was everywhere and whose circumference was nowhere. Allan Macdonald, Staffin's schoolmaster, was a short, vigorous, peppery man who spoke forthrightly, as though every phrase demanded emphasis: his conversational tone came close to a sustained shout, appropriate for addressing a convention of the hard-of-hearing or an auditorium of unruly youngsters. "I was born and brought up in Skye," he boomed. "Dunvegan. Forty miles away. I had very little choice when I left Portree school — that would be nineteen fifty-one — and went to Edinburgh University. In those days the career guidance system was very simple and basic. If you were academic, you were encouraged to go to university. You were given no guidance as to what you would do afterwards, and you simply ended up with your degree and more often than not you then went to do your teacher training because there was a shortage of teachers. When I got married I moved to Ayrshire. There was a house with a job there, and I wanted a house and I couldn't afford to buy one. I think maybe one of the things that made me want to move north again was that I felt that if I was going to stay in Ayr, my children were going to become southerners, and if I was going to have them involved in what I knew was the Highland way of life and Gaelic in particular, I had to make the move then."

He now had come to believe that even some of his fellow Highlanders succumbed to the vice so common elsewhere, and many were even confusing religion and Christianity. "Some have been very religious without being Christian," he said. "External appearances — like the Scribes and the Pharisees in the New Testament. 'Oh, what will the neighbors think?' or 'What will the minister think?' instead of being more concerned about the heart. God sees the heart. In the end of the day it's not the neighbors who are going to stand giving an account."

When I suggested that I did not understand the persistent hold of fundamentalism, Mr. Macdonald promptly roared that he was a fundamentalist. "The Highlander is a realist," he thundered, "and I think that the Highlander would not be happy with something that is vague and wishy-washy as nonfundamentalism can be. But fundamentalism — a belief in the sovereignty of God and the authority of the word of God, eternity, heaven and hell, creation. The Highlander is inclined to argue like this, this is the way I would argue, anyway: If God is God, then obviously man would expect him to leave a record which is reliable. And if you're going to offer me, instead of fundamentalism, a vague hope that maybe some of it is right, maybe aye and maybe why and maybe not or it might be or hope for the best, I think that's maybe one of the reasons why there isn't regard for Christianity in areas where you have this obtain. In the Highlands it's a self-perpetuating thing. If you have the Gospel being preached, then you will have more Christians who are brought up in this situation who believe it; they will go to be trained and they'll come back and they will preach it when they come back."

Mr. Macdonald said he regretted that so many incomers, totally alien to local culture and beliefs, had bought up houses on Skye, pricing local people out of the market. "I don't condemn incomers!" he exclaimed. "But I'll certainly condemn some of them, because they would like to take over. They would like to tell the local how wrong he is, the way things are done on Skye, how he, with his enlightened view, can do things much better. They can sometimes touch upon sensitive areas like what is the point of having Gaelic, for example, in your schools — it would be far better if you would concentrate on English. They might touch on another sensitive area like the Sabbath. I'll welcome the man who'll come and say, 'I like this place, and I like this way of life, and let's work together.' But I don't like the man who says, 'You're backward, you're behind the times, you need to do this, you need to do that.'"

I suspected that in William Pringle I would find the sort of incomer who would bristle at such talk, for Dr. Matheson, the Church of Scotland minister at Portree, had told me that Mr. Pringle spoke his mind. When I relayed this recommendation and asked if it represented the truth, Mr. Pringle promptly replied yes, and invited me to come see him at the Skye Wool Mill.

On the north side of Portree a sign at roadside invited people to visit the mill, and a large arrow pointed the way to a sizable building not far off the main road. The mill turned out to be a huge shop selling a variety of woolen goods — tweeds, sweaters, coats, slacks, jackets — and a leaven of souvenirs. From the shop I was directed to a cottage about fifty yards away. In the garden strolled a stalwart-looking fellow in a suit of wild tartan pattern, the country squire eccentric enough not to care if people stared. I was careful not to avert my eyes, and if Mr. Pringle thought my subdued costume strange, he was equally discreet. He invited me into the cottage and told me at once that everything there was venerable: the cottage was centuries old, he was born in 1909, and his wife was "over sixty-five."

For many years he had been chairman of James Pringle Ltd., a large knitting-and-tailoring enterprise, with factories in different parts of Scotland. During his chairmanship he had arranged for his company to buy a mill in Skye that had been standing idle for about twenty years. When he resigned as chairman, he decided that the mill was his responsibility, so he moved to Skye and took over. "I spent thousands of pounds putting in a complete new plant," he said. "I wanted to import technicians — dyers, loom-tuners, carders, foremen in all the departments pertaining to textiles. The district council would not help at all in providing houses for the essential personnel. I had them in caravans and all over the place. There were forty people in production, and that's excluding warehouse people and such. They were all crofters. You had a machine, say, for fifty thousand pounds, a machine with a certain output for an eight-hour day, and we weren't getting the output. I decided somebody was clocking people in in the morning at eight o'clock, and they were coming in at ten or eleven."

After waiting for that to sink in, he continued: "The island is self-contained in every way. They don't require money. The crofter lives off his croft plus some ancillary job that gives him the added income. No croft pays for itself, but at the same time they *can* live off the croft. They are a peculiar race, different from the Western Hebridean, who is a very active, working man. There's an endemic laziness with them that can't be called laziness. It's a *mañana* sort of existence — tomorrow never comes. The Skye man can beat everyone in improvisation. They can make an old machine run; they can take an old wreck and make it go again. But give them something on a steady, weekly, hourly basis — it's a useless proposition."

So, as he said, "I put a hammer through it, gave away the lot, cleared the place out, turned it into a sales warehouse supplied by our other factories. That was my experience; not a very happy one, but acceptable."

Though he waited for *that* to sink in, I was having trouble understanding his meaning, and he explained that he had reconciled himself to the fact that attempts to oppose the *mañana* spirit were hopeless.

Mr. Pringle then recalled for me, with greater pleasure, the days when he was a titan of industry, supervising big factories and a large sales force. He had believed in personal contact with customers, so he had traveled widely and gone frequently to America. "I built up a tremendous business during my short lifetime," he said. "And I still believe in ideas as big as a cathedral."

One of his pet notions was opposition to what he called "the segregation of school and industry." "Maybe sixty percent of the students here will go to university, and the rest are naught," he said. "With unemployment the way it is, they're being thrown on the scrap heap." He therefore had been advocating a Scottish college of technology for boys and girls to enter at age fifteen; the government would train the young rather than pay them to be on the dole. He had sent this proposal to education authorities and to all the Members of Parliament. The campaign had not succeeded — at least, not yet.

I asked Mr. Pringle if he was happy living on Skye, and

he seemed undecided between yes and no. "There is an innate jealousy here," he said. "If somebody has a little more than anybody else, you have to bring yourself to their level. All that I miss on Skye is people who think and speak as you do." The pronouns were a little confusing. He meant, of course, people who think and speak as *he* did.

At the Highlands and Islands Development Board in Inverness, I had heard of a successful industrial enterprise on Skye, a factory at Dunvegan producing electronic instruments. "You can take a whole week's production, put it in an envelope, and mail it," an official at HIDB said. "Donald MacLachlan set up the factory on Skye because he wanted to live there and needed to earn a living. None of his clients is on the island, so if you're being absolutely sane and sensible about it, the factory shouldn't be there."

When I phoned the factory, I was told that Mr. MacLachlan was at home. That sounded like a leisurely sort of entrepreneur, and I asked directions to his house and drove there. He lived in the village of Stein, in an old refurbished cottage next door to the oldest inn on the island, and he seemed very much at ease, a black-bearded man dressed informally, in old trousers and sports shirt. His account started from the beginning: birth in 1935, early years in Glasgow, studies in chemistry. After graduate school he lived in London and worked in electronic development. He had dreamed of living in the west of Scotland, and since he had friends who knew Skye he went there, in 1966. In those days the island was distinctly undeveloped. "When I came to Skye from London," he recalled, "the water didn't work because the ball cock was broken, and I couldn't buy a new one — there weren't any on the island. The first thing I did was unpack my old treadle lathe and turn myself one. Years ago it was terribly difficult to get hold of anything." In time, he found his dream cottage — a ruin, both ends of the roof gone, the interior a sea of mud — and started to rebuild it himself.

During his first six years on Skye he earned his living as a consultant to mainland firms on electronic component design. One day as he was sailing his boat, flying the flag of the Amateur Yacht Research Society — he knew quite a bit about boats and had won a competition for the design of a twenty-five-foot yacht — he saw another fellow, flying the flag of the society, who turned out to be a phoneticist from Edinburgh University. When Mr. MacLachlan said that he designed electronic components, the other man said that he was planning to spend £170 for an American transducer. The phoneticist happened to be a Scottish nationalist, and he jumped at Mr. MacLachlan's offer to make a transducer and keep the business in Scotland. "It took me about three months and about thirty attempts before it could do his job," Mr. MacLachlan said.

I asked him to tell me what a transducer was, and he defined it as "something that changes a measurement from one parameter to another, changing pressure to electric voltage." Later, I looked up the word in a dictionary, which translated transducer as "a device that receives energy from one system and retransmits it, often in a different form, to another." Mr. MacLachlan said that the phoneticist wanted a transducer to measure esophageal pressure during speech.

As he spoke, Mr. MacLachlan absent-mindedly fingered what looked like a length of black wire with a slight bulge at one end, and he suddenly realized that there was evidence in hand: the instrument he was holding was a transducer. Some transducers, he said, were very small indeed — two millimeters by ten millimeters. The one he held was a foot long and sold for about a thousand pounds.

After his first homemade transducer he decided to produce more, and by the second year was making a profit. Since virtually every transducer was of a different design, Mr. MacLachlan spent a lot of his time on product development for individual customers. He hired a helper, a ship's engineer

whose mother was from Skye and who had taken over his
mother's croft. About a year before my visit, the HIDB had
built a workshop at Dunvegan to Mr. MacLachlan's specifi-
cations, and leased it to Gaeltec, which the company called
itself, for a subsidized rent. Mr. MacLachlan was meanwhile
expanding the work force. "All except one were living on
the island when I took over," he said. "Most of them are
people who've been away; very few have been living on the
island continuously. A few are complete incomers. The way
I organize the thing, one needs to have a reasonably good
technical background. You need at least A-level standard in
sciences. I've got one — Sid — who was a graduate mechanical engineer. Another was a textile designer. Judith did half
of a degree course in chemistry and was working as a laboratory technician. Chris was a petroleum engineer or geophysi-
cist. Bob has a Ph.D. in bioengineering. He designed his own
artificial leg — lost one in a motorbike accident. Ian had
done an apprenticeship as a boilermaker on the Clyde. I
not only expect them to make things, but I expect them to
help in development, putting things together under the mi-
croscope, testing calculations. There's a Welshman who was
an R.A.F. navigator. He has three crofts along here, and he
works the crofts very hard, so he's off a lot of the time. I pay
basically at an hourly rate. A lot of the people are building
houses, and I have to organize things so that they can go
off when the weather is good." "Part of the perks" was how
Mr. MacLachlan described the arrangement allowing workers to take time off whenever they pleased.

He said that it was difficult to find qualified workers and
that it took six months before even they became at all useful.
"Lots of people come looking for work, and we don't generally take any who are not living on the island. There was
one exception. He was an anthropologist working with can-
nibals on Papua, and gave it up."

I asked if a week's production really would fit into an

envelope, and Mr. MacLachlan said it was very nearly true. The largest run of a single design would be about twenty units, and business was so brisk, since Gaeltec was the only company in Europe making transducers for measuring pressure within the body, that there had been no time to build up a backlog.

Was it true, I asked Mr. MacLachlan, that Skye people were given to a *mañana* philosophy? "There's a sort of natural selection here," he said. "I think the ones with that attitude tend to stay on Skye and not go away in the first place, because they haven't got the energy."

As I left, Mr. MacLachlan handed me a couple of brochures. One listed some of the things that miniature pressure transducers measured:

> Unsteady flow characteristics of stator and rotor blades in gas and water turbine development; Pressure distribution over ship hulls and propellors during varying drive conditions; Intracranial pressure after brain surgery; Arterial and venous blood pressure; Interaction between waves and structures in the design of off-shore oil rigs; The volume of rats' feet; Intra-abdominal, intrauterine and urethral pressure; Milking pressure in cows' udders; Air pressure on racing car bodies during track testing.

The other brochure, catering to my advanced scientific competence, added:

> Most of the devices we supply are tailored in some way to the user's particular requirement. Ask us about your measurement problem.

I did not have a measurement problem, but I did have trouble with that item about the volume of rats' feet. Surely this was not the garden-variety rat — and feet of same. The more I wondered, the more puzzled I became. So I wrote Mr. MacLachlan, noting that everything was more or less clear in my notes, but not in my head. In fact, I might need a transducer to make me swallow or understand that item about "the volume of rats' feet," or convince myself that I was not hallucinating. "Surely not garden-variety rats, the sort that run around on ships and in houses and perhaps even in gardens?" I wrote. "Is this a technical term for something else? I'd be grateful for your elucidation."

Back came elucidation: "The brochure you mention does indeed refer to garden-variety rat, the type that runs around on ships (or deserts sinking ones), as you described. The transducer was designed to be incorporated into a plethysmograph, and the volume obtained by measurements made thereon. I hope that this will convince you that you are not, in fact, deluding yourself, and look forward to hearing from you again."

"As you may have suspected, you would indeed be hearing from me again," I responded. "Your letter clears up one mystery, leaving entire another. WHY does anyone want to have the volume of rats' feet? What purpose does a knowledge of the volume of rats' feet serve? And what in the world of technology is a plethysmograph?"

The reply was prompt: "Rats' feet have been used in the study of arthritis, by noting the changes in the volume of the feet of arthritic rats over a period of time. A plethysmograph is a device (basically, a mercury bath with appended bits and pieces) for measuring changes in the volume of parts of the body due to changes in blood circulation. It would be used in conjunction with one of our transducers to give an indication of the changes in pressure accompanying the changes in volume as the arthritis pursues its course."

CHAPTER 16

At Dunvegan I had tasted lotus, and was in danger of forgetting that I was ever to depart, till Mr. Boswell sagely reproached me with my sluggishness and softness.

— Samuel Johnson

Dunvegan Castle, on the site of a ninth-century Norse fort, had, for perhaps eight hundred years, been the seat of the chiefs of Clan Leod. The castle had been built in stages, and the resulting dark beige stone conglomeration, ranging from the fifteenth to the nineteenth centuries, formed an astonishingly harmonious structure. For a long time this fortress, set firmly on the rocks of the shore, was accessible only from the water side, but then, to afford simpler access, a bridge was built across the moat.

Johnson and Boswell found here a sanctuary of what they came to consider luxury, refinement, and civilization. Boswell's *Journal* described the joy Johnson exhibited in the pleasures of Dunvegan, and reported him saying, "Boswell, we came in at the wrong end of this island." "Sir," Boswell replied, "it was best to keep this for the last," to which Johnson rejoined, "I'd have it both first and last."

Lady MacLeod, their hostess, told them of her plan to build a house upon a farm five miles distant so that the family could have gardens and live in true comfort, instead of being condemned to the severity of labor to make the rock convenient. Johnson objected, holding it the duty of the laird to have his seat at this castle, on this rock. "No, no; keep to the rock," Boswell chimed in. "It is the very jewel of the estate. It looks as if it had been let down by the four corners, to be the residence of a chief."

Since that day, with great labor, gardens had been developed here, and a long, attractive hedge bordered the path to the castle's front door. A collection box had a note asking visitors — who had to pay to enter the castle — for contributions as well toward upkeep of the garden. Nominally the castle was still the seat of the clan chief, but now he rarely kept to the rock and instead lived most of the year in London; he was a singer, his wife a pianist, and they earned a living by giving joint recitals. The singing chief was the son of Joan Wolrige-Gordon, daughter of Flora MacLeod, the twenty-eighth head of the clan. When selected to succeed his grandmother, the twenty-ninth chief changed his name from Wolrige-Gordon to MacLeod of MacLeod.

His castle was festooned with arrows and signs indicating a tour route beginning in the fifteenth-century tower, with the Business Room, where Flora MacLeod had dealt with finance. She was good at raising money and also at welcoming visitors. One exhibit was a framed certificate, dated June 1937, presented to Mrs. Flora MacLeod of MacLeod: "We, the MacLeod-Machlejds of Poland, pay homage and extend sincerest greetings to you as chief of the clan." The Polish version of the dedication was printed alongside the translation. Also on display was the charter, dated 1498, granted by King James IV of Scotland to the eighth chief of the MacLeods. As the accompanying caption explained, the charter related to lands in Skye and Harris, "in return for which MacLeod was to hold ready for the King's service one ship of 26 oars and two of 16 oars. The falcons' nests on the estate were to be reserved for the King." In a glass case was the drinking horn, its mouth rimmed with chased silver, traditionally used when a new chief took office. The horn could hold two and a half (some said five) pints, and the new chief had to quaff that much claret from the horn. To bring that gulp within the realm of drinkability, a false bottom had been inserted. Most treasured of all the exhibits was the Fairy Flag, a tattered and faded cloth remnant, carefully framed. By tradition, the flag could save the MacLeods three times, and it had already worked two salvific miracles. But there were suggestions of more extensive powers: spread on the marital bed, it would guarantee fecundity; hoisted from the ramparts, it would draw herring to the loch. The flag recalled the love of a fairy and William, fourth chief of the clan: when the lovers were forced to part, it was this banner that covered the child of their union. Only a whit less romantic was the portrait of Bonnie Prince Charlie, whose cover was not the Fairy Flag but woman's apparel that he wore during his flight, disguised as a maid to Flora Macdonald. Nearby were a pair of Flora Macdonald's stays and Bonnie Prince Charlie's own true waistcoat.

Hung about the castle were portraits also of former chiefs, including two paintings of Norman MacLeod, laird when Johnson and Boswell visited, and identified here as a brigadier general and as a major general. In 1785 he was named second-in-command of the army in India. As a caption put it, "While in India, the General had frequently to parley with that implacable enemy of Britain, Tippoo Sahib, Sultan of Mysore." Tippoo absented himself from hostility long enough to give General MacLeod a magnificent silver-hilted Persian sword of honor, and it was enshrined at the castle. In another gallery stood a bust of Emily MacLeod, sister of the twenty-fifth chief. Miss MacLeod died in 1896, the last Gaelic-speaking member of the family.

In his account of Dunvegan, Boswell wrote repeatedly of

the good manners and the hospitality of Lady MacLeod, noting that she entertained Johnson and himself "like princes." He wrote, "She has at the same time the greatest economy. She is butler herself, even of the porter."

MacLeod of MacLeod was not in residence, but Charles Heron, the family's former butler, was, at Rose Cottage, an old stone dwelling almost stereotypically perfect for its name. It stood on a side road near the castle, and the butler's wife, Catherine, a frail and delicate woman, came to the door and told us that her husband was working as a guide at the castle and that he would be home for dinner at any moment. Warmly welcoming and good-humored, she invited us to wait inside, and then, with little prompting, began talking about the Herons and the MacLeods.

At age twenty — she was born in 1904 — she had gone to work as a housemaid for Sir Reginald MacLeod, father of Dame Flora. Then, as Mrs. Heron said: "Charlie arrived on the scene. It took an awful time for him to ask me to marry. I didn't think he'd ever get to it. My mother didn't approve of me getting married. She didn't give me satisfaction in that. I was happy with Charlie, and I had to take the law into my hands."

I asked how large the staff had been when she went to work at Dunvegan. "There'll be five in the kitchen, and as many in the pantry, and we were three housemaids up the stair," she said. "I enjoyed every minute of it, and I look back on it a lot. It was hard work, but I enjoyed it. There was no labor-saving devices then. I ended up head housemaid. But I was happy with everybody and we were jolly people."

She remembered the time she and a table maid were the only people at the castle. "It was New Year's Eve, and this girl went off for New Year's, and didn't come home till six in the morning. And I was all alone. 'Well, if there's a ghost here,' I said to myself, 'I'm sure he'll say "Happy New Year" to you,' so I went up to the drawing room, and we didn't have TV, we had the other thing — wireless — and I had a glorious time. I never did see a ghost. I never met anybody but myself; I didn't see anything worse than myself.

"I had fifteen shillings a week, and you had to get your aprons and all and dress and shoes from your fifteen shillings. When I got higher up I got a decent pay. I was quite happy and I did my work and it was great fun for me and I think you just have to make yourself content. We're living in a different age, and the young today have bigger ideas."

Mrs. Heron went to the sideboard and brought out a copy of *Dame Flora,* a biography published in 1974. The book was enclosed in wrapping paper, and from an envelope inside the book Mrs. Heron extracted a letter that Dame Flora had written to her and to Mr. Heron:

My very dear friends whose lives have been intertwined for fifty years and more with my family — five generations of us . . . I wonder if you will recognise the Flora you know in *Dame Flora.* I am sure you will enjoy it, and of course you are part of those 96 years. From my heart I thank you. God bless and keep you both. Your oldest (I mean most aged) Friend

> Flora MacLeod of MacLeod
> *HOLD FAST*
> I know you will.

Inside the book's front cover was a dedication to Mrs. Heron, who "nursed my grandchildren and great grandchildren in your arms. I bless you for your long faithful friendship."

Mr. Heron, who was two years younger than his wife and managed to look even frailer than she did, arrived while we were admiring the book. I told him that his wife had said it had taken him ages to propose. What took so long? "To tell you the truth," he replied, "I always had the feeling that

I would like, if I could, to get her to be my lady friend. But I was quite backward."

"Slow in motion," she interjected, laughing.

"When I asked her if she would be engaged to me, she said, without any hesitation, that she would become engaged. It was the moon that dooed it. We were out on a moonlight night among the rhododendrons."

Mrs. Heron: "The rest were out with their boyfriends, and I hadn't any boyfriend."

Mr. Heron: "The other two housemaids were on duty, and I was on duty. Jessie said to me, 'Why don't you have a walk up the road to meet Cathy?' Well, I must have had the feeling and the interest to do it. I says, 'Right.' I'm walking up the road quite happy and wondering how she'll take this. Just at the church I met her. I says, 'Good evening.' She says, 'Good evening.' 'How about going for a walk?' I says. 'Yes,' she says. I'm wondering if I was hearing right. I'll never forget the lovely scene. As I was going up to meet her the moon was just coming round the corner behind the church. But when we actually got engaged it took us five years to get married. 'Yes,' she said, 'I will get engaged to you, but I will not marry you as long as my mother is alive.' I didn't press her; I didn't say anything. I was happy that she was willing to be engaged. One day she said to me, 'Are you still in the same intentions of marrying me?' 'Definitely I am,' I said. 'But I said to you I wouldn't get married to you while my mother is alive. Well, I'm going to tell you I'm going to get married as soon as I can.' She said why should she sacrifice our happiness together? We might as well join. So we married, in nineteen thirty-seven."

By then Mr. Heron had been with the MacLeods for nine years. "I came to London. I was just a single-handed footman. When we came up here there was a second footman with me, and there was also a piper who acted the duties.

I was never angry with my employers as a family, but there was many times I was angry with the butler before me. He was a devil, and he was always ready to catch me out. But I was fit for him. When I went for an interview for the situation, it was Captain Mitford that interviewed for help of Dame Flora and her father, Sir Reginald. One of the questions was 'Why are you leaving your present position? Are you hoping to better yourself?' And I said, 'Yes, that is my hope.'

"'Mr. Robertson, the butler, is one of my greatest friends,' Captain Mitford said, 'but he's a devil. He'll go for you, but you'll get the better of him. Just don't answer him.'"

"I called him Robin Redbreast," Mrs. Heron said. "He was small and cocky. 'Jump to it! Spring to it!' he'd say to the housemaids whenever he passed them."

She produced their visitors' book for us, bending for it with some difficulty. Mrs. Heron explained that she had fallen seriously ill three years earlier and had lapsed into a coma. "I was away with the fairies for three weeks" was how she put it. "I didn't know what had happened to me."

"When the ambulance was leaving, I went into it to see her," her husband recalled. "I said, 'I am placing her in your hands, God.' If there was ever a marvel of a lady alive, that's Cathy. The doctors, they didn't put it straight to me, but they didn't think she'd come back. She fought the trouble, and with spirit and determination she pulled through. The day she was critically and seriously ill, two doctors were seeing her. Doctor One came out and said, 'Charlie, we've done all we can for Cathy. Be prepared!' Our doctor, Doctor Two, came out, sort of smiling at me, and he said, 'Now, do you know, do you realize, how seriously Cathy is?'

"'Yes, I do.'

"'Well, you never said anything.'

"'I wanted to bear it myself.'

"'Well, you ought to tell your troubles to someone else, to

share your troubles. Now we'll just have to wait and see and trust.'

"He came forward and took me by the hand and he looked me in the face and said, 'While there's life, there's hope,' and I said, 'I have hopes.' And Cathy was so bright, cheery, and cooperative in everything, and they all loved her. It was that spirit and determination that brought her round."

I asked the Herons if they had regrets about devoting their life to service. "I wouldn't change it," Mr. Heron replied. "I've had my ups and downs, but the downs are mere details. I wouldn't even mention them. I'll always remember, as long as I live, dear Dame Flora; if there was someone strange at the castle, whom I had not met, I'd go along with her and she'd say, 'I want you to meet my most sincere and grateful friend,' not 'my servant.' "

CHAPTER 17

Raasay has little that can detain a traveler, except the Laird
and his family; but their power wants no auxiliaries. Such a
seat of hospitality, amidst the winds and waters, fills the
imagination with a delightful contrariety of images. Without
is the rough ocean and the rocky land, the beating billows
and the howling storm: within is plenty and elegance, beauty
and gaiety, the song and the dance.

— Samuel Johnson

THE ISLAND OF RAASAY, off Skye, had changed hands
many times since 1773, finally landing within the reluctant
grasp of the Department of Agriculture. In the eighteenth
century, Raasay — twelve miles long and two miles broad —
may have been home to as many as a thousand people. After
the clearances, only a few crofters and workers on the
owner's estate remained. Others emigrated or moved to the
smaller island of Rona, north of Raasay. Not till 1919 did
most of the people of Rona return to Raasay, occupying land
in the deserted townships.

A roll-on ferry now operated between Sconser, on Skye,
and Raasay. I drove onto the boat one morning, and went
up to the wheelhouse to have a word with the skipper,
Alistair Nicolson. His crew numbered two, one who collected tolls and the other who made himself generally useful.

During this trip the second mate demonstrated his agility by clambering onto the prow to remove a large sheet of plastic that had become entangled there and was flapping about like a sail.

Inviting me into the wheelhouse, Mr. Nicolson sat down and put his feet up on the wheel. From then until just before we landed, he steered the vessel with his feet while looking out at the water and devoting part of his attention to my questions. Since I had many questions, he suggested that when we docked I go along to Churchton House; he would have several hours to kill before the next crossing, and he would join me there. The directions were simple: leave ferry, turn left, and it was down the road, first house on the right. Raasay had no hotel, and Mr. Nicolson owned Churchton House.

I got there before he did, and his wife, who managed the guest house, asked me to wait in the living room. When Mr. Nicolson arrived he resumed the account he had begun on the ferry. He said that his grandparents and great-grandparents had lived on Tigh — a tiny island off Raasay, much smaller even than Rona — and indeed they had been the only inhabitants. Years after the clearances, when people were allowed to return to Raasay, the Nicolsons moved there.

When he went to primary school, in the thirties, there were more than sixty pupils, but now there were fourteen. Mr. Nicolson said that in about six years there would be only two or three. When I wondered aloud how many people lived on the island, he said there were a hundred and twenty-five, adding, "Not really living — they're dying."

"Aging?"

"Ancient. Half of the population is over sixty. There's only one couple on the island — the postman and his wife, who is part-time district nurse — who could conceivably still have children. They have two young children already." Only four people, all of them pensioners, lived in the northern end of

Raasay, north of Brochel Castle. The postman got to them three times a week.

"In the old days a young family could support itself on a croft," Mr. Nicolson said. "Now it can't even do that. The standard of living has gone up, and needs and desires are greater. You could still live off a croft if you went back to the old potatoes and fish and oatmeal two times a day and meat only on Sunday. I don't want to go back."

When I asked how many people were crofters, he replied: "Too few or too many, whichever attitude you take to crofters. Crofting is usually combined these days with work on country roads or with a shop."

Reviewing the families living exclusively from a croft, without other income, he counted aloud: "One, two, three, four, five, six, seven." The crofts ranged in size from two acres arable to fifteen — and a share in the common grazing. The sheep population had gone up, the cattle population had gone down, there were no longer any goats, and there were perhaps twenty or thirty deer left. But the lochs were underfished, he said. "Too many trout."

Mr. Nicolson, who was born in 1925, started work in the local sawmill in 1940, and the original forest planted by the estate was milled off during the war. Called up for national service in 1943, he was demobilized in 1946 and began forestry training. In 1950 he left for Kenya to work in forestry there, and stayed till 1964, when the country celebrated its independence. "I was disappointed to leave Kenya," he said. "It was a marvelous place to live — white raj, colonial oppressor, all that sort of thing. But I settled down here very well. There's lots of people who worked for the colonial government and came back and didn't make a job of settling and went off here and yonder. What I missed most when I came back was the ability to go places. I felt the constriction of an island. In Kenya, if I wanted to visit someone in the evening, a hundred miles away, I just got up and drove there. Here I was dependent on MacBrayne's [ferry] timetable. The only way to get a car off the island was when the tide was precisely right — you went onto the boat over a couple of planks, to suit a moving tide."

There was a steamer service, Mallaig on the mainland to the Kyle of Lochalsh to Raasay to Portree, but when the Kyle-Kyleakin — mainland-to-Skye — ferry began operating in a big way, the steamer service lost most of its customers. "They were running a monstrous-sized steamer at a monstrous cost," Mr. Nicolson said.

In 1962, MacBrayne's asked the people of Raasay if they wanted a ferry between Skye and Raasay. At a meeting to discuss a reply, Mr. Nicolson got up and spoke in favor. "I was practically booed," he said. "The old people said no, they wanted the old system, they wanted what they knew. At the time, there was a lot of money around for building pier facilities, and when the idea of the ferry finally took hold, the money was gone. It was stupid, really incredibly stupid, of the Raasay people to oppose the ferry."

For about eight years he served as a county councilor, and when regionalization was introduced he ran for the community council and lost. "The idea of regionalization was supposed to be increased efficiency, but all it's meant is increased inefficiency," he said. "It's just bureaucracy. The idea of regionalization was to save money, but bureaucrats have multiplied like the sands of the seashore. Where the whole thing has gone awry is at the district level. It's the districts that are either too big or the regions are too small. I would have said that one of the tiers is superfluous. Under the old setup, one man in Portree dealt with planning applications, did the whole shebang and shared a secretary with the social security officer, and nobody suffered. Planning applications were approved just as fast as they are now when there's a director of technical services, and I know he's got two, possibly three, underneath him, and an office staff.

There's about three of a staff employed on social services."

In 1975, when MacBrayne's finally began its ferry service between Sconser and Raasay — with government subsidy — Mr. Nicolson left the running of the guest house to his wife and signed on as skipper of the ferry. He and his wife together earned a healthy income, good enough to afford even a vacation to Kenya. "I told my wife, there's no point in piling up lolly if you don't enjoy it. We were going to go back before Kenyatta went and the whole place exploded."

When I suggested that most people in the islands seemed poorly off and that unemployment appeared a serious problem, he rejoined: "The whole of the Highlands suffers from this problem. What to do? They can talk about development boards all they like. Can you develop a place unless people develop it? Boards can't."

He said that to increase employment the government had encouraged the construction of a big smelter at Invergordon, on the mainland. Households flocked to Invergordon, and soon there were more people seeking employment than there were jobs. The same happened when a pulp mill was built on the mainland at Fort William. "You have to think of little cottage industries, and then you're up against transport. If you go into anything weighty or bulky you're up against it — the fearful transport costs. Now, with Common Market regulations, if you send up groceries from Glasgow you've got to send up two drivers."

Mr. Nicolson said that a couple of years earlier one of the incomers wanted to organize a Raasay society to bar development schemes that could change the character of the island. So there was a meeting, and the local people rejected the idea, since it was something new. Mr. Nicolson disapproved of the conservatism of his neighbors, but he appreciated the irony of incomers wanting to bar the way to other incomers.

He had no sympathy for those who bemoaned the prevalence, or even the presence, of tourists. "London is pulling in England, Portree and Broadford are pulling in the country — emptying the glens," he said. "There's a terrific demand for council houses in Portree. The glens are being inhabited now as holiday homes, summers only. Without tourism the islands would be a desert. If no tourists came to Raasay, the service over here wouldn't require anything bigger than an outrigger canoe. The local trade is peanuts; it would hardly keep the ferry in flags. If the tourist wasn't here to justify a large ferry, the local wouldn't have the boat to take his livestock on and off. If the tourists disappeared overnight, Skye would die on its feet. I reckon tourism keeps Skye alive, and all the experts and economists can say what they flippin' well like, it keeps these places in business."

Mr. Nicolson was a fluent Gaelic speaker, and I asked him how he felt about the state of the language, expecting to hear him say that it was a flippin' shame that Gaelic was languishing. "To stay alive, Gaelic would have to add three hundred thousand words from modern English," he said. "It's not on. And suppose we added only four thousand words. Then the native Gaelic speaker would no longer speak it. I like to live in the future, not in the past. Gaelic is all right for scholars and poets."

Telling Mr. Nicolson that I would see him on the ferry back to Skye, I set off on a tour of the island, beginning of course with Raasay House, where Johnson and Boswell stayed. In their day only the central portion existed; the symmetrical flanking wings had been added later. The buff-colored stone structure stood in splendid isolation near the sea, with a large lawn sloping down to a horseshoe-shaped bay, but the lawn was now overgrown with weeds, and the house itself was no longer a site of civility and joy but was desolate and abandoned. It had been thoroughly vandalized, and the windows on the ground floor were now — belatedly — boarded up.

Not long before my visit, the Highlands and Islands

Development Board, with the approval of the Secretary of State for Scotland, had purchased the building from Dr. John R. W. Green, who had acquired it almost twenty years earlier. Dr. Green, who lived in the south of England, owned not only Raasay House and its nine acres, but also Raasay Home Farm and its ninety-eight acres and farmhouse, the dry harbor, pier, and jetty, and an assortment of cottages, as well as mineral and sporting rights on Raasay, Rona, Tigh, and Fladda. Instead of developing or even maintaining his properties, Dr. Green let them sink into dilapidation, and when he resisted efforts to purchase them back he became known as Dr. No. His holdings were finally repurchased for £135,000, the sum fixed by the district valuer. Less than two years earlier, Dr. Green had sold the government Borrodale House, and this was to be converted into a fifteen-bedroom hotel. Between 1937 and 1960, Raasay House had been a hotel, and now there were plans to make it that again. There were other ideas afloat, but no rush to implement any of them.

Raasay's largest settlement was the village of Inverarish, little more than two facing rows of sad terrace houses with a line of shacks and sheds and occasional clotheslines between the rows. A large sign outside the island's one shop advertised four lines — groceries, hardware, draper's goods, and stationery. The stock was modest, which was understandable on so small an island with so tiny a clientele, though in summer, with the influx of tourists, there were sometimes queues, and three people served customers. No matter how many people waited, there was rarely any suggestion of impatience on the part of the clients or haste behind the counter.

When I came back to the ferry for the return trip to Skye, Mr. Nicolson was in the wheelhouse, sipping coffee and chatting with his crew. He seemed at ease with the world, and I asked if this impression was correct. "I'm content enough," he replied, "but we only get about one decent summer in twelve or fifteen. I remember 'fifty-five was a very dry summer, and towards the end of it you began seeing mature trees go brown because of the lack of water due to the shallowness of the soil. When the weather gets terrible I still want to get away. That wind's got an edge on it like a razor. It would be all right if we could only transfer this island to the South Pacific."

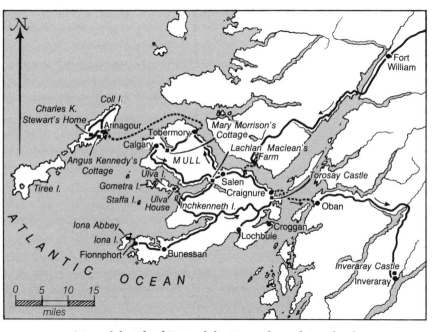

Map of the Third Part of the Tour Through Scotland

CHAPTER 18

Mr. Johnson had owned to me this morning that he was out of humor. Indeed, he showed it a good deal in the ship, for when I was expressing joy on being landed in Mull, he said he had no joy when he thought it would be five days before he should get to the mainland.

— James Boswell

AFTER DRIVING OFF the ferry onto Mull, we stopped for the night at the Craig Hotel at Salen, on the road to Tobermory, the largest village on this island of 367 square miles. Until recently, the hotel owners, James and Lorna McIntyre, lived in Strathaven, near Glasgow. He taught pottery in a local high school, and year by year he found teaching less rewarding. The McIntyres finally decided to start a new life, and bought the Craig Hotel, not because they dreamed of becoming hotel-keepers but because it would enable them to live on Mull. "My brother was over in Australia and said that everything's so vast that they'll talk about a beauty spot," Mrs. McIntyre said. "Here, everything's a beauty spot."

The hotel was a modest establishment — seven rooms, no private baths. Mrs. McIntyre had studied three years at a domestic science school, and she cooked while her husband served at table. The hotel register blossomed with clients' testimonials. "Better than my mum cooks," observed a student of Jesus College, Oxford. "Mega!" exclaimed another guest. One client wrote simply: "Home."

Mrs. McIntyre said that in March, when the tourists began arriving, people in the hotel business said to one another, "See you in October," for the season was too busy and too concentrated to allow for leisure. The McIntyres would have liked to visit local castles and museums, but during the off-season, when they would have been free to go sightseeing, Mull's museums and castles were closed.

"It's been a radical change for us," Mr. McIntyre said. "There's a lot of physical work, and it gets hectic — a seven-day week and twelve-to-fourteen-hour days. We've often felt, 'What are we doing?' It's when work overwhelms us, usually late at night, when we're practically on our knees. And then we have days when we have no one at all staying at the hotel. Then we can relax and the place becomes a home again."

"It's not a sort of nipping-around-for-suburban-coffee place," his wife said. "There are things we miss and people we miss. The thing we miss most is the choral society. There is one society here, but they sing during the summer, when we can't get away from the hotel. I used to be a square-eyes person. I'd watch anything that moved. How was I going to get along without TV — or time to watch it? But reception is bad here, and so is radio reception. We still collect records, and during the winter, when there were no guests at the hotel, we started family games again."

"The biggest problem is getting things done," Mr. McIntyre said.

"It's a mental attitude you have to accept," his wife explained. "If it's something urgent they're round in two minutes. If it's something that can wait, you wait. The only greengrocer comes three times a week during the summer. He calls you up; you don't have to call him. The freezer people come once a week during the summer and once a fortnight during the winter. Hale, the bacon people, come to the island every week. Bread and milk and eggs we buy at the shop across the road."

The mobile library called at the Salen school once a fortnight. Mull's dentist, who lived in Salen, made regular runs round the island, treating patients in his trailer. There was a doctor resident in Salen. "You can be ill whenever you like," Mrs. McIntyre said. "You don't have to make an appointment." A small cottage hospital stood around the corner from the hotel, but when anyone was seriously ill the doctor quickly ordered up an ambulance plane and had the patient flown off the island.

In a shed next to the hotel, Mr. McIntyre had installed a pottery workshop, and he sold as much of his ware as he had time to make. His wife warned that Mull had to be careful not to succumb to commercial fever and change into a different kind of place. "If they make it a get-off-the-boat-and-give-me-your-money-please island, it'll be the end of Mull," she said.

Just down the street lived Muriel and Ian McCrae. They had been on Mull twelve years, and after being with them a minute or two, it was easy to see that they were birds of rare feather. Muriel called herself Judy, and she called other people whatever came into her mind, speaking that mind plainly, though good-naturedly. She participated heartily in community activities, and when she ran a meeting — as she often did — she got things moving. In relaxed moments she whirled about like a windsock in a tornado, but more common was her dreadnought approach, racing under a full head of steam to engage the enemy or to answer a call of distress. The moment she heard that we wanted to rent a cottage on Mull, she was on the phone to a woman on the mainland who had a cottage down the street in Salen, and one minute later she was atop a ladder to the attic, pulling sheets from her store of linen and pressing them into my arms.

Ian McCrae's temperament was different. A retired physician, he was relaxed and soft-spoken, and if his wife was a straining dreadnought, he was a relaxed square-rigger, pleasantly becalmed. He reminded me of S. J. Perelman, a man of whom he had never heard, with similar exaggerations and understatements, and the same delight in the ridiculous. As soon as we sat down in the McCraes' cottage, which was directly opposite the post office, the dialogue swirled up around us.

Judy: "Ian started off in South Africa. I started off in Norfolk. We got married. We came up to the Highlands from Kent. We loved Mull and we started looking for a cottage. Spent about four or five years looking for it. It's so stupid when you're both a hundred and five years old and you want to be in the middle of things. We're more middle than we intended. You can be much more yourself here than in Kent or Lochaber, where we were after Kent. On Mull there's no class consciousness. That doesn't mean the road-sweeper doesn't realize the laird is somebody different."

Ian: "If you go to a dance or a *ceilidh,* you dance with anybody. You know them all by their Christian names. In fact, that's all that I do know about a lot of them."

Judy: "The west coasters are devious. They won't say no. You say, 'Will you come and sweep my chimney?' They'll say, 'I can't do it this week, I'll come next,' and they come two years later."

Ian: "There's no sense of perfection about anything. It's 'That will do.'"

Judy: "We're usually quite chummy here. Tobermory isn't chummy."

Ian: "Foreigners here are people who come from villages ten miles away."

Judy: "There are some people just arrived; they've bought the house of the doctor who was here before Dr. Jones. The old granny who came with them misses her bingo. They're people I feel sorry for, because they've got into a way of life they weren't used to."

Ian: "There's no organized sport. There's no football team. There's no field."

Judy: "There's a rugger team."

Ian: "I'm one of the very few people who ever ran the Derby. During World War Two, I was stationed with two antitank regiments at Epsom Downs. A friend and I used to run the racecourse, the same one the horses did. I've been sorry for the horses ever since. It's a heck of a long run uphill before you start. That was my chief contribution to the war."

Judy: "We had a friend from South Africa who visited us and told us we had forgotten to lock our doors. But we never lock our doors. I told our friend, 'In the front hall I found six eggs that someone had left me. In the kitchen there were six pancakes that someone else had left. If I'd locked the doors I wouldn't have had eggs and I wouldn't have had pancakes.' When the postman had a registered letter for us one morning he came right into the bedroom and sat down on the bed to get my signature. We get up as late as we can. This is a very busy house because of the site, and there are days when Ian says, 'It's no good. We have to move to Croggan.' That's as far as you can get on Mull. Nobody's there."

Ian: "There are doctors all over the place, the smell of iodoform everywhere."

Judy: "There's a Gaelic choir, but only a minority of them can speak Gaelic."

Ian: "This island has been called the colonels' island."

"Aging population?" I asked.

"Geriatric," Ian replied.

Judy: "As a joke, people say, 'Oh, she's English, poor thing.' Enthusiasm is being built up a bit for studying Gaelic. I'm not prepared to go to all that trouble when people can understand me quite well."

Ian: "The new people want activity, want to run things."

Judy: "Dr. Flora Macdonald says, 'The last off the boat runs the island.' "

Ian: "Don't try to reform them till you've been here for a few years. Take them as they are. Of course, they have changed since the old days. People here used to be so docile. When the laird wanted to hang someone, the victim's wife probably said, 'Go along, dear, do as he says.' "

Judy: "When we first arrived, people used to say 'Isn't it cold!' and I'd say, 'No, it was much colder where we lived on the mainland.' People didn't like that, so I took to saying 'Oh yes, freezing!' "

Ian: "The main tourist traffic is to Iona. You see so many tourists on the boat that you're sure the boat will sink, and the island as well. I've done a *locum* at Bunessan, where I get the tourists coming to Iona. Ninety percent wind up at the surgery at Bunessan and they've left their pills at home on the kitchen table. After the summer you find the place is yours again. Roll on, October, when the visitors and midges go."

We then feasted on homemade cakes and tea, and Dr. McCrae got out his volumes of Thurber to show his favorite drawings. Outside, the wind howled and the rain lashed.

Judy: "By Jove, the rams are getting restive."

Ian: "People in Kent think we spend our time in a hut with smoke coming out of a hole in the roof, and me weaving nets while she's knitting sweaters to keep me warm."

After Thurber, Dr. McCrae produced an excerpt from an eighteenth-century traveler's account in which the author prescribed charmel root as a cure for hangover. Dr. McCrae allowed that he had on occasion to deal with a case of hang-over — patient's, of course. Now if he could only find out what charmel root was . . .

I decided to find out for him. After searching fruitlessly in several dictionaries and promising myself to consult John-son's own *Dictionary* and the multivolume *Oxford English Dictionary*, I came across an account similar to that Dr. McCrae had shown me, in *The Present State of Scotland* (London, 1738): "The natives of Mull when the season is moist take a large dose of aqua-vitae for a corrective, and chew a piece of charmel root when they intend to be merry to prevent drunkenness."

In Johnson's *Dictionary* there was no "charmel." The O.E.D. provided the solution: "Charmele, obs. var. of Car-mele, Heath-pea. 1760 Pocock *Tour Scotl.* (1887) 89 They chew the root of an herb called charmele [*mispr.* charnicle] a . . wild liquorice."

On Mull, I was inclined to understand why people had hangovers, for I could appreciate why any release might seem welcome. There was rarely sunlight, and never a day without rain — to which hail was a frequent complement. Umbrellas never appeared, because the winds were too strong. Confirming the theory that misery loves company, we would listen to radio at night to hear the weather forecasts, and once there were warnings from all coastal stations. Many areas were to have gale force 8, several gale force 9, and some especially unfortunate places were in for storm force 10. Like a good chauvinist, I was proud to hear that Mull was going to escape the ignominy of mere gales and would have a proper storm instead. But there were also less perverse rea-sons for delight in this volcanic island with its mountains and moors and wooded glens: a grandeur to the scenery and a sense of quiet isolation, and this a mere mile and a half from the mainland.

Mary Morrison had come from Skye to this vale of beauty

and gloom about forty years earlier, taught primary school, and married. On retirement in 1975, she moved into a tiny house on an isolated croft, her only neighbors a son and daughter-in-law who lived in a larger house a few yards away. The Morrisons' croft was about a hundred acres, and they kept about fifteen cattle and fifty sheep. Summers, Mrs. Morrison's son ran cruises to the isle of Staffa. "You've got to work pretty hard to live pretty reasonable," Mrs. Morrison said.

She was a militant in the Scottish National Party, a determined woman set on helping the cause of Gaelic. "I had no English when I went to school," she said. "There was a definite repression of Gaelic — a class thing. The children of the doctor, the children of the minister, the children of the merchant, all spoke English. I was a crofter's daughter and spoke Gaelic. Today it's rather the reverse. People are envious of your knowing a second language."

To spread the good words she had been waging a campaign to have Gaelic taught in local schools, and when I asked how she went about it she replied, "Bashing the local authorities." They had promised to appoint an itinerant teacher, but when spending cuts were mandated, local officials said there simply was not enough money. Unfortunately, Mrs. Morrison did not know how to drive, or she would have done the job herself for nothing. "Sympathy without help" was how she characterized the attitude of authorities. "It's such a minimal cost," she said. "I imagine this whole service would cost only three or four thousand a year. We did a survey of the parents of primary and pre-primary children and we had a ninety percent return of parents wanting to have their children learn Gaelic."

Mrs. Morrison said that many of the retired people who settled on Mull were an asset to the community. "And then there are those who come off the ferry and sort of run Mull. Holiday-home people — they buy a home and use it only in the summer — are not welcome, but they put money into the economy. In the rural areas in Scotland and Wales, people buy up houses anywhere there's a green space. A lot of big tracts are now forests, and a lot of land is owned by individuals who don't do anything for it — they just stick a few sheep or deer on it."

She suggested that an outsider looking at the way she lived might think it was a life of privation — a hut in the middle of nowhere. "But I have the essentials," she said. "I have heating. I have my television. I'm perfectly comfortable and fed and get good home-grown vegetables and potatoes and rabbit and hare and deer off the hill. This is where I want to be and I find plenty to do and I can perhaps be of help to people around. I'm a cabbagey person. I have my roots where there's space around me. I help in the garden. I do the weeding, put in potatoes, whatever has to be done."

Donald Morrison, no kin to Mary Morrison, was a lean and wiry man, ninety-five years old, the oldest person on Mull, and he lived in Salen in a home for the aged. On the morning we went to see him, he was sitting in the men's common room with three other aged parties. "I was born and built on Mull," he said. "In the old days it was the sons that looked after the elderly people. There were no hospitals like this. There were poorhouses. Local people called them slaughterhouses. That's the way they go."

The nurse I had spoken to said that he loved to talk and that nothing pleased him more than a rousing discussion of politics. Sometimes political arguments got so heated that the staff had to intervene. I decided not to discuss politics, but instead to ask him about the history of Mull. In responding, his first sentence was "The bards have sung and the historians have written." Then he launched into an account, beginning in the 1840s, of the potato famine, about which he had heard from his father, and soon he got onto his own life story. He had left school when he was thirteen, and had become a crofter. Eventually he had six cows, two horses, and about thirty sheep. "In my day there was no thought about education," he said. "It was work and put off your jacket."

I asked Mr. Morrison if he had managed to earn a living. "Oh well," he replied, "we had the sort of living we had. The big men, the landlords, they were all right, but not us. Things haven't been moving very well in the Highlands. The landlord was an absolute monarch. He had his word and you had nothing to say. After the clearances, in the year of time of eighteen eighty-three, the landlords put up the rent awful, and the people could not pay it, the land wouldn't pay it. That went on till eighteen eighty-six, when the government passed an act to send out a royal commission to make a fair rent of the land. They went over all the Highlands and they made a fair rent with it. They done a lot of good. At that time. That lasted for a while. Since that day, you see, things have changed completely. There's not half the population that there was when I was younger. That's what they call rural depopulation. I don't agree with the capitalist system. If it was as good as what people preached and I heard, then why was it that one of the greatest sins committed under the heavens was committed in the Highlands under the capitalist system? That is the Highland clearances. The rottenness of the landlords slowly but steadily evicted the Highlander from this island glade into smoking cities to swell the ranks of the unemployed. That's what has happened. I'm quoting history just now. But very few people know anything about it. They have a summary, but not the act."

For centuries, the people of the Highlands and islands had lived within the patriarchal clan system, lairds and their people mutually bound by ties of custom, affection, work, and real or imagined consanguinity. Increasingly, the chiefs acquired a taste for the luxuries of the south, and when, toward the end of the eighteenth century, sheep farmers on the

Scottish borders offered high rents for land, the temptation was too strong to resist. Viewing their holdings as articles of commerce subject to the caprices of their pleasure, lairds turned to law to evict their tenants and subtenants. The despairing poor, believing their rights to the ancestral soil inalienable, and ignorant of how to scrape a living elsewhere, felt betrayed. With police and soldiers, landlords evicted the people from the glens. Sometimes, to enforce eviction orders, crofters' homes were set afire and people were forced to flee with no possessions except the clothes on their backs. Some sought refuge on the coasts, living in shacks and ditches and caves. Others, who tried to escape to the hills, were tracked down, bound like animals, and thrown aboard ships headed for the Western Hemisphere.

After the sheep clearances came the clearances of those who interfered with the pleasures of the hunt, when sportsmen, inconvenienced by the presence of crofters, arranged that the evictions should continue. Many of those driven from their homes migrated to the cities; others crowded into townships on the coast; and the rest left for the New World. Eventually there was a public outcry, even a beginning of desperate organized resistance. Finally the government established a commission to investigate the state of small tenants in the Highlands, and then in 1886 Parliament passed the first Crofters Act.

I asked Mr. Morrison, who was shaking with outrage at the memory of injustices past, what he would put in the place of capitalism. He looked straight ahead — I was sitting at his right — pressed his mouth even more firmly onto his pipe, and replied: "I would put people's communism as it was at the beginning. I would put pure communism. And what is pure communism? Do unto others as you would have others do unto you. That's pure communism. I don't know how it is today, but before the ages it was communism in the time of Christ. The land was not created for landlords or factors or anybody else, but when it was created it was given to the sons of men, and I say it should be that way yet. Capitalism was good for the well-to-do, but not for the working man. The only cure for the ills of the present day — I don't care what anybody says — is the distribution of wealth according to the theories of Immanuel Kant. I think he is a man for today. In my own opinion, unless there is more equal distribution of wealth, according to the theory of Immanuel Kant, there'll be no peace between labor and capital."

Mr. Morrison asked me if I realized that David Livingstone, whom he called "the missionary-explorer," had come from Mull. "He belonged to Ulva down there. His father lived in a cave there and then he got a croft and then he worked in cotton mills. You know the wages they had? Ten-hour day, two-and-six a week. That's the capitalist system. What do you say to that? How could they live? They were a big family, in one room eighteen by twelve. It's not what I say. I'm quoting history." As though he were declaring an official end to this chapter of history, Mr. Morrison added that David Livingstone "was found dead in Africa in a tent, on his knees, in the attitude of prayer; that was the end of David Livingstone, the missionary-explorer."

He told me that even in this century many of the poor on Mull had lived in tents, and that one of those people came to see him recently and told him about it. "And he was a strong fellow. He could twist my neck. Aye, that's the way it was."

Mr. Morrison acknowledged that there was more money about now. "But it took a long time before that came," he said. "When I was in school, the children, some of them, went barefooted in the wintertime in school. All that has passed away now."

He said that there had been changes as well in religion. "Nowadays we have got many kinds of religion: religion by the pack, religion by the ton, human materialism — look after the comfort of the body and let the soul look after itself. Yes, that's it. That is so."

I asked Mr. Morrison, whose first language was Gaelic, if he had had trouble learning English. "For years I didn't know my own name in English," he replied. "Gaelic is the third oldest language in Europe."

Interrupting, I asked what was the oldest. "I couldn't tell you," he said abruptly, putting me in my place. Then he began an account of Gaelic fables and ghost stories. "They used to frighten me. At *ceilidhs,* the old folk, the gray heads, were telling long stories about goblins and all that sort of thing and how they came out at night, and when we were coming home we would be running and keeping your mouth shut so that your breath would last longer. And even for a long time after leaving school I was afraid. But through successive years I forgot about it. Yes, that was the way, that was the way all over."

I feared that Mr. Morrison was getting tired, and I suggested that perhaps it was time for us to leave. But he told us to stay and voiced his disappointment that I had not expressed my own opinions on politics. Did I agree with his view of popular communism? What did I think about Kant? When I suggested that the Soviet system did not seem to work very well, he grew indignant. "Who said that?" he demanded. "I knew a man that was for five years over there, and I knew him as well as my right foot, and he was very pleased with them. And if it hadn't been for Russia during the war, where would we be today? Stalin was then called Marshal Stalin, but before that and at the time of the revolution he was called the cobbler's son in Georgia, a useless man that was fond of dancing and that was very fond of eating sugar candy."

CHAPTER 19

Dr. Johnson was not in very good humor. He said it was a
dreary country, much worse than Skye. I differed from him.
"O, sir," said he, "a most dolorous country!"

— James Boswell

FROM SALEN we moved north to Tobermory, which nestled
in a natural hillside amphitheater along a bay. High above
the harbor, in the Church of Scotland manse, lived Gordon
Holroyd. Born in Glasgow, he had spent most of his life elsewhere; indeed, he had moved about so much that he spoke
of himself as stateless. "There's nothing unique about Mull,"
he said. "Every advantage and problem you can find in the
Highlands you'll find on Mull. In the old days it was an
island, but when you drive on and off the ferry you're not an
island anymore. In the summer, MacBrayne's lands sixty cars
every two hours. It's more like a bridge than a ferry. The
population is soaring, after declining for a long time. It was
down to about fifteen hundred and now it's approaching
three thousand."

Mr. Holroyd said that people coming to live on Mull were
young retireds, ex-colonials, former civil servants. "They're
attracted by a quality of life that's still unhurried, unfussed.

For the years to come they may be creating an old-age ghetto."

I asked what sort of welcome awaited them. "In the Highlands you'll find if you're different you're wrong," he replied. "They're very courteous, kindly, hospitable, but they're still very resentful of people who come in from the outside and make a living here. It's deeply bred into them that the stranger who comes and earns his bread is depriving the islanders. It wouldn't make any difference if he came from Australia or Canada or Vietnam. If he comes and retires, that's all right. If he comes in and makes a profit, that's all wrong. You see, they feel *they* should have thought of it. There's a particular antipathy to the Englishman — the Sassenach. He speaks with a stranger's tongue, and the Scotsman with a public school accent falls under the same castigation. As for the tourists, fifty percent of the island will welcome them with open arms, and the other fifty percent live for the day when they all are away. Tourism is a rotten industry on which to base a life. I think it's insufferable. Once the tourists go home, from November until Easter, there aren't enough nights to organize everything: drama, camera club, gun club, Women's Rural Institute, historical society, bridge club, badminton club, indoor bowling, music appreciation society, night classes at school. The classes used to be mainly vocational, but now people tend to do academic subjects — higher English or French or mathematics. The scene here is changing so rapidly. Ten years ago I would have described this as a classless society. I wouldn't today. Neither would I want to be pressed into describing the stratification."

But then he suggested a threefold division: "Bohemians, indigenous, and dinner-at-nine . . . In the old days you could have counted on one hand the people who had *dinner* at night. Now you have to stop and think before you go knocking on a door at night which dinner party you'll be interrupting. The later the dinner, the higher up the social scale they think they are. The logical conclusion to which is that we'll be getting invitations to breakfast soon."

On Skye, other ministers had spoken of being born again. "If pressed, I'd say that," Mr. Holroyd acknowledged. "One has a change of heart. Nothing dramatic. One can turn round very quickly or very slowly, but you still wind up facing in the opposite direction."

I asked him what he preached about sin. "I very rarely preach about sin as such," he replied. "The Highlands had a very narrow concept of what constituted good and bad. The strength of the parish church, as opposed to the Free and Free Presbyterian, is that it always had a broader view, a bigger corporate intelligence prepared to incorporate new truths. We have no liturgy. The Free Church has no written liturgy, but it has a liturgy of habit and use. The Free and Free Presbyterian don't stray from the words of the King James Bible. I would use any word that happened to suit my context. There could easily be six terms rather than 'sin' — wrongdoing, misguided thinking, mistaken understanding, errors of judgment, errors of appreciation, errors of omission. One would try to be more specific than simply saying 'sin.' It's easy in a small place for people to care about everybody and yet to do nothing specific, and errors of omission can be at a very neighborly level."

Mr. Holroyd said that he was more interested in persuasion by reason than by dictate or fear, and he spoke of the Free Church "dangling them over the pit and letting them sniff the burning sulfur — an attitude I don't care for at all."

Noting that the Church of Scotland usually got on well with other churches, he added: "I defy anyone to cooperate with the Wee Frees Kirk. 'Impossible' would be the word you'd use for them. Oddly enough, I get along with the Free Presbyterians — just because we don't belong to the same ethos — just as I got along very happily with the synagogues in Glasgow."

The Free Church refused to permit debate about the word of the Bible, he complained, and he said that problems of Scriptural interpretation should be welcome. "By virtue of being debated, these things have a great relevance today," he said. "Anyone who just throws it at a congregation is appealing to a fairly narrow intellect, and that's what they'll have in their pews. It's the thinking people who are coming to church today; perhaps sometimes not the brightest, but they're thinking. Among the older people, however, you'll still find a lot of bigotry. They put a fence around what they've got, and they won't admit others. They're satisfied with too small a portion of what is viable and true."

From the manse we drove out to the neck of the island, where the land was pinched almost in two, to see Lachlan Maclean, one of a disappearing species on Mull — a farmer. In 1720 his forebears had been evicted from the island, and most of the family had emigrated to America; his father was the first in the family to return. When Mr. Maclean looked about him, he saw an island still declining. "You get a lot of people opting out and coming to Mull. They don't contribute an awful lot. As far as being a valid community, it's going down, though perhaps not as fast as before. The Lochbuie end of the island was once a self-contained community, with about sixty people. Today it has about sixteen souls in it, and only about three or four under forty-five. There used to be about fifty souls in Croggan, and about a hundred and twenty children used to gather there for local fêtes. The village, which had fifty people fifty years ago, today has two old ladies over seventy. Indigenous Highlanders are hard to find now. They're thin on the ground. There are more Mull people on one street in Glasgow than on the whole island of Mull."

Though many residents of Mull opposed the granting of building permits, fearing that the island would be spoiled, Mr. Maclean favored development. "If you want a bit of land to build a house, you'd have trouble to find it," he said.

"And after you find it you'll have twenty times as much trouble getting permission to build. People would complain about your spoiling the 'intrinsic beauty' of the place. These people want a Mull they would have liked to see — that never existed."

One big dispute had centered on the introduction of a car ferry. "I was one of those who campaigned for it," Mr. Maclean said. "My wife's father, Malcolm Black, was a third-generation sea captain from Mull. He ran the mailboat, and he said Mull would never survive without car ferries. And boy, was I told what sort of person I was for wanting a car ferry! These people who opposed the ferry were those who used to come here for a private Shangri-la, and they wanted cheap labor. When the ferry finally started, about nineteen sixty-three, Chrissie's father was captain of the first trip. And you should have seen the rush of those landlords, who had opposed the ferry, to be in the limelight — the people who said Mull would be inundated with orange peels and leather jackets. I'm afraid some of the Highlanders even kowtowed to them."

The Macleans kept about three thousand sheep and a hundred head of cattle, and also looked after about two thousand additional sheep for a neighboring estate. Two teen-age sons, whose hobby was making shepherds' crooks, were determined to go on being shepherds, and they had no desire to leave Mull or to try some other occupation. Mr. Maclean told us that his wife and their two sons recognized individual sheep, but that he did not have the knack. Beyond saying that one was born with the gift, he could not explain how it was that some had this ability and others did not.

But he boasted of another gift — a propensity to get involved in things that gave him extra work. Mull had twelve community councilors, and he was one of them. "You don't need to be smart in Mull to be anything," he said. "When you open your mouth, you're appointed." He said that his job consisted of being prodded by people so that he in turn would prod the district council, whose job then would be to prod the regional council. "Anything from our ferry services to public facilities — to make sure that we get our fair share. We always feel, rightly or wrongly, that if we don't keep shouting, we can easily be forgotten. I was very critical of regionalization at the start. Before regionalization, we were in Argyll County and our center of local government wasn't so far away. We knew whose ear to twist. Up to now, though, with regionalization, we've had a good share. The feeling was that places like this were so critical that they needed help. But to be quite fair about it, is a hole in the road in Mull as important as a hole in the road in Glasgow?"

As our car bumped along the route to Craignure, we had our own answer to that question. The road from Salen began with two lanes, and soon it narrowed to a single track, with long stretches in terrible repair. Lieutenant Colonel Albert Miller had invited me to visit him at Torosay Castle, and I walked past a receptacle, intended for admission fees and marked "Honesty Box," and rang at the door. The great stone pile looming over me was in the Victorian neo-Gothic style that had become known as Scottish baronial, and I was suitably intimidated. Colonel Miller invited me into the living room, a large, musty, disordered place, and then joined me beside the fire, stretching out his legs to warm them.

The colonel, now seventy-four and long since retired from military service, though not from military bearing, told me that he was born in Australia and came to Britain in 1916, when his father was a soldier in the First World War. "I fired the first shot in the war against the Italians, in the war in the desert," the colonel said. "I don't think they knew war had been declared. I fired my Bren gun, or whatever we had, but it didn't go off, so my sergeant really fired the first shot. I was a captain at the time, in the Eleventh Hussars. We started the war in Egypt, and we ended it by being the first into Berlin.

"I've got land and a certain amount of money in Australia. My grandmother used to say that the money was made in Australia, and she didn't like the idea that my mother and father lived in England. So when I inherited, I decided to use the income here, but not the capital. With my cousins I inherited my share of what had been my grandfather's estate, in Australia, which was very good, some of the best land in Victoria. I do go out to Australia from time to time, and it gets more and more expensive to go there.

"It was my wife's family that owned Torosay. Her great-uncle bought it from Colonel Campbell of Possil in eighteen fifty-six. Although Colonel Campbell married three times, and each time married a cousin, there was no issue. He then left it to a second cousin who had no issue, who left it again to a second cousin. The heir was Carter Campbell, and he had no interest in it and sold it to Arbuthnot Guthrie, who also had no children and left it to his nephew Walter Murray Guthrie, my wife's father. He was a delightful man, a very daring man. I think he was the first editor of the *Granta*, a Cambridge paper, and became the Member of Parliament for Bow and Bromley and died at the age of forty-one of diabetes."

I learned later that Walter Murray Guthrie had been appalled by the bequest, and had promptly offered Torosay for sale, proclaiming it a "substantial and commodious MANSION adapted for a family of rank," adding that the "SPORTING CHARACTERISTICS WERE VARIED AND UNIQUE AND PRESENTED A COMBINATION OF ATTRACTIONS SELDOM UNITED TO SUCH AN EXTENT IN ANY SINGLE PROPERTY, offering to the CAPITALIST and LOVER OF SPORT, an almost unparalleled opportunity of indulging his energetic proclivities." But when Guthrie visited the property, he withdrew his offer and commissioned a celebrated landscape gardener to exercise his energetic proclivities and design three Italianate terraces and a statue walk connecting the castle and the old walled garden. Over the years there were many notable guests, and the visitors' book was rich with their signatures: Jennie Randolph Churchill, Sir Winston Churchill, Nellie Melba, Lillie Langtry. One of the later entries read: "Torosay just visited by Concorde's sonic-boom."

The estate had descended to a daughter and to her son, David Guthrie James, who remembered meeting his great-grandmother, Lady Constance Leslie (1830–1925), at a family wedding three weeks before her death. "Grannie Boo" was then a shrunken figure who wore a bonnet tied under her chin with a black bow. In 1848, at her coming-out ball, she had danced with Lord Huntly, who told her, "If you live to a great age, my dear, you can tell your great-grandchildren that you danced with a man who once danced with Marie Antoinette."

David Guthrie James was the son of his mother's first marriage; Colonel Miller was his mother's second husband. "When my wife's mother died, my wife and I decided to come and live here rather than go to Australia," Colonel Miller said. "There are about fifteen thousand acres and the castle — fifteen thousand acres of deer forest or sheepgrazing, if you like. When my wife's great-uncle bought this place, it was basically a sporting estate. That was true all over Scotland. As the years went by the sports got a little less. Wildlife has decreased here. There is some agriculture, but it's at a great disadvantage. You have to work here twice as hard to obtain the same final reward. Because of the weather you can't plan ahead in agriculture or anything else. You have to wait until ten o'clock to know how the day's going to be. We can't produce the same size of animal, the same number of animals, as in Victorian times. In those days the balancing factor was rent; it was lower here than on the mainland. As the rents began to even out, you found your-self trying to do the same thing as farmers on the mainland, with inferior land. And though we had an island subsidy, it never quite made up for the disadvantages. Transport costs are so high. I used to reckon that the cost of living was twenty-five percent higher than it was on the mainland. People used to ask why we couldn't produce our own things, but when you have a very scattered population you can't make it economical. There's no gold in them thar hills."

Mull attracted people who wanted to get away from it all, and Colonel Miller thought that they may have come away because they had been failures at home. "They arrive here to do some piddling thing and they find it costs money, though some have made a success of it." He said that the same thing had happened in Australia in the old days. Those who came without capital failed, and those who came with capital succeeded. Colonel Miller said it was hard to find a genuine native of Mull, born and bred, but, then, "it's hard to find a Hawaiian."

He said that on Mull, family fortunes lasted about three generations. The first generation had a fortune and a family seat; the second generation had a family seat and no fortune; the third generation wound up with neither seat nor fortune. "Our family has been going for three generations, and it's our luck we're still able to carry on, but it's only because we've opened this castle to the public. That was the great leap forward. I also let stalking to the Germans, but that just about pays the wages of the gamekeeper. Many of the sports agents have gone bankrupt because they wanted to be big operators, and big is not beautiful. I can survive because I have a small number to deal with.

"The whole object of the trustees is to keep the land and castle in good repair. We are just trying to do what every landowner in England tries to do. During his lifetime he is there to look after the estate and hand it over improved, and of course due to legislation this is impossible. This is why we opened the castle and garden to the public three years ago, to avoid capital transfer tax. The target of the socialists is the landowner. There's no disguising that they'd be very busy trying to have confiscation of the land if they could do it. Obviously that will come, because socialism is only an introduction to communism. Especially in the Highlands, the absentee landlord was a tremendous target. But all these landlords were away because they had to earn money to support their estates."

Colonel Miller said that in a speech to the Scottish Landowners' Federation he had told his fellow proprietors that opposition to absentee landlords had led to estates being taken over by the Secretary of State for Scotland. And what was that august official, Colonel Miller demanded, but the biggest absentee landlord of all? At least other absentee landlords visited their estates two or three times a year, but the Secretary of State never visited his estates. Instead, he ran his property through factors — officials in the Department of Agriculture.

I had not found anyone with a good word for the clearances, not, that is, until Colonel Miller. The clearances had been a great thing, he said, obliging the Scots to emigrate and find abroad a prosperity they never would have achieved at home. People had been forced to leave for their own good. And it was not true that they were mistreated by landlords and agents of landlords. If people on the boats had tears in their eyes, was this not a natural reaction to leaving home — even if one was headed for a brighter future?

CHAPTER 20

To Ulva we came in the dark, and left it before noon the next day. A very exact description therefore will not be expected. We were told, that it is an island of no great extent, rough and barren, inhabited by the Macquarrys; a clan not powerful nor numerous, but of antiquity, which most other families are content to reverence . . . In the morning we went again into the boat, and were landed on Inch Kenneth, an island about a mile long, and perhaps half a mile broad, remarkable for pleasantness and fertility. It is verdant and grassy, and fit both for pasture and tillage; but it has no trees. Its only inhabitants were Sir Allan Maclean, and two young ladies, his daughters, with their servants.

— Samuel Johnson

THE RAIN poured down in torrents, and intermittently the storm swelled with the percussion of hail. From the road a turnoff led to the ferry pier. Cars were parked nearby and empty sheds stood open, but there was no sign of ferry or ferryman. It seemed for all the world that the problem of crossing had not diminished since 1773; Boswell wrote that "a servant was sent forward to the ferry to secure the boat for us; but the boat was gone to the Ulva side, and the wind was so high that the people could not hear him call, and the night so dark that they could not see a signal."

We drove back, and I went into the nearby primary

school. The teacher seemed startled by my intrusion into her one-room schoolhouse, but she recovered quickly and told me that there was a bell on the pier, and the way to summon Robert Cowe, the ferryman, was to ring that bell. She also said that I could use the school phone. Things *had* changed! Mr. Cowe answered almost immediately. Was that red car he had seen down by the pier mine? he asked. If I would just return to the pier, he would come right over.

Months before, I had written to Edith Lady Congleton, who owned the island, asking if we could visit, and she had invited us to come whenever we wished. But Lady Congleton had died just a few weeks before our arrival on Mull. I had then phoned Lieutenant Colonel F. Henry Howard, Lady Congleton's son-in-law, on the island of Gometra, immediately to the west of Ulva, asking *his* permission. He invited us without hesitation, and advised that if we met anyone on Ulva, just to say it was all right for us to be there.

Mr. Cowe brought us across in a rowboat with an outboard motor, explaining that the gearbox of the ferry launch was broken. Ulva House was only half a mile away, and we set out on foot. In any case, there was no sign of transportation; this island of about ten square miles hardly afforded employment for a taxi driver or car rental agency. Half a mile was no distance at all when road and path were dry, but the rain was still pelting and the path was an isthmus of mud and rocks in an ocean of mud without rocks. The rain soaked me, and mud oozed into my shoes. My wife had, foresightedly, worn boots.

Boswell described the house of Ulva's proprietor as "mean," and reported that the island was to be sold for payment of debts. But there was a new Ulva House, and it looked substantial and comfortable — two sizable stories and a third floor with dormer windows, a manor house of generous proportions and classic design. I rang the doorbell. A dog inside the house began barking, and finally a woman appeared and looked at us hesitantly, her face pale and drawn. I quickly explained what had brought us to Ulva. She came outside, stood with us in the rain, and began telling us about the terrible events. A few weeks earlier, her husband, the caretaker of Ulva House, had died suddenly, in the garden. Lady Congleton, who was eighty-four, had immediately taken charge. "She was a tower of strength to me," the caretaker's widow said. Then, eleven days later, Lady Congleton died. The caretaker's widow was left alone, in that large house, with no one but her dog, and she was still feeling the effects of shock.

I had hoped to see the inside of the house, but the caretaker's widow ignored every hint about how terrible it was to have so much rain and it was such a pity that she was getting wet. So we turned away — I full of petty sorrow for myself — and walked back through the mud to the ferryman's house. As the rain abated, Mr. Cowe scraped at the slime that had attached itself to the pier, and he seemed to have all the time in the world to tell us about life on the island.

Before taking the job of ferryman, he had been a full-time fisherman, and his boat was the family home. A house went with his new job, and his wife was delighted to be living on land. Daily he ferried two of their four children to and from the primary school; a daughter boarded at secondary school on the mainland, and a son of seventeen, who had been fishing since he was ten, spent his mornings fishing from the family boat. Mr. Cowe now did his own fishing at night. Lady Congleton had given him shooting rights on Ulva, and early mornings during the hunting season he had seen as many as six deer at a time swimming across Ulva Sound from Mull, and occasionally some of them were wounded.

Lady Congleton used to come down from Ulva House in a Land-Rover, leave the car at the pier, and return home on foot. When Mr. Cowe asked her why she walked, Lady

Congleton said that she was leaving the car for an employee: she herself was perfectly capable of getting home on foot. Once, in the last year of her life, he had offered his hand to help her off the ferry. "I'll ask for a hand when I feel I need one," she had said. "She was independent but straight," Mr. Cowe said, and told us that she had served as a magistrate and had also worked as a volunteer in workhouses for the poor. *Worked* in them; she had not played Lady Bountiful and made token visits.

When I asked how many people lived on Ulva, Mr. Cowe began counting aloud: "Two shepherds, a tractor man, a gardener, an estate manager, the caretaker's widow . . ." Finally he reached the total: twenty-two. "Before the clearances there were two thousand people on Ulva. Four or five hundred men went off to one of the wars." Lachlan Macquarie, who was to become a major general and governor of New South Wales, was born on Ulva in 1761. He was sometimes called the father of Australia, and his mausoleum on Mull was an attraction for Australian visitors.

By the time we were ready to return to Mull, the tide was so low that the rowboat was well below the lowest step cut into the pier on the Mull side. Mr. Cowe steered his boat along the shore nearby, and we clambered onto the rocks. They were slippery with seaweed, and we crawled along like crabs, gradually moving higher and finally climbing out onto the level ground beyond the seaweed.

Mr. Cowe had suggested that I might want to talk to Lachlan McNeill, who had worked on Ulva most of his life. "But whether he'll feel like talking to you I don't know," Mr. Cowe had said. Following directions, we started back along the road toward Salen and stopped near an isolated, decrepit trailer. When I knocked on the door, there was no reply. I knocked again, vigorously. Mr. McNeill opened the top half of the door and peered out, with a look that was not unfriendly, though it was not friendly, either. At last he let me come in.

His home was a mess. The bed resembled a heap of rags, and old books and magazines lay about in the débris of tins, paper, plastic, and rusty metal. He did not invite me to sit down, and I was just as happy to stand. We both stood there, wondering about each other. I asked him to tell me about Lady Congleton and about Ulva. "A very gracious lady, a good boss," he began. "She was very good to me."

Mr. McNeill said that he used to live in a house on the hill above the trailer. "The landlord at the time was putting us out, unless we'd pay a terrific rent, so she bought the cottage and gave it to me. The house burned down on me eight years ago. I had a log fire and went out for a minute, and some sparks started and the house went up quick. It went up in twenty minutes. Couldn't do anything. Couldn't even get to the phone. I retired at sixty-five — I'm seventy-five now. She kept me on working, mostly in the garden and fencing. I used to be a rabbit trapper and lobster fisherman. Before the war I got about four or five shillings for a box of forty-eight lobsters. There was no demand. After the war we were getting four pounds ten, three pounds ten a box. The boats began coming from Mallaig and wouldn't leave you the length of this caravan for your lobster pots. We used to take a thousand pairs of rabbits off some of the farms before that, and you were lucky if you'd get sixpence a couple. After the war, about five shillings a couple. That was very good — worthwhile turning out at that time. Then a plague of polecats cleared the rabbits, and in 'fifty-six the myxomatosis came.

"This is the worst summer I can remember — terrible. We used to have three bad days, three good days. Now we're lucky to have one good day a month. I'm at work all the time, and when I finish work I make my meal and I'm ready for a good day. I have two cats now to keep me company. And I have a good neighbor — comes in on my day off to see if I'm alive. I work pensioner's hours — nine o'clock till four — and I don't have to go on Saturday or when it rains. But of course everybody works pensioner's hours now."

Taking these words to heart, I waited till the next day for a visit to Inchkenneth. Coming from Salen, I had turned right along the seaside road to get to the Ulva ferry. This time I turned left, in the direction of the Iona ferry. Finally there was a side road marked "Inchkenneth." In the near distance the island lay low in the water, a great, dark, horizontal slab supporting gentle hills and modest plateaus; at the right rose a four-story building that looked like a hotel, and close to it stood a cottage, also of light beige stone.

The Macleans had long since forsaken Inchkenneth, but Andrew Barlow, who had bought the island, had written me that I would be welcome to visit. Following his instructions, I went to the old boatshed near the end of the side road, found the unlocked door at the back, and went inside. Burrowing into a pile of old bits of cloth in a wooden box, I extricated a field phone marked "Inchkenneth House," turned the crank, and waited. Soon Dr. Barlow came on the line, speaking from the island. It looked all right for a crossing, he said, though the wind was rising. He would come over to get me, and would I be good enough to go down to the water's edge and meet him.

That was not easy. The tide was out, and the rocks ahead were covered with slime and seaweed. I walked slowly, squooshing through the wet, just managing to keep my balance. It took so long to get to the edge of the shore that by the time I arrived, Dr. Barlow was waiting. He sat quietly, hunched in the stern of a small rowboat, the outboard motor still. I felt awkward, wondering how to start a conversation that extended further than "Good of you to come." The same awkwardness seemed to have overtaken him, and I attributed his silence to habits of solitude enforced by life on an island inhabited by only two people — his wife was the only other resident. Impatiently, I rejected any attempt to understand why *I* found nothing to say.

Clambering into the boat, I took the oars and unskillfully struggled to turn us around to get clear of land. Dr. Barlow started the motor, and against a choppy current we set off. As we approached the middle of the sound separating Inchkenneth from Mull, the sea grew rougher, and several times the boat seemed about to capsize. The McCraes had told me that Dr. Barlow was careful not to try crossing when the sea was dangerous, and I wondered if he had made an exception in my honor. But at last we reached quieter waters and slowly drifted in to tie up at a concrete landing. Mrs. Barlow was waiting, and we walked up to the large house. Dr. Barlow and I took off our outer clothing — he was thoroughly soaked — and we sat at the kitchen table while Mrs. Barlow made coffee. When I complimented her on the coffee, the most delicious I had tasted in months, she reached into a drawer and presented me with a catalogue of Thomson's coffees, noting that the variety she ordered from Glasgow was French Full Roast.

The second thing I wanted to know was what had led them — he was a retired pediatrician — to embrace the joys of separation from the rest of mankind. "Why does one do that sort of thing?" Dr. Barlow responded. "We were looking for somewhere fairly remote. We went to an estate agent and asked for details of remote cottages, and it was all a mistake, really. They took out the wrong drawer and sent us an illustrated brochure about Inchkenneth. It looked very attractive, and we thought it would be fun to see it. The first time we saw it, it was wet and bleak, and we thought very much against buying it. Then we met the people who were farming the island, and it was a lovely day and the sun was shining.

"The house was in a terrible state, and gloomy, and with a

leaking roof. It's still leaking, of course. We bought it from Jessica Mitford. Actually, it belonged to her parents, Lord and Lady Redesdale, who bought it in nineteen thirty-nine. Lady Redesdale spent a lot of time up here after the war — one of her daughters, Unity, was rather unpopular. Unity died about nineteen forty-nine, and Lady Redesdale died in 'sixty-three or 'sixty-four."

I remembered that Unity was an admirer of Hitler. Diana, one of her sisters, married Sir Oswald Mosley, leader of the British Union of Fascists. Deborah married the eleventh Duke of Devonshire. Jessica became an American and won fame as a journalist and author (*The American Way of Death*). Nancy, who went to France to live, was celebrated for witty novels (*Pursuit of Love, Love in a Cold Climate*) and for *Noblesse Oblige*, an extended appreciation of differences between U (upper-class) and non-U (other-class) speech.

"I think Jessica bought out her sisters' share in it," Dr. Barlow said. "It was on the market for several years without any takers. Before the Redesdales, it belonged to Sir Harold Boulton, an industrialist." In 1967 the Barlows bought the island, and everything on it, including boats, houses, and furniture, for £25,000. Since then, they had had an inquiry about their willingness to sell, and they had reason to believe it was from one of the Beatles. For the moment, the Barlows were not interested in selling.

Not long after they came to the island, the tenant farmer left, and then a couple of other farmers tried their hand. "It's too small to be a successful farm," Dr. Barlow noted. "Any farmer who isn't good wouldn't be able to make a go of it, and if he is good he would do better elsewhere." So the Barlows trimmed their ambitions. Where earlier they had sheep, cattle, ponies, and chickens, gradually they reduced the stock until now the only creatures left were the sheep grazed by a farmer who lived on Mull. He ferried the sheep across; the cattle used to swim across, prodded by the farmer in a boat alongside.

The Barlows had a vegetable garden and kept a stock of emergency supplies — spaghetti, rice, flour, butter, sugar, long-life milk, and canned goods. Both of them baked bread, and they brewed their own beer. There were tractors, water pumps, a gas refrigerator, a large electric freezer, and an electric generator. The generator ran on diesel oil, and one of the most difficult trials was getting fuel to the island. On Mull, opposite Inchkenneth, was a five-hundred-gallon tank, and a pipeline extended from tank to shore. Once the tank was supplied with oil, Dr. Barlow filled forty-five-gallon drums, which he then manhandled into a sea truck, a small landing craft that was larger than the rowboat and could cross in heavier seas. Dr. Barlow ferried the drums back to the island and stored them in the small house where Johnson and Boswell stayed. When we went on a tour of Inchkenneth, I counted thirteen forty-five-gallon drums there, and I wondered how Johnson would have reacted to the sight of the Macleans' home elevated to the splendor of an oil depot.

Dr. Barlow had turned himself into an expert mechanic who could fix all the machinery, and he also did rewiring, plumbing, and carpentry. Much of his labor went to maintenance and repair, but he and his wife spent a good deal of their time reading. Mrs. Barlow also drew, and back in London she painted landscapes based on her Inchkenneth sketches. There was no television set. The Barlows' son and daughter, graduate students at Cambridge, liked coming for holidays, but they were less keen on island life than their parents and never stayed long.

There was a rough-and-ready air about the big house. The large kitchen was strewn with crockery, pots and pans, and odd bits and pieces. None of the rooms seemed to have been disturbed by obsessive tidying, and it would have required a gargantuan effort to make headway at such a task. When

I asked how many rooms there were, Dr. Barlow replied: "Too many. We would have wished that there was just a cottage on the island." To satisfy my curiosity, they counted the rooms: ten bedrooms, four bathrooms, four reception rooms, kitchen. "The Boultons used to have a large staff," Mrs. Barlow suggested.

Built about 1850, the large house was made larger still about 1935. Sir Harold added the cottage so that his family would have somewhere to stay while workmen enlarged the principal dwelling. Now, when there were overnight visitors, they slept in the cottage. The Barlows had once spent a winter on the island instead of returning to London. "One knows what it's like," Mrs. Barlow said, "and one doesn't really want to experience it again."

During the summer, when tourists came to Mull, the Barlows occasionally saw people hanging around on the shore there, making clear that they wanted to find some way to get across to Inchkenneth. In summer the Barlows made about one foray a week to Salen to pick up fresh food, but in autumn, when the weather made travel more difficult, they went less often. "The tide goes up and down very quickly," Dr. Barlow said. "Unless one calculates very well, the boat is aground or miles out. Once we went across and couldn't get back."

I asked them if they could swim, and they said they could just manage. "The water's so cold, one wouldn't last very long," Dr. Barlow said.

The postman left their mail at the boatshed, and postal authorities paid Dr. Barlow about three pounds a month to deliver his own mail the rest of the way. For many years the Barlows had no phone, but then an underwater cable ended their isolation, though the phone was often out of order. Exposed wires had a distressing propensity to blow down, and the underwater cable was not immune to misfortune.

"Last year the cable was cut," Dr. Barlow said. "They were quite good about repairs; did it in two or three months."

As we walked about the island, Mrs. Barlow took to picking up débris that had been washed ashore. One of the first items she found was a large plastic bag, and in it she stowed the trash, almost all of it plastic, mainly containers that had held oil or detergent. It would have taken many more tours of the island to gather all the litter, but at least this was a beginning.

By tradition, Irish chieftains were transported after death to the small cemetery here and interred if it was too stormy to get to the more celebrated burial ground on Iona. I found no clear evidence of this tradition, so I made do with copying one of the inscriptions that was still legible: "Here lieth the corps of Donald MacLean of Broles who dyed the 25th of April 1725 aged 54 years deservedly lamented by all who knew and understood his virtuous and heroick mind." In the ruined chapel, several slabs had been propped upright. A Celtic cross stood above a stone incised: "In Memory of Margaret Lady Boulton widow of Sir Harold Boulton, Bart; died 18th Oct. 1938. Also her sister Helen Brown Lyonsor Merriani died 6th Oct. 1939." Near the large house was a small stone with a plaque on it, put there by Lady Redesdale in memory of her pet "Jose a faithful friend 1948–1959."

Because of tide and rising wind, Dr. Barlow was becoming increasingly nervous about getting me back to Mull without delay, and since the sea was now even choppier than earlier, we crossed in the landing craft instead of the rowboat. Before saying goodbye, I asked the Barlows if they were happy with their lonely lot. "One likes to get away from people sometimes," Mrs. Barlow replied. "If it's been a nice summer, one begins to regret that it doesn't go on longer. It think it must be about the most beautiful place in the world."

Her husband said: "There have been moments when we wished very much it had been something else — the sort of occasions when ceilings fell in. Everything seems to go wrong at times."

Would you recommend the life to others? I persisted.

"I'd recommend anybody who thought it was a good idea to try it out and see," he answered. "It isn't until you're really doing it that you know whether you'd like to live on an island."

Not long after my visit the Barlows decided that they finally had enough of living on an island. Their children lived in the south of England, the weather there was more clement, and — most persuasive of all — the job of maintaining the large house on Inchkenneth was overwhelming. So they put the island on the market, asking price £200,000.

CHAPTER 21

We were now treading that illustrious island, which was once the luminary of the Caledonian regions, whence savage clans and roving barbarians derived the benefits of knowledge, and the blessings of religion. To abstract the mind from all local emotion would be impossible, if it were endeavored, and would be foolish, if it were possible.

— Samuel Johnson

SINCE MY WIFE had to drive to Glasgow, I called Duncan McGilp at the Tobermory Garage to see about renting a car for myself. He said that at the end of each summer he sold all his rental cars, but he happened to have one car left, not in pristine condition; in fact, he said, it was in terrible shape. I found that he had spoken sober truth: the car was grimy, bits of machinery were strewn inside, a windshield wiper was missing, the fuel gauge refused to work, and the driver's window could not be cranked up or down. I had no choice, so I took the car and drove it back to Salen. In the dark it took me a long time to find my way out of the seat belt, and I wondered if this splendid vehicle would ever get me to Iona.

After trips to Ulva and Inchkenneth, I knew the road to Fionnphort, the hamlet on the Mull side, less than a mile across the water from Iona, and it was hard to miss the ferry: the road ended, and a boat lay alongside the jetty. After parking the car and wishing it well during my absence, I took my overnight case and walked across the boat ramp onto the ferry. In time, two other passengers came aboard — one an Iona woman, the other an American woman recently arrived to act as secretary to the Iona Community. She told me later that the Clydesdale Bank, the only bank with a branch on Mull, sent a mobile office to Fionnphort every Tuesday, so once a week she crossed and did the community's banking business.

Earlier, when I phoned, she had said that the abbey, which normally offered lodging, was closed to visitors for a few weeks. But on Iona I could stay at Finlay, Ross, the local supermarket. It stood just beyond the jetty, offering for sale clothes, food, stationery, and souvenirs, but no bread or vegetables or fruit. These could be purchased at the island's other shop, across the street. Most people on Iona appeared to divide their custom, as indeed they had to, between the two shops. There was one employee visible in the Finlay, Ross supermarket. She handed me two keys — one to the side door, to enable me to get in after shopping hours, and the other to a back room. Following me there, she deposited portions of Nescafé and Coffeemate, as well as cookies, tea bags, sugar, cup, saucer, plate, knife, spoon, and electric kettle. There was an electric heater in the room, and in the cupboard were two hot-water bottles. While I was out, that afternoon, someone added a tray with continental breakfast ready for the next day: portions of butter, jam, and marmalade, two rolls, and a napkin.

It was easy enough to get about on Iona, a mere three miles long and one and a half broad, with a main street, and a less-than-main street along the white shell-sand seafront. There were no sidewalks. The buildings were of stone, and a line of small houses stood along the seaside, with front gardens down to the water. Boats were drawn up on the shore, with others mounted on trailers. On the main street were the ruins of the thirteenth-century nunnery of St. Mary, the St. Columba Hotel (not ruined, but closed in this off-season), farmhouses, and a school. There was more than enough to fortify an initial impression of a gray island, bleak and uninviting, and to support Sir Walter Scott's description of Iona as "desolate and miserable." But there was also, on a low stone wall, a bronze plaque with Johnson's nobler tribute: "That man is little to be envied, whose patriotism would not gain force upon the plain of Marathon, or whose piety would not grow warmer among the ruins of Iona."

In 563, Iona was starting point for St. Columba's mission to the Highland Picts, and for more than a century following the saint's death the island was the center of the Celtic Church. Vikings repeatedly raided and devastated Iona. In 806, they murdered sixty-eight monks; and in 986, another sixteen. Toward the end of the Middle Ages a community of Benedictines lived there, but after the Reformation the abbey church and nunnery of St. Mary fell into ruin. In 1899 the eighth Duke of Argyll, proprietor of the island, gave the ruins to a group of trustees, principally of the Church of Scotland. Eighty years later the twelfth Duke of Argyll announced that in order to pay death duties he would be forced to sell Iona. At once there was apprehension that the island might be alienated in favor of some person or institution inimical to its traditions and to the wishes of its inhabitants. The National Trust for Scotland launched an international appeal for a million pounds, and finally a foundation purchased the island for £1,500,000. The National Trust for Scotland assumed the burden of running Iona, since no other agency had been found that was capable of safeguarding the island's interests, and the trust announced that Iona never would be offered for sale without the agreement of Parliament.

Triumphantly restored, the gray stone masses of the abbey

seemed ready for another millennium of prayerful service. Closely grouped, earthbound and squat, all but bereft of the lofty and graceful, the buildings appeared to huddle for protection against marauding infidels or simply against the indifference of a world without faith. Almost indistinguishable from its neighbors, and dating back to the sixteenth century, was a cruciform church surmounted by a low tower. Inside the church were the effigies of former abbots, the mortuary slab of a MacLeod chief, and a monument to the eighth Duke of Argyll, who died in 1900. Alongside the abbey stood St. Oran's Cemetery, by tradition the burial ground of more than sixty kings of Scottish, Norwegian, French, and Irish origin, the last being Duncan, victim of Macbeth. Nearby stood the buildings containing a museum and a library, a shop, and lodgings for staff and visitors. In the cloister was a modern statue — *The Descent of the Spirit* — of Madonna and child; on the back, in French, were inscribed the words "Jacob Lipchitz, Jew loyal to the faith of his ancestors, made this Virgin for harmony of men on earth so that the spirit may reign."

The great task of restoration was the work of the Iona Community, a singular religious fellowship founded in 1938 by George MacLeod, socialist pacifist and Church of Scotland minister in Glasgow. A religious order set up by a Presbyterian was an institution unusual enough to excite suspicion that this was a first step on the journey to Rome, and the community roused further hostility through its enthusiasm for political controversy. "It is not a return to Rome," the founder had insisted. "It is not a pacifist community . . . It is not a visionary movement . . . seeking helplessly to play at being Franciscans . . . It is on the contrary an exceedingly calculated movement within the normal purpose of the Church."

To judge by notices on the bulletin board just inside the entrance to the abbey, the purposes of the community were both distinctive and diffuse. Under the heading "Some Useful Addresses" there were plain signs of the times, including: Anti-Apartheid Movement, Amnesty International, Campaign for Nuclear Disarmament, Campaign Against the Arms Trade, Mobilisation for Survival (the address was The Abbey, Iona), Peace Tax Campaign, Third World First (in Oxford), and Scottish War on Want (Glasgow). Also posted was "The Peace Commitment of the Iona Community." It began: "1) We believe that peacemaking is integral to the Gospel." In the chapel was a printed list of those "for whom we should pray," with details of symptoms and problems, indications of action taken or advised, and summary of current status. "Dorothy — depression and post shingles —*Replaced*: Shingle pain recurs and is very troublesome. Barbara — drink problem — Letter of enquiry sent. Charles — in prison — No further word. Please pray. Betty, Hugh and Family — familial heart disease. Reasonably good. Betty very tired. Lorraine had flu. Aggressive neighbour has been a great strain on them all." The "Healing List" for one day included: "Sylvia — marriage breakdown, insomnia and depression," and "Nigel — severe back pain."

Brian Crosby, warden, or head, of the abbey, was in the ground-floor office, and we went upstairs to his small private office. He told me that he was a Canadian, that his maternal forebears were Highlanders, and that he had joined the community after studying theology at St. Andrews. There were now about a hundred and fifty members, including about twenty women and six Roman Catholic laymen. About ninety-five of the members, scattered about several continents, were ordained clergy, most of them involved in ecclesiastical activities. Among the others, there were a clerk, postman, teacher, social worker, librarian. One member worked in Glasgow as groundskeeper for the Rangers soccer team.

Members committed themselves to half an hour daily of

prayer, meditation, or study, in private or with their family. Ten percent of a member's disposable income went into a common fund expended mainly on Third World projects but also on help for widows of former members. Another mandatory discipline governed the use of members' time, "probably the worst observed and the least tangible," Mr. Crosby said. Members were expected to work for peace and to oppose weaponry. Mr. Crosby also spoke of "an extensive commitment to healing — prayer and laying on of hands."

The community ran two youth centers, and each year about fifteen hundred young people stayed there. "And you have about fifteen hundred different results," Mr. Crosby told me. "For many it's the first time they've experienced the faith being expressed in a way that seemed relevant to them — not only the worship in the abbey, but the whole relationship of daily living: eating together, working together, discussing." The community's guests were expected to work an hour and a half a day, washing, cleaning, making beds. Those in youth camps worked on projects such as caring for vegetable gardens, creosoting buildings, picking up litter along the road, cutting the lawn for the local schoolteacher.

"Politically, the community has been of the left, or at least left of center," Mr. Crosby said. "Giving a liberal interpretation to Scripture and ethics and doctrine. There's a very strong evangelical element, about the authority and necessity of the word of Christ, but there's no attempt to manipulate people or brainwash them. I've often said to a youngster bubbling over with spiritual fervor, 'Don't think it will always be like this, that life will be a bed of roses. Don't think you'll never be overcome by doubt.'"

With a skepticism I found difficult to conceal, I asked about the healing ministry, and Mr. Crosby said that on Iona it had a history of fourteen centuries, going back to St. Columba's renown as a healer. "It has an atmosphere of spirituality," he suggested, and said that he was aware of the danger of Iona becoming a Scottish Lourdes. "We've always refused to document cases of healing after prayer. We don't feel it a helpful attitude — talking up the results of prayer. But there's been a quite remarkable record.

"If you read and believe the Gospel, you have to do this," he insisted. "If one accepts the life of Jesus, then it's difficult to avoid the ministry of healing. After the third century it faded into an almost forgotten aspect of church expression. It was institutionalization that tended to reduce the spontaneous and the flow of the spirit. But nowadays, in recent times, in the past two decades, people have realized that they can't heed the Gospel and ignore the meaning of the ministry of healing.

"Prayer is not soliciting God's help," Mr. Crosby said. "Prayer is an offering of oneself to God. Any worship is an offering of ourselves to be the channel for God's love. It's not a question of poking God and telling him what to do. God has offered us the power to become his disciples, his instruments in the world."

We then had a spirited discussion — at times it seemed an argument rather than a discussion — about reconciling evil with a loving and omnipotent God. In the end we still disagreed. Mr. Crosby's argument, as he summarized it at one point: "Because the world is a free place, it seems to me the possibilities must be good and evil. It seems to me that with any other system you immediately begin to restrict and limit and predetermine what is going to happen. It seems to me you have to have the whole range of good and evil, from the death of infants to the most evident divine expression of good."

Apparently prepared to forgive my stubbornness, Mr. Crosby took me along for morning coffee with his wife and son and with members of the community staff. He and his family, he told me, were planning to leave Iona, and they were not sure where they would be going. What he wanted

to do was to be caretaker of an estate, a handyman responsible for repair and upkeep. The problem was that he seemed
overqualified, or perhaps not qualified enough. People would
feel that if someone with his background sought that kind of
work, it meant that he had gotten into trouble. But no, Mr.
Crosby said, he simply preferred manual labor to administration.

From the warden I went to the founder, and here I dis-
cerned no hint of second thoughts or regrets or ambitions
unfulfilled. White-haired at age eighty-five, tall and stately,
stiffly erect as though hewn from granite, George — now
Lord — MacLeod beamed down with what was easy to recognize as presence, and launched into an account orna-
mented with the studied emphases of someone who has re-
hearsed his lines and perfected his delivery. Pouring tea and
cutting portions of cake with pink icing, then sitting bolt
upright as he sipped and ate, he kept switching from the
particular — the making of Lord MacLeod — to the universal — the state of families, of society, of nations, of the
world.

His grandfather had been a popular preacher who worked
to improve the lot of Glasgow's slum-dwellers, but whose
most signal achievement may have come during his time as
an editor, when he rejected as improper a novel by Anthony
Trollope: Trollope had written about young people dancing.
George MacLeod's father had been a Presbyterian elder and
his mother a Quaker; their son had been confirmed in the
Church of England, had become a minister in the Church of
Scotland, and had received an honorary degree from a Roman Catholic college. Lord MacLeod therefore felt justified
in calling himself "an ecumenical disaster."

How things have changed! he went on. "Do you know that
there are now one million single-parent families in the
country?" What warped and difficult childhoods that caused!

"Five of my direct forebears were moderators of the

church," he said, resuming the personal account, then reverting once more to the broader view by noting that Bibles were selling better than ever at the Church of Scotland bookshop in Edinburgh. You had to give the charismatics credit for that, he said, adding, "Somebody said they're more airborne than reborn, but at least they're getting people interested in the Bible."

He — it was back to the personal again — had been brought up in the faith and had always attended church regularly. "Then I had an experience of a simple kind, of the reality of the Holy Spirit. I found that God was living, for me."

At Oxford, he studied law, then served during World War I in the Argyll and Sutherland Highlanders, which he called by their popular name, the Agile and Suffering Highlanders. After the war came theology studies at the University of Edinburgh. When asked to take over Glasgow's industrial Govan parish, he refused. In his place went his best friend, only to die of disease spawned in the Govan slums. So when he was asked a second time to take over Govan, George MacLeod felt he had to agree. "It was there, amidst all the terrifying unemployment, that I became very impressed with the courage of the unemployed, the way they looked after each other," he said. "If anybody was starving, they all brought food, quite regardless of whether they were Roman Catholics or Protestants. If anybody got in debt with their rent, up came somebody — all poor people — and paid the rent. If any boy got into trouble with the police, everybody rallied round the family and got the boy back onto his feet. Who was it who said that the great contribution of Jesus to religion was that he did away with it, in that he would have nothing more to do with the spiritual as such, but with the spiritual and the material the whole time? 'Feed the hungry, clothe the naked' is politics, politics, isn't it?"

The parish acquired an abandoned mill, and boys from the

parish used to go there on holiday. George MacLeod and members of the staff went to Iona for their holidays. "We got together one day and *we found ourselves saying,* 'Why not rebuild Iona Abbey?' Loud laughter, 'Ha, ha.' Then we went to the trustees of the abbey and said, 'Can we have the thing to rebuild?' And to my horror, they said yes. I thought they would say no. I wrote to the richest man I knew and asked him for five thousand pounds, which he could afford, to start rebuilding the abbey. He wrote back and suggested I go to a psychiatrist whom I would find on Bath Street, and for the sake of my soul I should go and see him quickly."

Who was this richest man? I asked, and Lord MacLeod replied, "I've forgotten his name." He gave me a knowing look, to indicate that he remembered the name but preferred discretion.

"So I wrote to the second-richest man I knew, and he hasn't replied yet. I don't think he'll reply now — that was forty-two years ago. Then I wrote to Sir James Lithgow, who was the man who owned the shipyard in my parish, and by this time I'd become a pacifist, through my mother's blood, I take it, and he was building battleships, so we didn't see much of each other. I wrote to him, and he said, 'Come on down and spend a night at our place.' After dinner he said, 'I've got one question to ask you. If I give you five thousand pounds, will you give up your pacifism?' And I said, 'Not on your life.' He said, 'Well, you've got five thousand pounds.' If I'd hesitated for one moment — gone!"

In 1938 George MacLeod and volunteer helpers went off to Iona, set up tents near the abbey, and got to work. "The Duke of Argyll wasn't keen on this business," he recalled. "So he said, 'You can't have any water; there's no water inside the holy acre.' So we sent some ... not water-diviners, but water-finders. They rang up every night to say they couldn't find water anywhere. Then they sent a telegram: 'Water found in the well.' Which was an extraordinary telegram to receive. It was the well right inside the holy ground. They just dug down and up it came — whoosh!"

The next summer another group of young ministers, plus masons and carpenters, came to rebuild the abbey library. "I picked up my newspaper the morning after we'd arrived and the heading was 'All Wood Requisitioned by the Government.' But a ship coming from Canada, in a storm, jettisoned its deck cargo, which was timber and which floated a hundred miles and landed on the coast of Mull opposite to Iona. All the right length. And we got a boat and went across and picked it up. One of the good things was we got the people of the island to come across with us and pick up all this timber."

Lord MacLeod said that it was a sign from heaven, and when I churlishly asked if his faith would have been even stronger if the lumber had landed directly on Iona, he shrugged off my suggestion and pursued his account. "My first year on Iona, I visited every household on the island, one by one by one by one, every house, and at the end of the summer was told that I was doing this in order to get people to cease going to the parish church, and to come to our community service. So the next year I didn't visit a single house, not a single house, intentionally I didn't enter a door, and at the end of the summer they said, 'MacLeod's getting all high and mighty — he used to come and visit us.' You can't win, you know."

A man wrote a letter to *The Scotsman*, an Edinburgh newspaper, to complain that Iona was being defiled by washing hung out on Sundays. "And I thought, where are we going to get from that sort of drivel?" Lord MacLeod recalled. The answer came in a letter reassuring him that cleanliness was next to godliness, and inviting him and the community treasurer to meet the writer for tea. She turned up saying that she had forgotten her checkbook, but then she tore off a corner of the paper lining a drawer and wrote a check — honored by her bank — for ten thousand pounds. "Since when I put out my washing every Sunday," Lord MacLeod said.

When I asked what he had wanted from the community, he replied: "What I wanted from the community we have got, which is a community that were interested in industrial areas. People came up to places like Govan and got in touch with the poor by living their lives and talking their talk." This reply, with its confusion of tenses present and past, seemed to indicate that he was torn between a view of what had been and what was now, and he agreed that he had described the community past, not present.

On my suggesting that he had a reputation as a radical, he said, "Well, I hope so, I hope so," and explained that he was a socialist because of "common sense." Part of this common sense was opposition to capitalists and munitions-makers; indeed, all those he lumped together as "moneybags." It was not the politicians who exercised real power, he said, but the moneybags.

About twice a month he traveled down from his home in Edinburgh to attend the House of Lords and register his independent views. There were about a thousand peers, he said, and though all were entitled to sit in the Lords, the majority never bothered. "The biggest vote ever was four hundred to forty, about entering the Common Market. And four hundred of them voted to enter the Common Market, and forty of *us* voted against the Common Market. And how right we were!

"Everybody's very friendly at the House of Lords. You can get the most extreme [opponents] sitting down and drinking a cup of tea together and screaming at each other."

I assumed that it was for his leadership of the Iona Community, and not for his perspective on power, that he was made a life peer in 1967, but when I asked him directly why he had been elevated to the peerage, he replied that he did

not have the faintest notion. He had chosen to be called
MacLeod of Fuinary, after a village that was the setting of
Norman MacLeod's *Reminiscences of a Highland Parish*
(1867). Lord MacLeod said that his great-uncle was minister
there in 1843, when the Free Church split off from the established church. To show that established ministers were,
despite evidence to the contrary, interested in the welfare
of their flock, his great-uncle had built a chapel to spare the
local people a six-mile walk on Sunday each way to and from
church. With the moderator of the church coming to inau-
gurate the chapel, the minister engaged two day-laborers to
build a track from the road to the door of the church. "They
were very pleased to get the job," Lord MacLeod said. "One
of them took his coat off and said, 'Excuse me, minister, but
are you the established church minister or the Free Church
minister?' 'Oh, I'm the established church minister.' 'Well,'
he said, 'I may be a poor man, but I'll never build a road to
help anyone get into the Church of Scotland.' And so my
forebear said, 'Before you put your jacket back on, come with
me.' And so he went this way and that way, up to the door
of the church, and said, 'Now, you build the road down and
help them to get out.'"

Mr. Crosby had suggested that I might like to talk to Iona's
Church of Scotland parish minister, and, without phoning
for an appointment, I went down the road to the manse and
knocked on the door. Harry Galbraith Miller welcomed me so
effusively that I knew there was some error. He urged me to
come inside, then suddenly turned and said that he had confused me with someone else. But he was no less hearty after
that; he pressed me to come into his study, invited me to sit
down, and began talking to me without asking who I was or
what I wanted, as though we were old friends resuming a
conversation. He sat in an easy chair, and he seemed bowed
under the weight of books. On all sides were shelves, floor
to ceiling, covered with books, and on the floor beside Mr.

Miller's chair were piles of additional books. As we talked, the day grew darker. Slowly his face disappeared and his considerable, blondish beard seemed to glow in the darkness, with nothing above it. Finally, when there seemed no wisp of the man left, and only a voice testifying to his presence, he got up and put on a light. I managed, eventually, to explain what I was doing on Iona, and he reciprocated by telling me about himself. He had been on Iona for ten years, and now that he was sixty-five years old he was ready for many more years of service. "I'm the permanent thing," he said, "because at the community they shift around every few years."

When I asked what the problems of his parish were, he replied: "Human beings are human beings all the world over, really. There are problems in a place like this, of course. You're at the very end of the line as far as communications are concerned. I write, I study, I have the parish to look after, and of course part of my parish is in Mull and there are no ferries in winter on Sunday, so you have to spend every second weekend away from home. I'm a pure philosopher and theologian. Mainly I write articles. Mainly I amuse myself. Mind you, when you have, as I have, to preach three times every Sunday, three sermons every Sunday, to congregations that include anything from archbishops to dimwits, you don't have a free mind you can devote to study. I'm constantly beset by the question 'What am I going to say?' I write out my sermons, partly because I find that if you want to speak with reasonable terseness and condensation it's almost essential. If you just trust to a genuine extempore speaking, you splurge round your subject. I tend to take four times as many words and six times as many sentences as you need to say it. There's no difficulty starting, but it's very difficult to stop with anything like a reasonable climax unless you plan beforehand. It also helps prevent you saying stupid things. You can write them down and strike them out. I don't

have ease of expression. It may take me an hour to produce
a paragraph. My ideas tend to clarify themselves as I write.
Sometimes I speak from notes and suggestions, and sentences that begin and never finish. You don't really get away
here with repeating sermons at all. I did it the other Sunday,
in the evening. One lady said, 'I heard this sermon before.'
I didn't say, 'So did I.'"

What do you preach about sin? I asked.

"President Hoover was against sin, or rather his preacher
was," he replied. "I'm tempted to wonder if I ever preach
about anything else. It's part of the presuppositions. Like
everything else, it has to be put in modern language, or
people haven't a clue what you're talking about. I prefer to
stress the virtues, on the principle of the small boy who objected to the Ten Commandments on grounds that it doesn't
tell you what to do but puts bad ideas in your head. The
average churchgoing person loves to hear sins denounced,
but they never take it to themselves. These things are best
done by a sideways kick when it's not expected.

"One of the most deadly sins today is the flight from responsibility. There seem to me a great many more young
people just drifting about the world without recognizing any
great need to take their share of pushing it along. Of course
they're aided in this, or rather driven to it, by the appalling
unemployment.

"Among the young, the most prevalent sin is hypocrisy.
They think they're very sincerely seeking for faith, for a true
religion, and they're not really doing anything of the sort.
They're just running away from anything that would be dangerous — they might be converted. It's much more comfortable to seek God than to find him. If you accept him, you
get a great feeling of comfort — you've discovered your identity again, you've got some meaning and purpose, and a great
sense of no longer fighting against something you know sub-
consciously to be stronger than yourself, something you know

you can't defeat in the long run. But it's also to put yourself under an authority that demands literally everything. And I think it's this that people run away from. There is in every heart a great fear of God until you've actually experienced his goodness and his grace. As long as you talk about God, you don't need to come to a decision."

He said that he was disturbed by people discussing religion at the drop of a hat, on and on. "We've talked about it long enough," he would say. "Will you make up your mind?" In his sermons he often told the story — "and it's probably true, even if it was meant as a joke; there are lots of rags in my mind" — of the graduate student who was asked how his thesis was getting on. "The preliminary procrastination is almost finished," the student replied.

Don't you have doubts? I asked.

"Oh, we all have doubts, often," he replied. "But this is an interesting thing, as far as I can make out, and I'm preparing to write an article on this whole thing called doubt. I'm just about reaching the point where there's room on the plate to put something on it."

I could not resist interjecting, "You mean you've almost reached the end of your preliminary procrastination?"

He nodded, smiling, and continued: "I have very little patience with people who boast about their religious doubts — they're a sign of weakness and deafness. 'There are none as deaf as those who won't listen.' We all have doubts, and some ones due to nothing deeper than that our liver is out of order. When doubts come, they mustn't be crushed down or we mustn't pretend they're not there. They must be fought through, or they'll fester. I don't know if I've had any doubts about God himself. There were times when I wished I had. There were times when it would have been more comfortable if there weren't a God — when your conscience is bothering you and it would have been very nice to know there wasn't a God."

When I asked how he reconciled evil with the notion of God, he said, "I know all the theoretical answers in the books, that evil serves a purpose. And it remains a mystery. To me the real problem is the suffering that human beings inflict on others. To take the classical example these days, the great concentration camps of Germany in the thirties and forties. I cannot even begin to put myself inside the skin of the people responsible for creating and working under this system. That men can bring themselves so to act. And for this I have no answer."

I asked Mr. Miller what his attitude was toward the young who came to the Iona Community. "A mixture of many things," he replied. "Part of it is a sort of sadness and a kind of pity. When people come to me and start criticizing the community, I refuse to enter into the criticism, because I say that theologically I differ quite widely from the theology of the community. I find their theology shallow, and they think of me as ethereal and unworldly. I suppose they'd even tolerate fundamentalists, and it can range to the most liberal churchman type of theology. Anything really goes there. They're just there. I know it's confusing to a lot of these young people who come. They don't get any picture of a community with definite purpose or place where they're going. Brian [Crosby] would be very similar in his theological outlook to myself. George More, the subwarden, is a man whom I have a great respect for, but his battle cry is 'Down with religion!'"

Mr. Miller found that the older people who came to Iona were pretty well fixed in their views, and not half as stimulating intellectually as the young, who were interested, excited, ready to commit themselves. "The older ones are more inclined to have crankish theories to cram down your throat," he said, "and I cram my theories down theirs. This island draws the religious crank — all kinds of people, the ones that have the second sight, the spiritualists, the people who believe in fairies; they all come here because Iona is a special place."

When I asked about the start of the Iona Community, Mr. Miller suggested that Lord MacLeod was "a bit of an actor, and determined to be the center of any group in which he found himself." He told of the time that Lord MacLeod was standing on the jetty on the Mull side of the ferry crossing and saying that he could sense the change that came over people who visited Iona. At that moment, a group of rough-and-ready girls from Glasgow passed by, girls who had just visited Iona. One girl was saying to another, "You can carry your own bloody case." When Mr. Miller, who was standing nearby, suggested that this did not seem to suggest that everyone was changed by a visit to Iona, Lord MacLeod responded, "Oh, I can assure you that when she came here last Saturday she would have used stronger language than that."

Mr. Miller told also of being at a gathering that Lord MacLeod attended. "Everybody was standing around with a glass of sherry. George was standing in the middle of the floor, holding the center as only George can do it. He said, 'You know, we had a group of American ladies just after the rebuilding. I got them to the west door and I thought I'd impressed on them the magnificent achievement of rebuilding. "Dr. MacLeod," one of them said, "if there's one thing I like, it's looking at old ruins." ' So I said, 'Maybe it wasn't the old stones she was talking about. Maybe it was you.' That was the only time I flattened George completely. But he got his own back. I was returning from Mull as he was landing in Mull. He saw me, and I heard him say to some people who were going to Iona, 'You should take a look at the parish church. Quite distinguished architecture. Medieval.' I said, 'It should suit the minister. They tell me he's quite medieval.' He went on another twenty paces, turned back, and said, 'I would leave out the "medi-." ' "

"On another occasion, I knew he was on the island, but he

wasn't in church on Sunday morning. In the afternoon, when I got to Mull, he'd beaten me to it. I said, 'Oh, I heard you were on Iona.'

"'I wasn't in church this morning,' he said. 'I disagreed with what you were going to say.'

"He maintains that Christianity is meaningless unless it is involved in the political situation. I maintain that religion ceases to be a touchstone of any political situation unless it is above all political situations. But I don't think either side maintains its position completely. I've heard George criticize his own left-wing beliefs very pungently, and I wasn't above getting involved in some political situations."

By the end of my visit it was dark outside, with not a glimmer of moonlight. Mr. Miller suggested that the county council should pay residents for leaving curtains open in order to illuminate the streets. As I returned to my room, I realized that Iona's public lighting consisted of two lamps at the jetty. The rest was darkness.

On the ferry returning to Mull, there was only one other passenger. Driving back toward Salen, I felt that I was moving from the world of commitment to that of skepticism, and I was comforted by the thought. As I traveled along the coast road, a flock of sheep came rapidly down the hill at right and crowded onto the single-track road, heading for my car. With the precision of a ballet company, the flock divided into two groups and pranced past me, right and left. Then came two dogs and a young man. I hailed him, and guessed correctly that this was one of Lachlan Maclean's sons. With an embarrassed smile, he confirmed his father's account that he and his brother planned to go on being shepherds because they liked working with animals. Then he strode on, a stylish cap perched jauntily on his head, a shepherd's crook in his hand, self-assured and in control of his flock.

I found myself wondering about George More and his

battle cry of "Down with religion!" Eventually I did the honorable thing and phoned him — by this time he had retired and was living in Glasgow — to ask what he meant. "It's a complaint against the tribalism that is satisfied with mutually exclusive religious systems," he said. "The great game is to make your religious group succeed against another's. But the great Biblical insight is that God wants certain things done. He wants certain things — called the Kingdom of Heaven — done."

CHAPTER 22

Here, as in Skye and other islands, are the laird, the tacks-
men, and the under tenants.

— Samuel Johnson

WHEN I BROUGHT the car back to Mr. McGilp and asked
how much I owed, he said he would not dream of taking
money for an old wreck and thought he had made it clear
that the car was not one he would normally rent. We had a
pleasant to-and-fro, and finally, under duress, he agreed to
accept five pounds for two days' rental.

Since I was planning to take the ferry to Coll the next
morning at eight-forty-five, I stayed at a hotel in Tobermory,
down the main street from the pier. Breakfast would not be
served until eight-thirty, so the waitress the night before left
water in a thermos — by morning it was barely lukewarm —
with tea bags, cold cereal, milk, and sugar. It was not a good
start to the day. I got to the pier early and went aboard the
sixty-eight-foot launch that took passengers out to the larger
boat that stopped at Tobermory en route to the islands of
Coll and Tiree. The larger boat, the *Claymore*, was too big
to tie up at the Tobermory dock.

When the captain of the launch came aboard, I was astonished to see that it was John Warnock, who ran a service

station and oil agency near the pier. I had thought him pretentious for dressing in yachting uniform, complete with yachting cap, but when he turned out to have a sideline as captain of the *Loch Nell*, I felt abashed. There were two others in the crew, and though the launch could take thirty-five passengers, only three turned up for this trip. "Nippy," said Mr. Warnock when I greeted him.

"It's nae much a day," said the crew's older mate. He went away and returned almost immediately to expand on his greeting. "Aye, it's poor weather." That made me feel much better, of course, for I recalled the fate of young Donald Maclean, the laird of Coll, who piloted Johnson and Boswell to Coll. "We parted from him with very strong feelings of kindness and gratitude," Boswell wrote, "and we hoped to have had some future opportunity of proving to him the sincerity of what we felt; but in the following year he was unfortunately lost in the Sound between Ulva and Mull; and this imperfect memorial, joined to the high honor of being tenderly and respectfully mentioned by Dr. Johnson, is the only return which the uncertainty of human events has permitted us to make to this deserving young man."

When I recalled how narrow was the sound between Ulva and Mull, I wondered how it would be possible to negotiate the much longer passage between Mull and Coll. Having planned to travel several days earlier, I had phoned the piermaster on the morning of the day to ask what the prospects were. "I wouldna' advise going," he had said. "The weather's verra bad." In fact, it appeared that whenever the weather was bad enough, the captain of the *Claymore* skipped Coll and went straight to Tiree — unless the weather was so bad that he did not venture forth at all.

The veteran mate had further encouragement to offer. "It's going to rain like blazes, I think," he said. My spirits soared anew. He went off to deal with some ropes that were proving unruly, but returned quickly, apparently experienced at identifying timorous victims. "I've seen it go from dead flat calm to force ten in an hour," he said. "It's during this moon. Maybe it'll settle down with the new moon on Monday."

Minutes later we were in the outer harbor, alongside the *Claymore*. The two other passengers and I walked aboard through an opening in the side of the *Claymore*, almost level with the deck of the *Loch Nell*. Before dashing to the cafeteria-lounge, I stopped to review the cargo: two cars, two trucks, and two calves looking bewildered and forlorn.

Soon I was comfortably ensconced behind hot coffee, roll, butter, and jam. Having assuaged my appetite, I decided that scientific curiosity demanded that I try *Claymore* porridge. It was not bad. As I ate, the young woman at the cafeteria counter kept polishing the metalwork at her station. From loudspeakers came the shrill sounds of Highland music, interrupted by calls for "Agnes." As it reached the open sea, the *Claymore* started rocking a bit, but the waves seemed gentle. I counted thirteen passengers, then, with good luck, found a fourteenth, and when I found a fifteenth I felt confident about prospects of reaching Coll. The *Claymore* could take three hundred passengers, and it carried a crew of twenty-seven.

The first one off the boat at Coll was a woman with a great number of untidy parcels and misshapen bundles and sagging suitcases. I discovered later that this was the laird's wife. Mrs. Wheeler-James, my bed-and-breakfast landlady, was waiting on the pier, and she drove me to her house, showed me to my room, and suggested that I call on Angus Kennedy, whom she described as an old piper who lived in a remote cottage near the sea. She offered to drive me to the beginning of the path that led through the bog to his cottage and assured me that I would be able to walk the rest of the way — though not in my city shoes. Her own Wellingtons were an almost perfect fit, and thus accoutered, I clumped into the car after her. She drove out along a bleak road, pointed to where she said there was a path through the bog, and asked me if I could see the roof of the Kennedy cottage in the distance. I just managed to convince myself that I could. Follow the path, she said. "You can't miss it." Those fatal words again. When she drove off, I plunged into the bog, sinking almost knee-deep, the mud splashing up above her Wellingtons. Soon I was reduced to guessing where the path was. In some places there were planks laid along the route, almost buried in water. I made the mistake of stepping on a plank and promptly slid to one knee in the mud. Hoping that I had not lost the path, I kept going in what seemed the general direction of the Kennedy place. Its roof was now certainly not visible. Finally, almost despairing of finding my way, I spotted a woman dressed in a long plaid overcoat, with a green wool cap fastened atop her head with a blue kerchief. Oblivious of my presence, she was scooping up bits of wood. I approached carefully, trying not to frighten her. Suddenly, with a start, she saw me looming there. I quickly explained that I was looking for Angus Kennedy. She was his sister, and lived with him. Leading me through a wasteland of débris, she showed me into the cottage I had managed to find, with some help.

It was yet another play by Beckett. The inside of the house looked as though it had never known the transports of broom or duster and had never allowed itself to be shorn of any imported glory: whatever had entered had stayed, there to decay. A man who looked the part of a Beckett tramp stood by the window, peering out toward the sea, and he turned slowly and stared at me with curiosity. He was dressed in an old pea jacket, with an odd belt cinched around his ample waist. On his head was a wool cap, blue and red and green dots, around his neck a camel-colored Jaeger scarf. His sister kept on her overcoat and headdress. Both of them wore Wellingtons.

"I've lived here all the days of my life," Mr. Kennedy said, once I had reassured him about my intentions. "Did you see that old house over there?" he asked, gesturing toward the front door. His movement suggested the presence of a structure outside, one that I had not seen. "I was born there and I've been here ever since."

Mr. Kennedy said that he was seventy-four years old, and his sister, Katie Sproat, was sixty-nine and widowed. There had been seven children in the family — two boys and five girls. Their father had been a tailor who made clothes for men and women. "People came from all over the islands," Mr. Kennedy said. "He made a pair of trousers, cloth and all, for two shillings. It's fishing I was doing. I did not like school. I thought it was unpleasant sitting there all day."

"You took to the fishing and left everything," his sister said.

"I still do a little fishing," he said. "I'd still go back to it if I could. Before the war we'd be getting sixpence — you were lucky to get ninepence — a pound for lobsters. Just now they're up to three pounds a pound."

Mr. Kennedy told me that he still had two boats, one about twenty years old, the other about twenty-five. "By God, there's plenty to do, making up the gear," he said. "You lose a lot of creels if the weather's bad." He complained that the cost of fuel for the boats was "extortionate." For heating the cottage he cut peat, and there was plenty of it in the bog. "Now people are too lazy to cut peat. The peat is clean, and the coal you get is filthy."

The Kennedys were the last people on Coll to get electricity — just a year earlier. Before that, they used a paraffin lamp. "It gave good light," he said, "as good as that" —pointing to an electric bulb. They still got their water from a well. I asked what the yearly rent was for this land, on which they grew potatoes and vegetables. Ten pounds, he said. For how much land? "I'm not quite sure," he responded. "Between rocks and bogs I think it'll be about thirty acres."

He had last visited the mainland about eight years earlier.

"Oban and these places," he said. "It's time I was going again to see what they're doing. But I like to be looking at the sea. Any time I go away to the town for a holiday I'm pleased to get back. When you get to the town you're closed in, you're boxed in."

The Kennedys read newspapers, and they were shocked by what they read. "There's murders and sex and robberies, things that were never known," Mr. Kennedy said. "Another thing that was a bad thing for this country — when they did away with hangings."

"We would think that if you lived in the town somebody could come in the night and kill you," Mrs. Sproat said.

"No policeman in Coll," Mr. Kennedy added. "One in Tiree. He comes over now and again, just to sign the book to show he was here."

"There's the drugs and drink," his sister observed.

"Oh, a good clean drink is all right," he said, "but the drugs — that's what's causing the damage. It's a changed world. I think that the children of today are brought up in cotton wool and glass cases. I don't think it does them any good at all. Young people today don't work at all. I think young people today is getting life too easy."

I asked about his reputation as a piper, and Mr. Kennedy said that now he rarely played the pipes. This led him to muse about changes that had overtaken the island. "There are not so many people left here," he said. "They're scattered all over the world. In the old days you could do with very little money in a place like this, but then when you needed money there was no work, so a lot of them cleared off. I suppose America's like Britain. There'll be rich and poor, and the ones who are rich are too rich, and the ones who are poor are too poor."

When I set off to return through the bog, Mr. Kennedy came along for about the first hundred yards, stepping forth confidently. He suggested that I head for the trees in the distance, and from there I would see the road. Like Johnson, I hardly would have characterized the twelve sprigs as trees, but I was thankful even for small mercies. As I walked along, still uncertain of my way, a helicopter flew overhead, and I felt like the hero of John Buchan's *The Thirty-nine Steps*, who wandered across the moors while a plane droned overhead, apparently keeping tabs on him. I reached the road eventually by aiming for pylons I could see in the distance. Then I started back along the single-track road toward the village of Arinagour. It was a long road, with no sign of habitation. Mrs. Wheeler-James's boots somehow became too big for me, and walking in them became more and more difficult. Suddenly, almost without warning, I was engulfed in a hailstorm, with no shelter anywhere. I put my hands to my head to shelter *it*. After about five minutes, the storm ended. Then it began again. By the time I reached the Isle of Coll Hotel, in Arinagour, my trousers were dappled with mud from the bog, my jacket was soaked, and I was soaked.

At the hotel bar I found the local builder in desultory conversation with Alastair Oliphant, the hotel's owner. Mrs. Oliphant was away on the mainland, so her husband was doing everything on his own, serving drinks and preparing bar lunches. I seemed to be the only one interested in food, and while I waited for Mr. Oliphant to serve my lunch, I began recovering from the minor ordeal by bog, weather, and Wellingtons. Two fellows came in from work on the road and ordered beer. "Quite quiet, the road, after the rush hour," one of them said, and it turned out that the rush hour had been six cars. The builder, who identified himself to me as Pete, had been on Coll for three years. Almost everyone was friendly, he assured me, adding, with a suggestion of approval tinged by regret, "Nothing happens."

Mr. Oliphant nodded assent. He told me that he came originally from Glasgow, his wife from Sussex. He had been working as an electrical engineer, and when he and his wife came to Coll for a holiday, they liked the place enough to want to stay, and bought the hotel in 1962. It was terribly rundown, and they had improved it considerably. I learned later that the man whom people on Coll referred to as "the Dutchman" had subsequently tried to buy the hotel, but Mr. Oliphant had turned him down. The Dutchman, Jan de Vries, was a wealthy businessman who lived near Amsterdam and had bought a lot of property on Coll. Mr. Oliphant quoted him as saying, "I have given up all my executive duties; I have retained a few directorships."

Confused about rival hegemonies on the island, I wondered who was now the laird. Was it the Dutchman or was it Charles Kenneth Stewart? "The Dutchman is the Dutchman, the laird's the laird," Mr. Oliphant replied, and offered a brief history: "About a hundred and fifty years ago the Duke of Argyll sent his factor out to see if Coll and Tiree were worth buying. The factor reported that Tiree was worth buying, so the duke bought it. Then the factor bought Coll for himself. The factor was a Mr. Stewart."

Mr. Oliphant said that the current Mr. Stewart now rented from Mr. De Vries some of the land he had sold him: "The Dutchman owns the land, Kenneth Stewart pays rent to the Dutchman, and the Dutchman pays feu duty to the laird." Feu was the traditional rent — in money, grain, or service — paid by a vassal.

That cleared up everything, and I went back to my feast of chicken soup, cheese sandwich, strawberry cheesecake, and coffee. Not a thing except the water used in the soup and coffee originated on Coll. That evening, since there was no place else to buy a meal on the island, I was back for another imported bar snack. The TV in the bar lounge was on, tuned to BBC-1, the only channel that could be picked up on Coll. "That's rather useful," Mr. Oliphant said. "There's no argument about what to watch; it's BBC-One or off." He told me that the island had joined Scotland's electricity grid just three years earlier and that electrification had been held up for months by the airstrip war.

Mr. Oliphant explained that the laird owned the land on which there was an airstrip, and the Dutchman used to land there in his private plane. When the laird and the Dutchman fell out, the laird objected to the Dutchman's landing on his airstrip, and he announced that it was only for ambulance planes and for service flights; that is, for a feeder airline that occasionally flew to and from Glasgow. That left everyone else out, and the only else was the Dutchman. So Mr. De Vries looked around for a stretch of level ground that he could use for *his* strip. He finally found a farmer with a suitable field and paid for construction of an airstrip. Then civil aviation authorities closed down the laird's airstrip, which had become overgrown with vegetation. But thanks to heavy rains, the Dutchman's strip was waterlogged and also unusable. Not one to admit defeat, Mr. De Vries took to arriving by private helicopter or, sometimes, aboard his yacht. While the battle raged, with rights of way disputed, the installation of electrical cables had been delayed.

When I reached the Dutchman by phone, he told me that he was still involved in "international business." He had first come to Coll in 1963, and now he visited about six times a year. Others had told me that he used his property as a shooting estate, employed a full-time gamekeeper, and brought business associates for visits. When I asked Mr. De Vries about life on Coll, he proved reluctant to reply, explaining that he made it a practice never to discuss what he was doing on Coll. Saying that he was about to leave for "the Baltic states," he promised to call me from Helsinki. I never heard from him.

But the laird and his wife were more amiable, and I went out to see them in their old stone house on the moors. In the living room an open fire burned, and there were books lying about, one of them a massive history of the family.

Mr. Stewart said that the Macleans sold Coll in 1856 to John Lorne Stewart, factor to the Duke of Argyll. Perhaps it was true that John Lorne had acted dishonorably in buying the island for himself rather than for the duke; Mr. Stewart was simply not sure. Nor did he know the price.

Mr. and Mrs. Stewart then volunteered a detailed genealogy, proceeding by leaps and hesitations and eventually reaching Catherine McNab Stewart. "She had married Henry Paul of Woodside, which is in Glasgow," Mr. Stewart said. "Their son was Henry Moncreiff Paul, and *his* son was Brigadier General Ernest Moncreiff Paul. He was my grandfather, and he added Stewart to his name. Then his son, my father, dropped the Paul. He was Henry Moncreiff Stewart. If you inherit a property through a female line, you often change your name by deed poll."

By this time I was deeper into genealogy than I had expected to be, but the Stewarts were going strong, and Mrs. Stewart turned to her husband and said, "I can never understand why your father dropped his name and your grandfather added his name."

Mr. Stewart ignored the interruption, continuing, "Father and grandfather died in nineteen forty-two, within six months of each other, my grandfather of old age, my father as a prisoner of the Japanese. I inherited."

As though still struggling to get a foothold on the slippery trunk of the family tree, Mrs. Stewart turned again to her husband and said, "Your father was Colonel Henry William Moncreiff Stewart and you are Charles Kenneth Moncreiff Stewart." She settled back in her chair and smiled contentedly, happy to have confirmed that detail. Her husband nodded, and added that it was his great-great-great uncle, the Stewart who had purchased Coll, who founded the line. There was no portrait of him at the house, but in the living room was a likeness of the divine who was Henry Paul's father. "He married a Moncreiff," Mr. Stewart said. "That's where all the Moncreiffs come in. In nineteen thirty-four my father and mother got this house, which was actually a schoolhouse. There were four schoolhouses on the island, and then three were shut. We have three daughters — Fiona, Fenella, and Nicola — and Nicola is eager to go to agricultural college."

Prior to the time of the present laird, the estate was entailed; that is, the property had to descend to a specified line of heirs and could not pass to others. But economics was a dismal science, farming a hazardous business, and profit elusive. Mr. Stewart, who was now fifty-five years old, had the entailment annulled so that he could sell a portion of his holdings. When I asked how big the estate was, Mr. Stewart said that the island had twenty-four thousand acres, and he had owned eighteen thousand. Then he wondered if the island had eighteen thousand acres of which he had owned fourteen thousand. In fact, as I learned later, the island did indeed have eighteen thousand acres. "The running costs were getting so difficult, they made it harder and harder to make ends meet. So I sold about twelve thousand acres. Mr. De Vries bought about eight thousand, and we sold another farm of about four thousand. Now we own only about three thousand acres and farm about five thousand that De Vries owns. He wanted a holiday place. Holland's a small country, and the Dutch islands are overrun by Germans. I haven't regretted selling or disposing of the land, but I only mind selling it to this man De Vries. He's not interested in the welfare of the island. When he came here at first we had great hopes, but he doesn't look after his tenants."

"He's got five empty houses on the island," Mrs. Stewart added. "He's terribly greedy. He wants to buy control of everything for himself. So everybody goes to the east end, and that belongs to Mrs. Erskine and she never says no to anything, so the place is overrun with caravans and caravan sites. There should be a happy medium."

Mr. Stewart had fallen out with the Dutchman, not only over airstrips but also over money. "A lot of landlords renew rent every five years," Mr. Stewart said. "I think he was putting the rent up about four hundred percent. At that time the home on the farm was more or less derelict. His lawyer suggested arbitration, so we went to arbitration and he lost, so the rent was put up about thirty-three and a third percent."

The next evening I called on Archibald MacLean, a retired policeman who lived down the street from my bed-and-breakfast. He was treasurer of the local Free Presbyterian church, and was doing the church accounts in a room crammed with the sort of trinkets awarded as prizes at fairs or sold at seaside resorts. Mr. MacLean took off his glasses, padded about on his stocking feet — socks of thick, gray wool — and finally sat down with me before the open fire. He was a hefty man — on the police force he was known as Big Archie — and it seemed to me that the alleged perpetrator of any alleged crime would have had unalleged second thoughts about tangling with him. He stood, as he put it, "a little just over the six feet," and he weighed 231 pounds.

Mr. MacLean told me that his father had been a farm laborer in the employ of Charles Edward Stewart, laird at the time. "There used to be a lot of people on the island, between three and four hundred," he said. "There were about fifty kids at the school. Plenty of wholesome food. At one time this was a great island for cheesemaking, and now it's for raising cattle and sheep, and the cheesemaking is finished. There are now about one hundred thirty people on the island, mostly old-age pensioners. People leave here and go to the mainland and get jobs and get married and only come back at holiday time, and that's what's leaving the island so depleted. There's almost as many cars as there is people.

"In the old days I used to go quite a bit with telegrams to the coast guard out to the east end of the island. I used to get about two shillings to take a telegram to Sorisdale, and the north side about one-and-six. I gave all the money to my mother. The money was always there, and we never put a hand to it without permission. I think my father had only about fifteen shillings a week, and there were six of us, two sisters and four brothers. We were really happy, because there was more contentment then. They don't seem to have the same regard to one another and the same spirit of helpfulness they had in those days. Nowadays you won't get any work done unless you pay out. In those days the crofters helped one another, and they were good churchgoers. They regarded the law of God and the giver of all good things.

"There's no man perfect in this life. I've consciousness that God is able to forgive me for my sins. There is rest for the people of God, but there is no rest for the wicked. The word of God is a mirror to those who want to learn. And if we look at the work of God, we'll see if we're doing what he commands us to do. The way I look at it, we're created into this world, and man's chief end is to glorify God. It's by the Almighty that we live, move, and have our being. He gives us all these, and we accept his blessings day by day."

Mr. MacLean told me that he had served over twenty-five years in the Glasgow police. "We had a lot of 'drunk' and 'breach of the peace' and 'found in possession of stolen goods' and 'housebreakers.' Not a great deal of violent crimes, but assaults, stabbing assaults, and burglary assaults. I was in the East End of Glasgow."

"A rough area?" I asked.

"Yes, indeed," he replied. "We had those two gangs, the Belly Boys and the Norman Street Conks. The Belly Boys were Protestants, and the Norman Street Conks were Catholics. They used to fight with knives, bottles, or sticks or bits of iron or anything at all. Irresponsible young men that maybe didn't want to work, and loafed about at billiard tables and football matches and knockin' about street corners playin' football and all that. I always intended, if I was spared and well, I wouldn't spend all my time in Glasgow; I'd return to my native place. Life is much quieter here than what it is in Glasgow. I looked forward to the freedom to be off the leash."

He now cultivated his garden — cabbages, turnips, parsley, parsnips, potatoes, and lettuce — using seaweed as well as manure for fertilizer. Breakfasts he prepared for himself, and then he went daily to his sister's house for dinner at noon and high tea in the afternoon. "I would like to travel a bit, maybe a cruise — Australia, New Zealand, and out there the Holy Land," he said. "But to live in any other place? No. Although there's trouble everywhere. There's no safe place to be. Life is cheap nowadays, and yet they don't want to bring capital punishment to these crimes, and I think that's wrong. It'd be a deterrent, anyway. There used to be two or three murders a year; it was very rare in Scotland as a whole. Nowadays it's a daily occurrence."

CHAPTER 23

He maintained that Archibald, Duke of Argyll, was a narrow man. I wondered at this; and observed that his building so great a house at Inverary was not like a narrow man. "Sir," said he, "when a narrow man has resolved to build a house, he builds it like another man. But Archibald, Duke of Argyll, was narrow in his ordinary expenses, in his quotidian expenses."

— James Boswell

IN HIS *Journal*, Boswell wrote: "The Duchess of Argyll, I knew, hated me, on account of my zeal in the Douglas Cause. But the Duke of Argyll has always been very civil to me, and had paid me a visit in London. They were now at the castle. Should I go and pay my respects there?"

The Douglas case involved claims to the Hamilton title and fortune, and the Duchess of Hamilton, a celebrated beauty, argued that her son was the rightful heir. Boswell forthrightly, intemperately, supported the rival claimant, and in an allegory treated the Duchess of Hamilton with contempt.

By 1773 the Duchess of Hamilton, widowed fifteen years earlier, had remarried, and she was ensconced at Inverary Castle as wife of the fifth Duke of Argyll. "I mentioned how disagreeable my company would be to the Duchess," Boswell wrote. "Mr. Johnson treated this objection with a manly disdain. 'That, sir,' said he, 'he must settle with his wife.' "

And so the two travelers went to the castle. They were shown about and given what Boswell described as "a little low one-horse chair" to drive through the grounds. "Mr. Johnson was much pleased with the remarkable grandeur and improvements about Inverary. He said, 'What I admire here is the total defiance of expense.' "

At dinner, Boswell was made uncomfortably aware of what he called "the Duchess's peevish resentment." "I was in fine spirits, and offered her grace some [soup]. I was in the right to be quite unconcerned, if I could. I was the Duke of Argyll's guest, and he had nothing to do with the Duchess of Hamilton's foolish anger."

When the duchess asked Johnson why he made his journey so late in the year — this was October 25 — he replied: "Why, madam, you know Mr. Boswell must attend the Court of Session, and it does not rise till the twelfth of August." In his *Journal*, Boswell reported:

> She said, with spite, "I know *nothing* of Mr. Boswell." I heard this, and despised it. It was weak as well as impertinent... I shall make no remark on her grace's speech. I indeed felt it as rather too severe; but when I recollected that my punishment was inflicted by so dignified a beauty, I had that kind of consolation which a man would feel who is strangled by a silken cord. Dr. Johnson was all attention to her grace. I never saw him so courtly. He had afterwards a droll expression upon her dignity of three titles: Hamilton, Brandon, Argyll. He called her a Duchess with three tails.

The Duke of Hamilton, who had enjoyed this title as a peer of Scotland, was at the same time Duke of Brandon in the English peerage, and the duchess, having acquired her first two tails from him and her third from Argyll, was eventually the mother of four dukes. Horace Walpole, the eighteenth-century wit, wrote that the Duke of Hamilton had been so infatuated with his wife-to-be that, while playing cards at Lord Chesterfield's, he "made violent love at one end of the room, while he was playing at Pharoah at the other end; that is, he saw neither the bank nor his own cards . . . he soon lost a thousand." Two nights later, the duke's passion could brook no further loss. He sent for a parson, and when that principled cleric refused to join the duke and his love in solemn wedlock without a ring, the duke threatened to summon the archbishop. Finally, the parson did as he was directed, using a curtain ring.

It was, incidentally, hardly giving the good lady her due to speak of only three titles. She had been sought in marriage also by the Duke of Bridgewater, father of British inland navigation. When she rejected him, thus cutting short her chances of a fourth tail, he was mildly discomfited and said he would marry her sister.

Ian Campbell, the twelfth Duke of Argyll, was in the direct line of succession to the Duke of Argyll who had been host to Johnson and Boswell, so I wrote asking if I could call on him at the castle. After all, I was not a partisan of the Douglases, I had never written an allegory, and I would offer no soup. His Grace did not reply, but his secretary, Mrs. K. Short, did. She wrote:

> For the Duke's part, he ventures to suggest that Johnson's and Boswell's visit to Inverary was not perhaps their happiest one, certainly in Boswell's case, where he was received very coolly by the then Duchess, as you will know, and of the many distinguished visitors to Inverary Castle over the centuries, these particular ones strike the least sympathetic note with the present Duke; in fact mention of them is inclined to make him wish to "take to the hills"! He therefore feels that there is little he could add and trusts that you will understand that he believes a meeting would not be productive.

Since the castle was open to paying visitors, I decided that my wife and I — she had by now rejoined me — would go there anyway, and also see the town of Inverary. When the castle was under construction, in the middle of the eighteenth century, the town surrounding the old castle was uprooted and moved to its present site. For moving the town and deciding how it should be rebuilt, the duke of that unsettling time was sometimes called the first town planner in Scotland.

Set beside Loch Fyne, Inverary was now almost completely devoted to tourists drawn by the castle. Tearooms and souvenir shops vied for favor, and in summer the town was inundated by crowds milling up and down the streets. The Argyll Arms Hotel, at the town's entrance, was where Johnson and Boswell had stayed, and one room was now designated as that occupied by Johnson. It was on the third floor, inside a towerlike section, and afforded a splendid view below of the Anvil Coffee Shop and the Arch Filling Station. At lochside was the town's monument to the dead of World War I: the statue of a kilted soldier, with a plaque reading, "In memory of those young loved lamented here who died in their country's service 1914–1918." A note added, "These are they which came out of great tribulation."

The drive through the castle grounds began at the main street and was clearly signposted to a parking lot in front of the castle. On the cover of *Inverary Castle*, a booklet sold in the duke's gift shop, the Gothic-revival structure appeared in heavenly blue, but the reality was a harsher gray. Construction of this great stone pile began in 1744 and was completed in 1788. About a hundred years later, the eighth duke added conical roofs on the turrets and raised the roof to make room for an additional story with dormer windows. On the front lawn were the barrels of several cannon, the handsomest, according to a caption almost entirely obscured by shrubbery, forged by Benvenuto Cellini, an Italian, for a French king, and recovered from a Spanish vessel sunk in the harbor of Tobermory, just off the Scottish island of Mull. The Duke of Argyll had led a salvage expedition in 1955 and had to rest content with the cannon he found instead of the gold that proved elusive.

Busloads of tourists were arriving at the castle, and the visitors came trooping in, filling the entrance hall, spilling over into the state dining room, shuffling on to crowd room after room. Groups were being shepherded about by castle guides in kilts of the Campbell tartan, and doors had to be shut between successive groups so that the intelligence imparted by one guide would not drown out the account of another. In one room were sheets of paper with a notice reading, "The Duke of Argyll hopes that all his clansmen and clanswomen will sign this register which will be kept at Inverary with the older family documents."

The present Duke was twenty-sixth chief of Clan Campbell, and also, as *Inverary Castle* indicated, Marquess of Kintyre, Marquess of Lorne, Earl of Campbell, Viscount of Lochow, and Lord of Inverary, Mull, Morven, and Tiree, as well as Master of the Royal Household in Scotland, Admiral of the Western Coasts and Isles, Hereditary Sheriff of Argyll, and Keeper of the Royal Castles of Dunstaffnage, Carrick, Tarbert, and Dunoon. Modestly, *Inverary Castle* omitted mention of his additional eminence as Keeper of the Court Seal of Scotland, Earl of Cowal, Viscount of Glenilla, Baron Sundridge, and Baron Hamilton.

Having attached myself to the first group of tourists admitted when the castle reopened after lunch, I listened with pleasure to the commentary of the guide. He began with an account of Guy Fawkes night of 1975, when a fire had seriously damaged the ornate French interior, now restored. On the table in the state dining room stood what he described as a twenty-four-pint punch bowl, gift of Queen Victoria to the eldest son of the eighth duke, who was to become the ninth duke and who married Princess Louise, fourth daughter of Queen Victoria. The bowl was used every New Year's Day. There were also four German silver-gilt sailing ships, or nefs, moored on the table. One of them, with superstructure removed, turned out to be a vessel for wine, which could be poured through the bowsprit. The guide said that the custom after dinner had been for the ladies to leave the room. Reaching into a closet, he brought out a chamber pot and said that this was then passed around for the men to use.

In the adjoining hall hung a portrait of the Duke of Cumberland, commander of the English forces that defeated the Scots at the Battle of Culloden in 1746. The Duke of Cumberland was known in Scotland as the Butcher of Culloden, but Inverary Castle was dedicated to him. What had once served as a library was now the China Turret, housing a collection of Oriental and European china. The guide recalled Johnson's saying that no expense had been spared in building the castle, but he directed our attention to the ceiling, whose decorations looked like plaster, though they were only papier-mâché and cost a mere twenty-five pounds, eleven shillings, and sixpence. "This gave the lie to what Johnson said about 'in defiance of all expense,'" the guide suggested. I was astonished to hear mention of Johnson, in view of the duke's sensitivity on the subject.

In the armory hall our group learned that the ceiling was ninety-five feet high and that in winter the two facing fireplaces burned ten tons of logs a week. One display case contained an assortment of sheaths for dirks, some sheaths with slits in which Campbell warriors kept knife and fork, the lust for savagery vying with a hunger for gentility. One sheath bore in Gaelic the invocation "Give me a drink of blood — the thirst is on me."

When the guide came to a portrait of the former Duchess of Hamilton, of Brandon, and of Argyll, he said: "As Dr. Johnson rather rudely called her, 'the duchess with three tails,' but he didn't get on with her." This was, of course, untrue; it was Boswell who did not get on with her. I was astonished to hear the name Johnson invoked yet again, but I held my tongue, lest the thirst were on this guide. When I learned that the motto of the duke's family was *Ne obliviscaris* (Do not forget), I began to understand why the twelfth duke, two centuries after the event, felt honor-bound to be upset about Boswell.

Before her marriage, the current, single-tailed Duchess of Argyll was Iona Colquhoun, and our next stop was at Rossdhu, her childhood home on Loch Lomond. Her brother, Malcolm Colquhoun, son of Sir Ivar, chief of Clan Colquhoun, was at home when I called, and he evidently bore no grudge against Johnson and Boswell. He received me in his office, on the second floor of the stately Georgian house, dressed casually in open-necked shirt and no jacket. Occasionally one of the phones beside him jangled insistently, and he did his best to transfer the calls elsewhere. Malcolm Colquhoun, who was born in 1947, was son of the eighth baronet and thirty-second chief of Clan Colquhoun, and he said that the man who welcomed Johnson and Boswell to Rossdhu was his great-great-great-great-great-great uncle. This was Sir James, twenty-third chief of Colquhoun, who had supervised the completion of Rossdhu, using for wings and portico stones from the old castle. When I told Mr. Colquhoun that Boswell had been in love with Sir James's daughter Kitty, he said this was news to him.

The Colquhoun estate covered forty-eight thousand acres, and the family still owned the islands — "about twenty-five or so" — in Loch Lomond. "One or two are inhabited," he said. "A couple of cottages on them." He complained that in Scotland there were no laws of trespass: "By and large anyone can go anywhere they like." As a result, people were forever landing on his islands and having picnics, and there was not a thing he could do about it. "You'd have to have a navy, and an army as well," he said.

I asked how the family had acquired its great estate. "Like everybody else, we probably stole it," he replied. And how had the Colquhouns managed to hold on to these ill-gotten gains? "We always managed to support the right people," Mr. Colquhoun suggested.

For the past seven years the house had been open to paying customers, and about twenty-five thousand people a year came to Rossdhu. "It hasn't helped in the slightest," Mr. Colquhoun complained. "It's made it worse. We try to minimize the loss." Then he added, "There are some tax advantages. Income can be set against expenditure."

While he stayed behind to tend the phones and an electronic calculator on which he could tot up losses, I set off to admire the house's treasures. One room boasted a collection, designated "Unique," of boxing prints assembled by Sir Iain Colquhoun, lightweight boxing champion of the British Army, 1912–1913. The Moor and Loch Room was crammed with stuffed animals in glass cases, trophies of John Colquhoun (1805–1885), heavyweight champion of the hunt, who bagged most of his game in the neighborhood. Among his prizes: barnacle goose, white-fronted goose, whooper swan, black-throated diver, red-throated diver, shelduck, Slavonian grebe, shag cormorant. Also on display was a reproduction of a painting of John Caldwell Calhoun (1782–1850), who died a natural death, having served the United States as vice-president from 1825 to 1832. The name Calhoun, pronounced the American way but without voicing the *l*, came close to the approved pronunciation of Colquhoun in Scotland.

In defiance of pronounced ambiguities, the family had managed to trace itself back to the twelfth century, with special pleasure in the fortunes of the fourteenth century, when the Fair Maid of Luss, who owned these lands, brought them in marriage to Sir Robert Colquhoun of that Ilk, chief of a clan that fought for Robert the Bruce. Whenever the chief of Clan Colquhoun girded his loins for battle, he dipped a wooden cross in goat's blood and sent it off with a horseman, who galloped through the countryside summoning the faithful by shouting the name of the rallying place. In 1592 Sir Humphrey Colquhoun neglected such innocent rounds in favor of dalliance with the wife of the chief of the Macfarlane clan. The Macfarlanes, without benefit of goat, set off in pursuit, and Sir Humphrey was laid low by an arrow shot by one of his own people — probably his brother and heir. The corpse was then hacked to bits and served up to Lady Macfarlane.

In 1603 great numbers of the Colquhoun clan fell victim to the ferocious MacGregors, and the surviving Colquhoun women rushed off to win the sympathy of James VI by bringing him the bloody shirts of their dead kinfolk, and also, apparently, a few shirts dipped in sheep's blood. Two months later the MacGregors returned to the assault and massacred the Colquhouns yet again. Thanks, however, to Campbell treachery, the MacGregor chief was captured and executed, along with eleven clansmen. The name MacGregor was officially proscribed, and it was only in 1775, by Act of Parliament, that it was restored to legality.

From Rossdhu, Johnson and Boswell traveled south along Loch Lomond in Sir James Colquhoun's coach to Cameron, once the property of the Colquhouns, but in 1773 the seat of the Smolletts. That Johnson and Boswell should have sojourned here with Commissary Smollett seemed natural to Patrick Telfer Smollett, the present-day owner. "In those days anyone traveling north or south stopped right here, and spent one night here and one with the Colquhouns," he said. The house that Johnson and Boswell knew had changed considerably through nineteenth-century additions such as false turrets and false windows. "In eighteen sixty-five it became a Victorian monstrosity," Mr. Telfer Smollett said, with a modicum of pride.

He told me that Commissary Smollett — a commissary was

a judge in a court dealing with probate and divorce — was his great-great-great-great-great-great grandfather. Tobias Smollett, the eminent eighteenth-century novelist, author of *Roderick Random, Peregrine Pickle,* and *Humphry Clinker,* was his many-greated uncle. Tobias's sister Jane succeeded to the estate, married Alexander Telfer, and insisted that her husband take the name Smollett. "That's where the Telfer crept in," the contemporary Telfer Smollett said.

Cameron House had a collection of Tobias Smollett first editions, as well as frankly populist exhibits. "We decided we must have two gimmicks," Mr. Telfer Smollett explained. He and his wife had therefore furnished one room with model airplanes, and another, called "Whisky Galore," with whisky bottles. Above the entrance to this room was a sign reading: "Visitors are reminded that no bottle on display contains alcohol. Some bottles contain a poisonous fluid used for display purposes. Please do not touch."

I asked what the poison was. "Tea," he said. "It was my wife's idea."

The estate's wildlife reserve — visitors were invited to drive through the area, but not to get out of their cars — was *his* idea, as was the zoo where animals were not supposed to get out of the cages. He had always loved animals, and when he married Georgina Fox he already owned quite a few prairie dogs, marmots, and foxes. "They were all loose here; there was no one about," he said.

It was when he visited the Canadian Rockies and saw bears wandering around that he hit on the notion of a wildlife reserve for Cameron. Now visitors could see not only bears roaming loose, but North American bison, Tibetan yaks, deer, and Highland cattle; in the zoo were raccoons, wildfowl, monkeys, arctic foxes, and binturongs.

When visitors driving through the reserve made the mistake of stopping, the brown bears liked to let the air out of tires with a swipe of their claws. The bears seemed to relish the hiss of air escaping. They also liked to steal windshield wipers. Soon after the wildlife reserve opened, a Swedish girl stopped to photograph a polar bear, and the bear grabbed her arm and bit it. She slapped the bear across the face and drove off, to be rushed to the hospital. Mr. Telfer Smollett expected a lawsuit, but all he got was gratitude. Very few people can say that they were bitten by a polar bear, the girl exulted. Sometimes, by burrowing under the fence, an animal escaped, and just in case anyone proved less indulgent than the polar bear's victim, Mr. Telfer Smollett carried lots of insurance.

Schoolchildren flocked to Cameron from all over the region; during the week I was there 5190 children were expected. "Tomorrow," said Mr. Telfer Smollett with an air of trepidation, "forty-eight buses, all at the same time." He conceded that most of the youngsters were well-behaved, but whenever he saw two or three teachers on their own, he knew he was in for trouble. "The sort of thing the children will do is jump on a peacock's tail to get a feather," he said. "So we run about like a clucking hen trying to save everybody."

The Empress Eugénie of France and the last Emperor of Brazil came here, and they were on their good behavior, as was Churchill when he arrived. "We have had more solid talk here than at any place where we have been," Johnson told Boswell, and no animals let the air out of their coach wheels.

CHAPTER 24

To describe a city so much frequented as Glasgow, is un-
necessary. The prosperity of its commerce appears by the
greatness of many private houses, and general appearance of
wealth.

— Samuel Johnson

THE PRINCIPAL of the University of Glasgow went to the
window of his office and looked out at the metropolis. "Ad-
mittedly, the city has now been almost ruined by concrete,
high-rise buildings," Alwyn Williams said. "When I was here
in nineteen fifty to 'fifty-four, as a junior lecturer, Glasgow
was still a sort of baroque Victorian. As a geologist, I appreciated the way they used the sandstone, which they would
have been doing quite well in Johnson's day, of course. They
used the yellow, honey-colored sandstone and the red sandstone from Mauchline, which would have been one of Rob-
bie Burns's stamping areas."

Before he cast himself as an administrator, Dr. Williams
specialized in paleontology and worked at what he described
as tying up the Scottish and Irish rocks with the Appalachian
rocks. "That's the link there was," he said. "Four hundred and
fifty million years ago this bit of Scotland, Scotland and
northern and western Ireland, formed part of the Canadian

shield, which was a piece that got knocked off and stuck onto Europe."

Dr. Williams said he had no idea why he was asked to exchange his geologist's hammer for an executive's gavel. While at the University of Birmingham he received a letter from the Secretary of State for Scotland asking permission to send his name forward to the queen for appointment as principal of the University of Glasgow. At that stage Dr. Williams could have declined, but not once the queen made her appointment, for one did not refuse anything to the queen. Afterward he had second thoughts, but finally decided he had done the right thing.

"I like the people," he said. "The average Glaswegian is highly articulate, with a well-formed sense of humor. It's pawky humor, dry and pithy, the New York kind of humor compared with the shaggy-dog Texas humor. He's very, very quick in retort, very good at debate, and he will use flowery language to a lesser degree than others. The people here are extremely generous in their sympathies, unaffected in their approach to other people, and quick to sense when relationships are strained, when there is a need to help conversation along, when there is a need to help somebody who is feeling isolated, ill at ease in company. In business they fancy themselves as hard men, maybe to cover up a streak of sentimentality that can be exploited to their disadvantage."

Johnson wrote approvingly of the University of Glasgow's study calendar — a single session and single recess each year, rather than the Oxford-Cambridge system of more than one term and recess. At Glasgow, students could apply themselves to study without repeated interruptions. But now, in common with other Scottish universities, Glasgow followed the English pattern. "What we have to bear in mind is that the old system of one session was geared to the lad and the lass who went to work in the factory or in particular went back and worked on the farm," Dr. Williams said. "This would give you the complete run from June, the ripening of crops, through to the harvest period into October. There was a break one weekend in November — Meal Friday, Meal Monday — when the students were given time off to go back to their homestead to collect their barrel of salted herring and their bag of oats."

"Yet when I have allowed to the universities of Scotland a more rational distribution of time," Johnson wrote, "I have given them, so far as my inquiries have informed me, all that they can claim. The students, for the most part, go thither boys, and depart before they are men; they carry with them little fundamental knowledge, and therefore the superstructure cannot be lofty."

"My contention is that the student leaving us is a much better-rounded man than his counterpart in the south," Dr. Williams insisted. "He has a wider base on which he's built his knowledge. When they leave, they're men, not boys."

Boswell wrote that "we had not much conversation at Glasgow, where the professors, like their brethren at Aberdeen, did not venture to expose themselves much to the battery of cannon which they knew might play upon them."

"My guess is that the principal of that day was not necessarily all that impressed with Johnson," Dr. Williams suggested. "He was much more concerned, as indeed I am today, with things like how does one pay for a gallery, and what does one do about running a museum. We've spent, to us an enormous sum of money, one and a half million pounds building a gallery. We found ourselves three hundred thousand pounds short. And we had been left what is the largest collection of Whistler works in the world — mainly because he quarreled with everybody else and got to know us toward the end of his days, when there wasn't time left for him to quarrel with us, too. And he left us everything through his sister-in-law Rosalind Birnie Philip. She was well aware of the fact that we did not have the accommodation to look after the collection appropriately. So she divided the collection up into two or three. The major part she gave to the university on the understanding that it never left the university for exhibition: she disliked London so much. But she then bequeathed another major part of the collection to us on the understanding that we could sell some or even all of it in order to build the gallery. So we ended up by building a gallery, and we spent nearly seven hundred thousand pounds out of our own reserves, putting off the evil day when we would have to possibly sell Whistler paintings. And we were advised by our professor of fine arts, McLaren Young, who was the world's authority on Whistler, that there were eleven canvases which could be sold. When it was found that we were going to sell Whistlers, all hell was let loose. The culmination of it all is that I've been mounting a campaign in order to collect as much money as possible."

Just that morning *The Times* of London had published an editorial declaring that "the collection as a whole, which includes the entire contents of Whistler's studio at the time of his death, has a value for scholarship greater than that of its parts, and it should be kept together unless that is quite impossible."

Principal Williams promptly decided to take advantage of the opportunity offered by the editorial, and wrote to *The Times* suggesting that people who wanted the Whistlers to stay together could contribute money. He told me that the outcry over the plan to sell the paintings had originated in London and that he had written an earlier letter telling critics "where to get off, on the grounds that it seemed suspiciously to me as though they were not so much concerned about the Whistlers as about being sure that we were in a position where they could always borrow them. Otherwise they would have given us money a long time ago to build the art gallery." Some weeks later the whole crisis was resolved when enough money came in to ensure that the Whistlers could stay intact.

About an hour's drive from the university, hard by Mauchline and its red sandstone, was the village of Auchinleck, and
not far from it the large estate that had belonged to Boswell's
father, Lord Auchinleck. Johnson and Boswell stayed here
on their way from Glasgow back to Edinburgh, and a small
sign — "Auchinleck House" — now stood at the entrance to
the grounds, with open gates practically ordering me to visit.
I drove almost a mile along the rutted, neglected road lined
by large stones, and stopped before the large, gray Georgian
residence. There were two full stories, a basement with windows at ground level, and an attic as well. The whole place
was derelict and falling into ever-greater ruin. In many of
the windows the glass was broken, and weeds luxuriated in
the cracks of the stone steps rising to the front door. At the
foot of the stairs one of the decorative stone urns from the
banister had fallen from its pedestal and lay in rubble and
undergrowth, like the statue of a maximum leader toppled
after a coup d'état. The explanation, however, resided not in
politics but in economics.

A modern James Boswell had inherited the estate about
ten years earlier and had improved some of the farm buildings, but, because of a shortage of funds, had neglected
Auchinleck House, where no one had lived for twenty years
now.

Nor were there many signs of life or industry in the village
of Auchinleck. I had phoned ahead to Gordon Hoyle, and he
was going to show me round. "It'll take an hour and a
quarter, an hour and a half," he had warned. Mr. Hoyle, who
was in his eighties, had a draper's shop, and when I called
he came right out, got into the car, and pointed the way to
the south end of Main Street, where a sign indicated the
Boswell Museum. We parked, and then in the rain Mr. Hoyle
and I slowly circled the outside of the building while he
intoned a circumstantial account, stone by stone, of epochs
in the construction, decay, and reconstruction of the old

Barony kirk, now transformed into the museum. He reeled off dates for stages of rise and fall and rise, year by year, century by century, his hands tracing airy arabesques as he itemized achievements and defeats of the millennium. I wanted to hurry him along, but, after all, he had warned me it would take time.

When we reached shelter inside the museum, Mr. Hoyle was no less determined that I should miss nothing. Arming himself with a bamboo pointer and a lantern, he led me on a slow round of the interior, annotating exhibit after exhibit, detailing the provenance of each piece — china and silver with the Boswell coat of arms, snuffboxes with secret hinges, a cabinet that had belonged to the eighteenth century's James Boswell, Boswell family portraits, a Boswell genealogy, and a section devoted to the memory of William Murdoch, not a Boswell but nonetheless a distinguished son of the parish and an inventor of gas lighting. This seemed a peculiar intrusion into the Boswellian precinct, but it was not the only offender, as Mr. Hoyle made clear in identifying the final canvas. "This is the portrait of an unknown man by an unknown artist," he said. Sensing my perplexity, he explained that a benefactor had offered it, and since there was space on the wall, the museum had gratefully accepted.

Finally, having exhausted the vein, Mr. Hoyle was ready to reply to my questions. It turned out that he was not a native of Auchinleck, not even a Scot. A Yorkshireman who had married a Scotswoman, Mr. Hoyle had settled in Auchinleck in 1946, and his passion for Boswelliana had crept up on him. The affair began when he and a friend, John Paterson, assumed the thankless and unpaid job of seeing to it that the entrance to the Boswell family mausoleum, adjoining the old Barony kirk, was kept secure and in good repair. "We didn't want people going down and disturbing the coffins," Mr. Hoyle explained. "It was a love of conserving something. But it cost time and money, so we wrote Lady Talbot of

Malahide, who owned the mausoleum, and said it was about time she did something about repairing the place."

Lady Talbot was a descendant of Boswell, and her home at Malahide, near Dublin, was site of the discovery of a trove of Boswell papers. Alerted to her responsibilities, Lady Talbot offered the mausoleum, where six generations of Boswells were interred, to the National Trust for Scotland, but the offer was declined.

Mr. Hoyle then, in 1970, had another idea. "Suppose we found the Auchinleck Boswell Society — each put a pound in; a pound apiece won't kill anybody," he suggested to two antiquarian friends, Mr. Paterson and the stationmaster since deceased. So the Auchinleck Boswell Society wrote to Lady Talbot, asking her to give it the mausoleum. "She hemmed and hawed for a few months," Mr. Hoyle said. "Then she gave us the mausoleum, although it belonged to her godson, as a present. She also gave us two hundred pounds of her own money and fifty pounds from her godson. This was fine. It started us off."

There was more to come. Lord Auchinleck had erected the mausoleum and he had renovated the church, but a great-grandson, in the first half of the nineteenth century, had built a new church less than a hundred yards distant, and the roof of the old church was removed. The building fell into ruin, till only walls remained. Then the local grave-diggers wrote the church session that, because of the danger of walls collapsing, they would no longer care for graves in the churchyard. Fatalistically, the session prepared to demolish the remains of the old church. But Mr. Paterson was a member of the session, and he persuaded his colleagues there to donate the ruins to that other body of which he was a member, the Auchinleck Boswell Society. With government help, the society set to work to restore the church to a semblance of its early nineteenth-century self and to convert it into the Boswell Museum. The churchyard itself belonged to the local county council, so the society asked for a three-foot-wide right of way to the church. "Now we have the title deed to the church, the mausoleum, and the roadway," Mr. Hoyle said with pride. "It all belongs to us."

In 1978 the museum formally opened; since then, prospective visitors simply applied at the draper's shop on Main Street. Mornings, when a shop assistant was on duty, were the best times; Mr. Hoyle could leave his business with clear conscience and savor the joys of instruction in Boswellian minutiae, never hurrying, never failing to give each acquisition its due. When I mentioned Boswell's ties with Johnson, Mr. Hoyle suggested that the two were indissolubly bound to each other. "It's like a horse and carriage," he said. "Like a marriage."

The three-man Auchinleck Boswell Society had long since swollen into a fellowship of about two hundred and fifty, many of them Americans. "We've gone from strength to strength," Mr. Hoyle said. Annual membership cost £1.50 or $5.00, and life membership £15 or $45.00. The society held an annual dinner in the neighboring village of Cumnock, as near as possible to August 18, the day that Johnson and Boswell set off on their Highland tour. At the 1979 dinner, Mrs. Robert Boswell gave the museum twenty pieces of silver engraved with the hooded hawk of the family arms. Mr. and Mrs. Buchanan of Glasgow donated what the society's *News Letter* Number 20 described as "a very fine old buttonhook." While Mr. Hoyle averted his eyes, I made my token offering to the contribution box and my exit along the hard-earned right of way. Having acquitted himself of his duties to the Boswells, Mr. Hoyle wished me good hunting on the trail of the hooded hawk.

It took a little searching to find the next shrine, for, though road signs were plentiful and explicit, and though Rosslyn Chapel and Rosslyn Castle stood a mere seven miles from the heart of Edinburgh, the buildings enjoyed an air of seclusion. Chapel, open to the public, and castle, hidden from the road and padlocked, stood beside the village of Roslin, a small settlement that for complex historical reasons did not enjoy orthographic unity with its two notable landmarks. Dorothy Wordsworth visited in 1803 with her brother William, and she wrote: "Went to see the inside of the Chapel at Rosslyn, which is kept locked up, and so preserved from the injuries it might otherwise receive from idle boys! But as nothing is done to keep it together, it must in the end fall. The architecture within is exquisitely beautiful."

Sir Walter Scott's *Lay of the Last Minstrel* added a distinctly commemorative note. One verse:

> There are twenty of Roslin's barons bold
> Lie buried within that proud chappele;
> Each one the holy vault doth hold —
> But the sea holds lovely Rosabelle!

His poem became so popular that coaches were soon leaving Edinburgh daily to bring tourists en masse. But where were the coaches of yesteryear? When I arrived at Rosslyn, staff — John Taylor, curator of the chapel, and his assistant — outnumbered visitors. The curator, a short man, and his assistant, a tall man, were drawn up intimidatingly in the entrance lodge, side by side like an undernourished Tweedledum and an overnourished Tweedledee. I paid the admission fee, mumbled a request for a guidebook, and haltingly confessed my interest in the chapel. Mr. Taylor began by informing me that he lived in the former inn, a few yards away, and that his family had resided there since the beginning of the century. A number of illustrious guests had been kind enough to scratch their names on the windows, and a plaque on the façade commemorated the visits of other famous people, including Johnson and Boswell.

Mr. Taylor then delegated his towering Tweedledee to

escort me round while he stood solitary watch. My guide informed me that the carvings I was going to see were remarkable, the work of specialists from France, Italy, Portugal, Spain, and even Scotland. As we entered the chapel, he said that he used to be a choirboy here; like a choirboy he relished pointing out the impudences of some of the carvings, for example the one-man band, the bagpiper plainly carved by a foreigner, since the bag was slung under the wrong arm, the imp watching the priest, the other imp watching the congregation, and the fox dressed as a friar preaching to a congregation of geese.

The late sixth Earl of Rosslyn liked to think of the chapel as the Bible in stone, and there was plenty of evidence in less impudent carvings: expulsion from the Garden of Eden, birth of Christ, Christ at the carpenter's bench, Christ in the temple, crucifixion, descent from the cross, resurrection, St. Peter at the gates of heaven, God in radiant glory with kings prostrate at his feet. My guide then told me of the chapel's master mason who wanted to carve an intricate pillar and went off to Rome to see how it was done. While he was away, his apprentice carved the pillar, and when the master returned he was so furious that he grabbed a mallet and killed the apprentice. And so, high in the chapel hung a stone head with a scar on its forehead, and in the opposite corner a stone carving of the master mason's head. The pillar itself was a wondrous achievement, with spirals of foliage and intertwined dragons, and no sign of an apprentice's immaturity.

Wonders were everywhere to behold. One series of carvings illustrated the seven mercies: helping the needy, clothing the naked, visiting the sick, visiting prisoners, comforting the fatherless and destitute, feeding the hungry, burying the dead. And there were the seven deadly sins: pride, gluttony, anger, sloth, luxury, avarice, and lust. In 1688 some of the statues suffered for their sins when a mob attacked the chapel, holding it popish and idolatrous. Byron was to write:

Oh Roslin! Time, war, flood and fire,
    Have made your glories star by star expire.
Chaos of ruins! Who shall trace the void,
    O'er the dim fragments, cast a lunar light,
And say "Here was or is" where all is doubly night.

When Queen Elizabeth II and Prince Philip were coming to visit the chapel, in 1961, the Earl of Rosslyn was asked to submit a list of those he planned to present to the royal party, and it took a flurry of correspondence for him to win approval for his suggestions. Motive for the court's misgivings was not made public, and one was left to suspect that the royal family feared offense to Bolshevik sensibility, since the earl's list included his mother, become Princess Dimitri, having married Prince Dimitri of Russia, a nephew of the lamented czar and brother-in-law of Prince Yousoupoff, who had helped to dispatch Rasputin. The earl had additional trouble when he refused to reveal to the lord lieutenant what gifts he planned to give the queen and prince; the earl insisted that half the pleasure of a gift was the surprise, and he finally got his way.

I asked Mr. Taylor what Peter St. Claire-Erskine, seventh earl and tenth baronet, was up to. He said that his lordship was a student at Bristol University and that he was interested in a career with the police.

On that note of incongruity, I had come to the end of the line, and I set myself to reviewing the lessons I had learned. My journey had brought me greater sympathy with a stubborn and compliant people, thoughtful and foolhardy, abstemious and indulgent, tolerant and suspicious, traditionalist and innovative, good-humored and dour, and my conclusions were hesitant and firm.

I found myself resisting every conclusion, as stubborn voices within me contended, one insisting that there were undeniable things to say about the Highlanders, the other ridiculing such claims as naïve and taking exception to every statement.

"Is it not possible to admit at least that this is an amiable people, solicitous and helpful, given to civility and good humor and softness of manner, more inclined to self-depreciation than to vanity, rarely pompous, with a strong feeling for equality?"

"Surely you can't be serious," the other voice countered. "Don't you see how hazardous it is to sum up a single person? Attempting to draw conclusions about two people is twice as difficult, and how in the world can you hope to say something valid about hundreds of thousands? All you do is compound your errors. This is hardly the way to be rational, and it's certainly no way to be scientific."

"But we do it all the time. We have the evidence of our observations no less than the strength of our intuitions and the corroboration of others. Must we passively subside into mute senselessness, none the wiser about what we experience? You can hardly argue that these are not hardy, thrifty, proud, unsophisticated, but sensitive people. Are you so entrenched in theory that you can't admit that they have a highly developed sense of history, of offenses endured, of defeats and persecution and injustice? Won't you concede, at least, that they consider themselves second-class citizens, neglected by distant government and oppressed by domestic burdens: poor land, harsh climate, lack of employment opportunities, distance from industry and markets?"

"You're missing the point. It's not that they're less than hardy, or that they're spendthrift, craven, or insensitive, but rather that all this is the purest subjectivity, as fickle as intuition; it's not demonstration, not proof. Your conclusions may be superficially convincing; the important thing is not the aura of conviction but the substance of truth. Continue the way you're going and you'll wind up saying that Italians are emotional, Englishmen cold, Frenchmen amorous, and Germans methodical."

"And what do you think you're being, except persnickety, stubborn, and pedantic? If the result of travel is inability to recognize plain facts, there's not much hope for you. *I* managed to see, even if you pretend you didn't, that this was no primitive, unlettered people; this was not a society in which class distinctions were oppressive, with great disparities of wealth; this was not a land alien in spirit and exotic in manner. You did manage to notice — or didn't you? — the beauty of hills and lochs and glens, even the stark grandeur of barren moors. You did have a small taste of the miseries of climate — wind and rain and cold — as well as the pleasures. Do you deny the reality of depopulation? Can you ignore the fact that many of the unfortunate as well as many of the most enterprising Highlanders and islanders emigrated — still emigrate — in order to pursue professions or simply to get jobs? You did at least, I trust, hear people speaking English. Did that suggest nothing about the decline of Gaelic? You were aware of changes in the observance of the Sabbath. Doesn't that say something about a decline in religious traditions? What about the people in the older generation bewailing those in the younger generation, complaining about the erosion of faith and standards and neighborliness, and about the inroads of envy? Well?"

"If *you* would only leave impressionism where it belongs — on a canvas — we'd be a lot better off. Every conclusion you reach cries out for contradiction. For every tolerant Highlander, another is intolerant. For every person who moans about the young, there's another who doesn't. If many recall the indignities of the past, others have no idea what the past was like."

How I, distancing myself from this internecine strife, longed, as this dialogue continued, for a party of the third part to arbitrate! Then I remembered Dr. Johnson, and fled to him for counsel. *He* was not forever teetering between yea and nay. *He* reached conclusions about *his* trip, and I quickly hunted up a few of them:

· "I sometimes met with prejudices sufficiently malignant, but they were prejudices of ignorance."

· "The clans retain little now of their original character, their ferocity of temper is softened, their military ardor is extinguished, their dignity of independence is depressed, their contempt of government subdued, and the reverence for chiefs abated."

· "Who *can* like the Highlands? — I like the inhabitants very well."

Against this majestic assertiveness, a small voice insinuated its skeptical presence: "Do you really take Johnson, who lived for the joys of contest, who practiced the wiles of debate, who argued that black was white — not that I'm taking a stand on that issue — as authority?"

I listened wearily and relapsed into silence, convinced — well, almost convinced — that my trip could be identified by a time and a place, but that the end was not a conclusion.

INDEX

INDEX